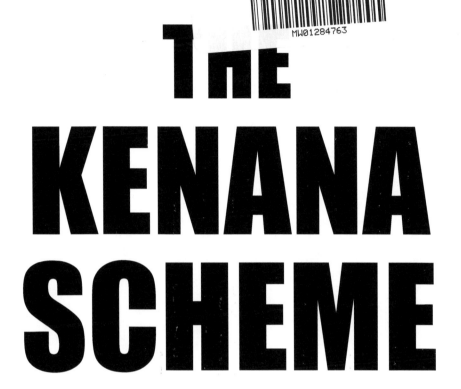

The
KENANA
SCHEME

AN ANTHROPOLOGICAL CASE STUDY OF SOCIAL CHANGE, ECONOMIC DEVELOPMENT, MIGRATION, AND DISPLACEMENT IN AFRICA

HASSABALLA OMAR HASSABALLA

To the Nomads and
Peasants of the White Nile

Photographs by

Ithar Hassaballa Omar Hassaballa

Haroun Suliaman Haroun

Hassaballa Omar Hassaballa

A Note on Spelling

I have not adopted any standard for the transliteration of Arabic words but followed an approach that can easily be identified by Arabic speakers.

TABLE OF CONTENTS

CHAPTER TWO NOTES.. 66

CHAPTER THREE

THE ECONOMIC AND SOCIAL LIFE OF THE LOCAL INHABITANTS OF DAR MUHARIB PRIOR TO THE ESTABLISHMENT OF KENANA SUGAR SCHEME................. 69

CHAPTER FOUR

KENANA SCHEME AND SETTLEMENT SCHEMES
IN THE SUDAN 133

CHAPTER FIVE

KENANA ORGANIZATION OF THE SYSTEM OF PRODUCTION

CHAPTER SIX

STATISTICAL PROFILE AND SOCIOLOGICAL CHARACTERISTICS OF THE KENANA POPULATION IN 1984–1985

CHAPTER SEVEN

SOCIAL SERVICES IN THE KENANA SCHEME..................... 233

CHAPTER EIGHT

LIST OF TABLES

LIST OF FIGURES

PREFACE

THE KENANA SCHEME

AN ANTHROPOLOGICAL CASE STUDY

OF SOCIAL CHANGE, ECONOMIC DEVELOPMENT,

MIGRATION, AND DISPLACEMENT IN AFRICA

The problems of underdevelopment and stagnation in Africa, south of the Sahara, become more critical as time goes on. These complex problems of persistent underdevelopment are the result of numerous factors, but imperialist domination and the colonial mode of production are the root cause. The political, economic, social, and administrative institutions formulated by the colonial powers were designed to benefit the colonizing country. Local resources of the land and the people were ruthlessly devoted to the extraction of cheap raw material to be shipped abroad. The consequences were enormous, especially the sharply defined process of polarization of the population of the colonized country into the few rich and the poor deprived majority. Even more dangerous is that until today politicians, planners, and developers are still following their colonial predecessors' approach to development.

The Kenana Scheme in the Sudan manifests this extractive approach through its combination of the technology of the multinational corporations and petrodollar funds invested by Arab companies in a site comprised of Sudanese natural and manpower resources. The project site lies 320km south of Khartoum on the clay lands of central Sudan. The Kenana Sugar Project was designed in accordance with the "breadbasket strategy" to boost agricultural production for export. This was a primary goal of the previous government (1969–1985). To achieve it the government gave astonishing concessions in water, land lease, tax and customs exemptions to the multinationals, and the Arab companies. According to the Sugar Agreement of 1972, 150,000 Feddans were leased for ten piasters per Feddan (symbolic rent) to the Kenana Sugar

Company without duties or charges to the nomads and peasants who were the traditional users of the land. Lonrho Company was given the contract to transform the land and organize the inception of the Kenana Sugar Estate.

The cost of construction and development of the Kenana Scheme was estimated at $150 million in 1973, but actual costs exceeded one billion dollars when it was completed in 1980–1981. The project attracted thousands of skilled and unskilled laborers, expatriates, officials, migrants, and immigrants. At the same time, the nomads and peasants of the region were forcibly evicted from the scheme area because there was no place for them as livestock keepers and cultivators in the new industrial and market setting.

Government intervention, commercialization of agriculture, and the penetration of the market economy brought tragic, adverse, and undesirable changes to the region. The indigenous people were forcibly driven out of their homeland, and the environment was caught in a rapid cycle of degradation because of the massive clearance of acacia forest and bush. The traditional socioeconomic order, political and cultural life were destroyed, and self-sustaining economic formations were replaced by a giant capitalist enterprise which offers seasonal employment to a work force far smaller than the population, which formerly drew its livelihood from this region.

Today, many countries around the world are witnessing food shortages, and the high prices for obtaining that food. Many multinational corporations and forign countries expressed their interest in investing in agricultural development in Sudan to close the food-population gap in their countries. It is imperative this time to respect the property rights of the traditional users of the land in rural Sudan, and not to be victimized and alienated as it happened in the previeous development schemes in Sudan.

ACKNOWLEDGMENTS

I would like to express my gratitude to the Economic and Social Research Council, which financed and sponsored my fieldwork, and to the Kenana administrative staff, who allowed access to the Project. My appreciation is also expressed to the Ford Foundation for financing a fellowship at the University of Washington to enable me to write my Ph.D. thesis on which this book is based.

In the Economic and Social Research Council, I would like to thank Dr. Ibrahim Hassan Abdel Galil, Dr. Mohammed M. Abdel El Salam, Dr. Atif A. Saghayroun, and Dr. Bodour Abu Affan, and from the University of Khartoum Dr. Abdel Ghaffar M. Ahmed. All gave their valuable discussion, help, and assistance during the course of the fieldwork.

My appreciation is expressed to a considerable number of Kenana staff, especially the Administration Manager, Dr. Hassan El Amin. These include Sayed El Amin Hamid, Salah Bushara, Engineer Mamoun M. El Amin, Engineer Maryoud M. El Sunni, Engineer Ahmed Musa; also my thanks are due to Ahmed M. El Nashi, M. El Asha, Hamid A. El Awad, M. Abdalla, Omar El Sayed, El Bedri Mirghani, Isam El Din Suliaman, Fadulalla, Wad El Nayir, Khalid, Imad, Wad El Mahadi, and Dr. Bashar Suliaman, for their support, solving of problems I had encountered at the field site and the provision of information I needed.

A special word of appreciation is due to the nomads and peasants of Dar Muharib region. Here I would like to thank El Shaykh Musa El Khanferi, El Shaykh M. Yousif, El Shaykh Musa Ghanim, El Shaykh Ibrahim Hassabu, El Shaykh Musri, El Shaykh Bakhit M. Bakhit, and El Shaykh Ramadan Tiya, for their hospitality, cooperation, and for allowing me to live in their camps and villages to engage and participate in the dry and wet season socioeconomic activities.

At the University of Washington, I am very much indebted to Professor Edgar V. Winans, who inspired, supervised, and directed my work from the early start of my study. Also, a special word of appreciation goes to him for his extensive comments on the first draft. Being a student to him, I found support, assistance, and thoughtful guidance.

My gratitude is also expressed to Professor Eugene Hunn, Professor James B. Watson, and Professor Farhat Ziadeh, for their valuable discussion, insight, views, and comments.

My gratitude also goes to the family of Debra Boyer and George Yeannakis in Seattle for their hospitality and support.

Finally, my thanks go to my wife, Kawthar, my son Mujahid, and my daughters Ithar and Ruaa for their dedication and support.

CHAPTER ONE

INTRODUCTION

ENTRY TO THE FIELD AND PROBLEM

I got interested in studies of social change, development, and transformation when I was a graduate student in the Department of Anthropology, University of Washington. When I returned to the Sudan in June 1982, I went to visit my family and relatives in the Southern White Nile Province. I found that most of the Arab speaking nomads and the peasants had been displaced, which resulted in a massive out-migration from the region, while the few left behind were relocated in villages that spell expulsion instead of accommodation. But the most devastating blow to these indigenous people was that they can no longer use their pastures, sorghum fields, camps, or village sites because the land had been expropriated and was at the disposal of the Kenana Sugar Company (KSC) to establish the largest sugar scheme and refinery in the world.

Working as a researcher with the Economic and Social Research Council in Khartoum, I gained the approval of the council and my supervisory committee at the University of Washington, Seattle, to conduct a fieldwork to assess the socioeconomic implications of the Kenana scheme under the auspices of the E.S.R.C. Because the Kenana Sugar Project has "restricted entry" to researchers and scholars who are not part of the Kenana field staff, I had to wait for a couple of months for the Kenana administration to give the go-ahead.

Prior to the beginning of the fieldwork, I did the preparation concerning reviewing the literature, defining the research problem, formulating the hypotheses, and making operational definitions. When the study was approved by the Kenana scheme administration, I made a two-week trip to carry out a "pilot survey". After that, I came back to gain approval of the full designation of the research Instrument, questionnaires, and other necessary methods to gather the data. Once I was in the field site, I was helped by the administration manager, public relations manager, and his assistant to find accommodation near the center of the proposed area of study.

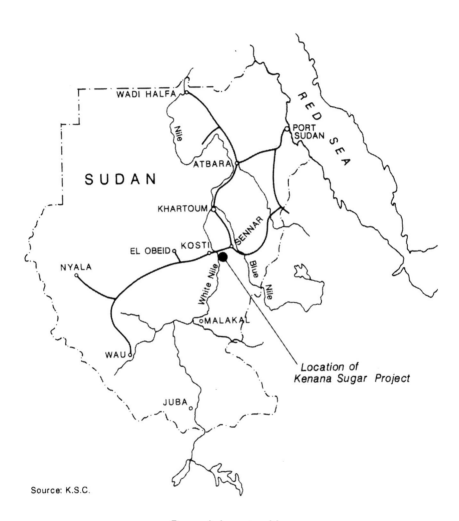

Figure I   Location Map

Source: K.S.C.

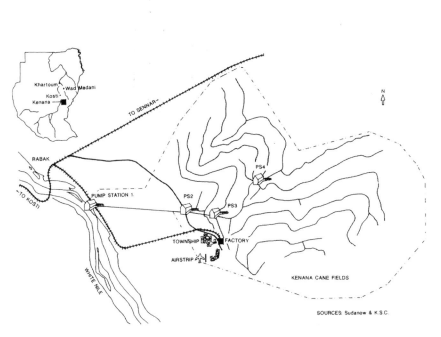

Figure 2 Location of Kenana Sugar Project

The study lasted for twelve months from February 1983 to February 1984. Once I settled down, my goal was to gain more information about the scheme itself. For the broader setting, I did not have any difficulty since I was brought up in the region among a family from the White Nile Baggara Arabs, engaging with them in herding, collecting water, agricultural family labor, and the annual nomadic movement between Southern Sudan and the White Nile Province. I had a "close encounter" with the geography, ecology, environment, language, culture, modes of production, tribesmen, and their shaykhs.

To know the process of change in the region, information about the scheme, its establishment, goals, and future plans are crucial. In a quest for more information about the Kenana Scheme, I had an interview with the General Manager of Sugar Production (GMSP). At the end of the interview I asked him if I could examine some of the files or reports for overnight. He stated that the files and reports were either confidential or for internal use only. Thus, for internal information on the Scheme I depended on some of the Scheme departments, and division circulars, and interviews with key field staff in Kenana, but as time went on, access to some of the information became easier.

In studying the Kenana Scheme community, I categorized the society into five groups:

1.   Officials: Sudanese and Expatriates

2.   Seasonal Laborers

3.   Small Businessmen and other Migrants engaged in the service sector

4   Nomads

5.   Peasants

I employed a field assistant and five enumerators to help conduct the interviews. According to Spradley's approach (1980), "The Development of Research Sequence" in doing enthnography, some tasks are better carried out before others, especially if informants and social situations make access to some depend on others.

So we started things off by gathering information through questionnaires followed by in-depth interviews, participant observation, taking field notes, and using a cassette recorder and a camera to record the ongoing activities. These are the same methods of data gathering we used with every group in the Kenana setting. Unobtrusive observation was used once in a while when the situation demanded it. The most difficult group to interview and gather data from was the expatriates who are part of the officials. The expatriates either don't want to get involved, or they want to be left alone. Although there was no difficulty in gathering information from the nomads and peasants, a lot of them showed frustration and anger, and this was understandable because of the socioeconomic crisis they were facing at this time.

The five enumerators worked with me for six months, while my field assistant worked with me until the completion of the study. In a normal working day, we started early in the morning. We would come back with filled questionnaires, field notes, interviews, etc., in the evening, we start right away checking the questionnaires to make sure they were all correct. We also would go over field notes for correction and comparison. Late at night I would start organizing the daily work including elaboration of condensed notes into an expanded record, and also working on the field journal.

This study is based on four conceptions.

1. Integrated rural development programs, and the breadbasket strategy launched to increase agricultural production and hence boost the export-oriented economy, resulted in environmental and ecological deterioration, aggravation of rural poverty, creation of socioeconomic problems, and above all, landed the Sudan as a food importer instead of being an exporter.

2. Government intervention and forced commercialization of large-scale irrigated agriculture in the rural areas deprived the indigenous

population of their rights of using the land as pastures or fields and gives these rights to private investors.

3. Rural development spearheaded by the multinational corporations, Arab companies, and government bureaucrats has generated serious conflicts of interest between investors and the traditional users of the land. In dealing with this problem, the government forced the indigenous people off the land and hence destroyed self-sustaining economic formations, which resulted in massive out-migration of a considerable number of these traditional communities. The people are now either foraging in far distant areas, or congregating in slums at the edges of towns, looking for subsistence, while the few who are left behind in the new development setting are living in a subhuman situation.

4 When the government forcefully intervenes to change the traditional mode of production and its economic foundation, local inhabitants will be divorced from the means of subsistence. As a result, they will be exposed to starvation and misery, which will contribute to economic and political instability in the country.

Studies of social change have been characterized by limitations in contributing to the body of theory that can be accepted as a united theory of social change. Scholars who tackle the subject often end up formulating their own theory, which cannot be applied to other societies. The approach, theory, and process of change described by a scholar is difficult to apply to another society, not only because societies are different in their aspects of life, but also because this results in them reacting differently to elements and processes of change. In trying to study such a complex process of change in Kenana region, I have to deal with the effect of the new technology on the region. There is also the field staff, expatriates, administration, and migrants from different tribes from Western and Southern Sudan. Then, locally, the impact and process of change that is brought by the development project to transform the lives of a considerable number of nomadic tribes as well as peasant societies in the White Nile Province. Only after starting studying the scheme, officials, seasonal workers, small businessmen, nomadic tribes, peasant societies and the changes they are undergoing, I came to know the benefit of some of the studies carried out by ethnographers, who focused their observation on a single society.

Since the region, the field staff, migrants, nomads, and peasants are undergoing a rapid process of change, the analysis must be reviewed in terms of change and society transformation. In the following chapters, the main features of change and transition are discussed under the titles of environment, ecology, domestic social organization, politics, and mode of production.

THE PHENOMENON OF SOCIAL CHANGE

The phenomenon of social change is complex and inevitable to all types of societies, whether prehistoric, tribal, or modern. However, the factors that are capable of precipitating a given process of social change, its scope, direction, consequences, and speed are markedly different from one type of society to another. The factors that can contribute to the complex process of social change include a historical accident, a catastrophe, war, confiscation of land, new technology, education, government, civil disobedience, the action of political and voluntary organizations, planned economic development, population pressure, and so forth.

In clarifying the concept of social change, scholars have given many definitions, which are meant to describe the phenomenon. For example:

Social change, it is now held, may originate in any institutional area, bringing about changes in other areas, which in turn make for further adaptations in the initial sphere of change. Technological, economic, political, religious, ideological, demographic, and stratificational facts are all viewed as potentially independent variables which influence each other as well as the course of society (Amitai & Etzioni 1964:7).

Sociocultural change includes significant alterations (1) in social organization: the size, formality or informality, kinds of relationships and systems of statuses and roles that characterize groups, including whole societies; (2) in cultural definitions: the knowledge, beliefs, values and norms that guide action, thought and feeling; and (3) in the material products of Sociocultural action (Biesanz & Biesanz 1973:406).

Social change is largely governed by total social setting into which a variable factor or factors have been introduced...By way of summary, social change and the factors which accompany social change are complex, variant, and nonrepetitive, to borrow MacIver's felicitous phrase. More simply, Henri Poincare has said that history does not repeat itself. In some measure, each specific social change is unique, a distinctive product of a time and place. But not wholly unique. Otherwise, social science could not exist (Green 1956:617).

According to Engles "...the final causes of all social changes are to be sought...in the modes of production and exchange" (Cited in Amitai & Etzioni 1964:7).

The phenomenon of social change has been surveyed, studied, and analyzed by many philosophers, political scientists, anthropologists, sociologists, historians, and economists. Despite this, one of the most important facts about the studies and theories of social change is that there is not yet a universal acceptable theory of social change.

It is not possible to give a brief account of the different theories of social change developed by different scholars, for it would be voluminous and beyond the scope of this study. However, it is important to give a bird's-eye view of the most significant theories that underlie crucial features of the process of social change.

Some scholars have adopted evolutionary theories to explain social change. Many early anthropologists followed Darwin's theory of biological evolution to conceptualize that different societies are tested in the evolutionary ladder of natural selection, and if they prove to be adaptable and useful to the community, they continue and survive. According to this theory, human history is ever developing into higher forms, from magic through religion to science, or from savagery through barbarism to civilization. A reverse type of evolutionary theory called "primitivism" argues that man is sliding from an original state of virtue into evil, going backward instead of forward. Contemporary cultural evolutionists, like Leslie White, argue that culture is an independent power that is characterized by greater use of physical energy sources resulting in increasing control of the environment.

Dialectical theorists conceive of the course of history as an upward spiral; each stage of evolution contains its own weaknesses and contradictions, which must be resolved through conflict before the next stage can be reached (Biesanz & Biesanz 1973:407).

The concept of conflict and struggle is considered to be the core element in the studies of the dialectical theorists, because they see conflict as inescapable in all societies. Conflict originates because of opposing interests in the economic and political spheres, struggling for access to scarce resources.

Cyclical theorists of social change say that there is no shorter or longer path that man or society can take to achieve perfection. Every civilization will flourish and decline. An important element in the cyclical theory of social change is the "Rise and Fall" phenomenon discussed at a very early time by Ibn Khaldun, and recently by Sorokin and others. Societies or civilizations are treated as living organisms and are said to go through the stages of birth, youth, decay, and death, giving rise to a new society.

The particularistic theorists of social change believe that transformation in societies can happen because of determinant factors like ecology, geography, religion, or technology. But the particularistic theorists are divided on the issue of whether man plays a crucial role in the process of social change. Some of them believe that social change can occur because of forces beyond man's control. Others, such as Weber, give man a leading role in the process of change.

The sociological theorists generally take a multidimensional approach to the explanation of the phenomenon of social change, where there are a number of factors. If these are not directly responsible for a given social change, they facilitate it. These factors range from education, transportation, communication, demography to industrial and development programs.

In the advanced and developed nations, social change is planned or directed and hence the consequences of it predicted. To put it another way, these countries can promote and control the processes of social change. According to Vasudeva (1976), this is due to the fact that there are some forces that can accelerate the process of social change: a new-felt need and awareness, effective means of communication, transportation, science and technology, education, confrontation with other cultures, cultural exchange of men and material, the appearance of dynamic and effective leadership on the scene, etc. (Vasudeva 1976:4).

Also, he points out that among some of the factors that resist social change are: fear of the new, ignorance, traditions, ethnocentrism, and vested interests. He also added that:

In the developing countries, however, social change comes limping, owing to cultural anaemia (Ibid 1976:2).

However, resistance to social change in the developing nations, or "the slow limping process" of social transformation, can hardly be based on ignorance, traditions, ethnocentrism, or even cultural anaemia. The fact of the matter is that any patterns of change that have swept these nations from the time of the colonialists until the post independence era are bitter and inhuman. The colonialists as well as the present authoritarian governors have practiced exploitation and oppression against the indigenous population. It is no wonder that the process of social change is slow in these countries, and people are reluctant to accept new innovations and development programs, because of the victimization and the suffering involved from the colonial era until today.

Change in a society may be either through violent or non-violent means. The violent social changes come as result of catastrophes, wars, and revolutions, while the peaceful changes come as the result of planning social change, like the introduction of the technological innovations and socioeconomic development programs. But sometimes, socioeconomic development programs can be categorized as violent. For example, when the central government intervenes to force commercialization of irrigated-agriculture in rural Sudan, which is the theme of this book.

DEVELOPMENT PROGRAMS IN THE SUDAN

In the past, the traditional economy of the Sudan depended on three main activities: trade, agriculture, and nomadism. Trade centers flourished along the Nile, for instance Sennar-Berber, or at such places as Swakin in Eastern Sudan and El Fasher in the west. The Sudan was well tied to the trans-Saharan traffic, Arabia and Indian Ocean trade, which led the above mentioned centers to flourish commercially. In the traditional economy, agriculture was practiced by cultivating the Nile silt-banks (gerf), using flood irrigation, water wheels driven by animals (Sagia), and counterweight traditional lever pumps, operated manually (Shaduf). In the clay plains of the Sudan and the South, cultivation depended on rainfed agriculture. The pastoralists and livestock keepers lived in a region extending from the northern fringes of the Sahara to the deep swamp grassland of the South. Although pastoralists had different ethnic origins, their concern was to have large herds of camels, cattle, sheep, or goats. The livestock-keepers engaged in seasonal movements to seek fresh pastures and water for their animals, and also to avoid flies and infested areas of diseases.

Prior to the emergence of large-scale irrigated projects, agricultural land, pastures, and other natural resources were communal to all members of the tribe. The most important characteristic of these societies during that time was their ability to preserve the structure of social order through a feedback system turning on self-sufficiency.

In the 1920s, the Colonial Government established the Gezira scheme. Once the project started the process of production, the Sudanese economy changed drastically. With the construction and development of the Gezira scheme, the National Sudanese economy witnessed the following:

1. The start of a series of large-scale irrigated projects, which became the dominant pattern of Sudanese programs of development until the present.

2. Displacement of tribal users of the land, without having studied alternative plans to accommodate them after their land was expropriated, and hence creating a landless class.

3. Dominance of cotton over grain as the backbone of the economy, which strengthened the linkage between the Sudanese economy and foreign interests. This was an unequal economic relationship that exploited and will continue to exploit Sudanese natural and human resources if the linkage equation is preserved when designing new programs of development.

4. Designing the path for Sudan as an export-oriented country and hence caught in a vicious circle of underdevelopment and structural dependency.

5. Creating bureaucratic and administrative elite who not only has common interests with colonialists, but holds their development policies as a "sacred shrine" from which they cannot deviate in launching new development programs.

6. Concentration on export crops has put greater pressure and practical constraints on the use of human and natural resources to produce grain, which is the staple food in Sudan. In the long run, this has led to the present emergency shortage of food, to famine, and to disguised starvation.

More land was put under irrigation during the 1940s, especially the Blue and White Nile pump schemes. Also during this time (1944), the British started mechanized agriculture in the Gadambiliyya. In the post independent era, the country committed itself to a ten-year plan of economic and social development (1961–1962 to 1970–1971). Although it was interrupted in 1964 because of the October Revolution, projects like Mangil extension, Khashm El Girba and two major dams of El Girba and the El Roseires were completed. In 1970, under the auspices of the central committee of the Sudanese Socialist Union, the five-year plan of economic and social development of the Democratic Republic of the Sudan was declared to cover the period between 1970–1971 and 1974–1975. This included a number of development projects. As the year 1975 was approaching, the Sudan was facing a $100 million shortfall due to the low world demand for cotton and the climbing development expenditure, which was attributed to the increasing demand of import requirements. The five-year plan was extended to cover the period from 1977–1978 to 1982–1983. The most important characteristic of the six-year plan is the designation of the "breadbasket strategy" with the main objective of boosting cash and staple cropping in the rural central rainland of the Sudan. This had the two goals of self-sufficiency internally, and increasing exports as part of the program to strengthen the national economy.

Vast territories were put under cropping, after capital was provided by the Arab states. As a result, Arabian companies and multinational corporations penetrated the rural areas with the help of the government to push commercialization of agriculture. The allocation of four million Feddans by the government to include various rain-fed mechanized agriculture and the irrigated schemes of El Rahad, El Suki, North-West Sennar, Assalaya and Kenana, only worsened the socioeconomic conditions of the rural people, who were forcibly driven out of their traditional land to give way for the construction and development programs that proved to be pockets of colonialism and a burden on the Sudanese economy.

To many development theorists, backwardness and underdevelopment in the third world countries, especially, Africa south of the Sahara, are deeply rooted in tribalism, illiteracy, primitive institutions, traditional attitudes, and population pressure. In contrast, the real sources that are responsible for the persistence of underdevelopment are:

The characteristics of the political, economic, and social institutions created during the colonial era that shaped the export section itself are the primary factors, inhibiting the anticipated spread of modern technology (Seidman 1974:8).

For the sake of stopping persistent underdevelopment, poverty, and starvation, and creating balanced socioeconomic development and equitable distribution of the national resources, a careful reconsideration and vigorous evaluation of existing programs should be adopted by the new government (replaced the military regime in April, 1985). It is necessary to end corruption and mismanagement in order to turn the economy around. According the Uma Lele (1978), development should be carried out to improve the living standards of the masses of low income groups, and the development process should be self-sustaining.

KENANA SUGAR SCHEME

In 1971, the idea of establishing a large-scale sugar project and refinery was developed when the Sudan was importing thousands of tons of sugar. The construction and development of a successful giant sugar project would satisfy the increasing need for the commodity at home and strengthen the national economy by exporting sugar and earning foreign currency. In 1972 after preliminary investigation and geographical surveys, three sites were located for the proposed Kenana Project. These sites were:

1. West bank of the Blue Nile from El Roseires to Singa,

2. East bank of the White Nile from Malakal to Mangala,

3. East bank of the White Nile from Malakal to Kosti. The third site was chosen to be specifically the area between El Jebelein and Rabak on the east bank of the White.Nile, on the grounds that it was more appropriate in terms of water reliability, land topography, a reliable source of power, adequate transportation that links the project and other regions of Sudan, and the availability of seasonal laborers.

The Kenana Sugar Scheme lies 320 kilometers south of Khartoum, 30 kilometers from Rabak, and 36 kilometers from Hajar Assalaya Sugar Scheme. It is connected to Kosti (40km), the largest town in the province, through a concrete arched bridge over the White Nile and hence to Western Sudan.

The Kenana Sugar Company Limited (KSC) was incorporated in March 1975, with the purpose of developing and operating an integrated cane-estate and sugar refinery on land that had been used by Muslim nomads and peasants in the Dar Muharib area as their main source of subsistence. The Kenana Sugar Scheme is a combination of western technology controlled by multinational corporations, Arab petrodollar funds, and Sudanese natural, and manpower resources. Although in 1973, the initial cost of implementing the project had been put at $150 million by Lonrho, the British company; it escalated to over one billion dollars when operations finally started in 1980 to 1981. The rapid escalation of the cost of the Kenana Project was attributed to world inflation and poor Sudanese infrastructure, but the Arab investors who provided the capital think otherwise. They believe that the multinational corporations have taken them for a ride. As a result, suspicion, tension, and conflict of interests began to develop between the multinational corporations and the Arab companies. Lonrho and other multinational corporations were forced to withdraw and the shareholding and power structure in the Kenana Company was revised.

The total size of the Kenana Sugar Project is 150,000 Feddans, of which 80,000 Feddans are under cane cropping. The Scheme is irrigated from the White Nile. Four pump stations lift water at the rate of 34 million gallons an hour to reach the head of the estate at 42 meters above the river level. The Scheme developed the so-called long-farrow irrigation method which sometimes extends to 2 kilometers long. The cultivation of 80,000 Feddans allows the harvest of 17,000 tons of sugar cane, which is crushed in the Kenana factory to produce 1,700 tons of white refined sugar every day, with maximum capacity of 330,000 tons of sugar production per year.

The Kenana Sugar Scheme is managed and administered by Kenana Sugar Company (KSC) composed of public, private, and foreign shareholders. The completion of the Kenana Scheme brought advanced technology, expatriates, officials, rural migrants, and refugees to the area of Dar Muharib, which became the center of attention in the White Nile Province and throughout the Sudan. During the production season the Kenana work force reaches 15,000 of which 8,000 will be laid off during the off-season. However, Kenana employees, whether permanently or seasonally employed, or even migrants working in the service sectors, have a chance for regular or temporary earnings for themselves and their families. The indigenous population of the area have very little chance at all, since they lost their land and grazing rights to the Kenana Scheme.

SOCIAL CHANGE AND SOCIETY TRANSFORMATION IN KENANA REGION

Prior to the development projects and technological advance in Dar Muharib area, the nomads, Baggara Arabs, and peasants were the indigenous population of the area, which lies in the central clay plains of the Sudan. The region is located in the southeastern part of the White Nile Province. For centuries the nomads and the peasants used the open Savannah woodland to pursue pastoral nomadism and agriculture. They were self-sufficient in a non-monetized economy and preserved their tribal sociocultural order. These economies were well-adjusted to the environment around them. There was work all year round to utilize the range of natural resources and the different seasons of the year to the best of their knowledge by using family labor and voluntary working parties (Nafir) during times of peak labor demand.

In the dry season, from November to May, the Baggara Arabs of this region, who rear cattle, sheep and goats, leave Dar Muharib to engage in a long nomadic movement with their livestock to reach the swamp grasslands in Southern Sudan. They begin returning north to Dar Muharib region with the beginning of the rains in the south. In the wet season, from June to October, they herd their livestock and cultivate in the Kenana region. It is at this same time that the peasants of Dar Muharib and their families cultivate their sorghum field before they move to their dry season villages at the banks of the White Nile after harvest.

With the establishment of the Kenana Sugar Scheme and the commercialization of agriculture in the region, nomads as well as peasants have been displaced and forcibly driven out of their ancestral homes that they occupied for generations. They have received no compensation or aid for this devastating loss. The indigenous population of Kenana region was simply forced out, and they were left on their own to suffer the catastrophic consequences. The Kenana Project is the kind of scheme, which is imposed from above, with no endeavor intended to build consensus or to consult with the traditional population of Kenana. This is having far-reaching results. According to Marx:

The expropriation and eviction of a part of the agricultural population not only set free for industrial capital and laborers, their means of subsistence, and material for labor; is also created the home market (1976:910).

The traditional users of the land have little choice. They must either leave the area or stay and try to fit in the new market economy even though they do not have the means or the opportunities to participate. As Green stated:

As a money economy replaced a barter economy and as labor became more free to offer itself to any employer, economic organization grew detached from the control of traditional culture (1956:623).

CHAPTER TWO

GEOGRAPHY AND HISTORY OF THE WHITE NILE PROVINCE

GEOGRAPHY

SIZE AND LOCATION

The White Nile Province is one of the central provinces in Sudan. To the north lies the Province of Khartoum, to the northeast lies the Province of Gezira, to its east and southeast is the Province of the Blue Nile, to the south, the White Nile Province has boundaries with the Upper Nile Province, and to the west lies the Province of Northern Kordofan, and to the southwest it has boundaries with the Province of Southern Kordofan. The northern limit of the White Nile Province is latitude 15° 8' and southern limit is latitude 12° 8' and with longitude of 31° 32' and 32° 56'.

The White Nile Province has a total size of 38,816 square kilometers out of the total Sudan area of 2.5 million square kilometers. Sudan has eighteen different provinces, with much variation in climate, water resources, density of population, agriculture, and urbanization. The White Nile Province, although not of large size in comparison to other provinces, is rich in terms of fertile lands, permanent sources of water, and density of population that provide the working force of the agricultural development schemes, and light industry, in Kosti, Kenana, Assalaya, and Ed Deum. White Nile Province enjoys a diversification in economic activities and production. It has an area of 535,000 Feddans under mechanized cropping to produce sorghum (dura) millet and oil seeds (sesame and groundnuts). As a result, White Nile Province is one of the main grain supplies in the country. It is also famous for its oil seed crushing factories. A total area of 450,000 Feddans is under cotton. Because of cotton grown in the Province, there are a number of ginning factories in Kosti and Rabak, also there are textile industries in Kosti

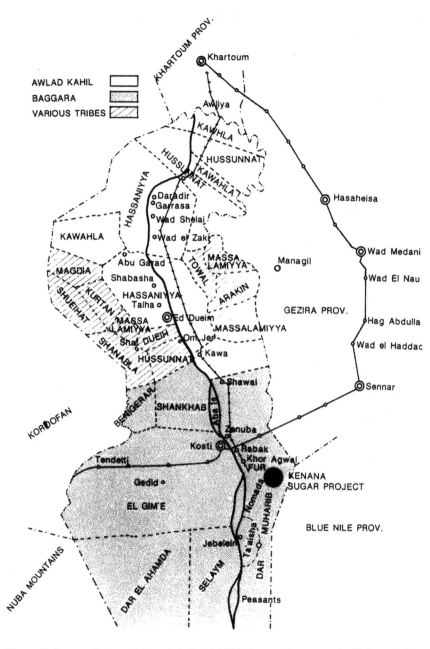

Figure 3 Source: Adapted from J.A. Reid 1930; Some Notes on the Tribes of the White Nile Province. Sudan Notes and Records, Vol. XIII, Part II, pp. 149–213.

and Ed Deum that produce 9 million feet of cloth annually. It is one of the most productive provinces for white sugar in Sudan because of the twin sugar schemes in the area.

Kenana and Assalaya, altogether produce 440,000[1] tons of white sugar annually, while the rest of the sugar factories in Sudan (El Geneid, Khashm El Girba and North-West Sennar) produce 226,000 tons of white sugar annually. Also, the White Nile Province leads the country in cement industry, producing 100,000 tons of cement annually at Rabak cement factory. One of the most important reasons that led this kind of industry to flourish in Rabak town is the closeness of the cement raw material southeast of the factory site at Rabak. The area is also rich in traditional farming (400,000 Feddans) and nomadic pastoralism. The Baggara and Jammala keep 1.2 million cattle, 0.6 million camels, 2.5 million sheep, and over 1 million goats. Towns like Rabak and Kosti have a reputation as among the most important livestock markets in Sudan, mainly because these towns are not far away from the nomads, besides, they have access to all seasons roads and railways that connect them to the biggest towns in the east and north: Sennar, Wad Medani, and Khartoum (Amir 1980:19).

CLIMATE AND NATURAL VEGETATION

Landscape and relief forms are significantly affected by the type of climate that exists. There are two important landscape features in the White Nile Province. The first is the area of the stabilized dunes (Qoz) in the northwest of the Province. The second is the so-called "clay plains" that constitute the rest of the Province. But the most important of natural features of the landscape in the region is the White Nile, which makes the region one of the most cultivatable and livable areas in the Sudan.

The important features of the climate in the Province are the long dry season (November to May) and the short wet season (June to October), with the maximum rainfall in July and August. The White Nile Province lies within the savannah belt. Its northern territories receive rainfall of 200mm, and the southern fringes receive rainfall of 600mm. But recently, because of the wave of desertification and drought in the country, especially the season of 1984 to 1985, in the Province, like other parts of the Sudan, rainfall is less than half the usual annual average. As a result 4 million people have been displaced from Kordofan and Dar Fur. The displaced people headed toward the "green provinces" White Nile, Gezira, Khartoum, and the Blue Nile.

The natural vegetation, to a great extent, depends on the type of soil and the amount of precipitation. In the wet season, the northwest of the White Nile Province gets poor rain in comparison to the rest of the region. So it is a semi-desert area with sparse thorn scrubland and short grass. The rest of the Province is green in the wet season. It supports a vegetation complex known as the "open savannah woodland" with acacia trees, and short to medium grass. During the dry season, most of the grass either is grazed by animals or destroyed by fire (Lebon 1961:10–11).

Throughout the regions of the White Nile Province, there is no dominant grass, but there are many species, including Cymbopogon giganteum, Cymbopogon nervatus. Sorghum purpureosericeum. Rottboellia exaltata, Sehima ischaemoides. Schoenefidia gracilis, and other herbs like Ocimum basilicum and Fagonia cretica, (Kenana Reports on Agriculture). Also in the wet season the acacia trees throughout the region look fresh and green. The type of acacia that are found in the region are Acacia Senegal (Hashab), Acacia Mellifera (Kitter), and Acacia Seyal (Talih). The region of Kenana is known as the short grass country, where these kinds of acacia are dominant. The annual rainfall for Kenana region is 400mm. Kenana region lies between the north semi-desert and the south tall-grass acacia forests, which include, Balanites Aegyptiaca (Heqliq), Acacia Sieberiana (Kouk), Hyphaene Thebaica (Dom), and Borassus Aethiopium (Daelib). As one travels from the north to the south, the vegetation and acacia trees become thicker.

ROADS AND THE TRANSPORTATION SYSTEM

The well known route of transportation in the past was the White Nile. It was used as a route of travel by the Nilotic people in their canoes and rafts. In the 1830s, the route to the southern region was opened for missionaries, merchants, and slave traders. These people used wooden boats to go down the river. As the steamers were introduced during the Anglo-Egyptian era, the town of Kosti came to be the biggest river port in the Sudan. Since independence, most of the commodities and equipment going south are shipped from Kosti. The White Nile is a very important transportation artery between Khartoum and Juba with a navigable distance of 2,220 kilometers, which has made it vital for communication between Northern and Southern Sudan.

The White Nile Province is also linked to the national railway networks. The railway runs from Sennar to Rabak and Kosti. From Kosti the railway goes to Kordofan and Dar Fur. In 1976, a 30 kilometer railway was extended from Rabak to Kenana factory to facilitate the transportation of sugar.

One of the oldest roads was the route from Sennar, used during the Funj Kingdom; it goes to Kordofan and Dar Fur via the White Nile region. Also ancient are the roads that follow the White Nile banks north and south.

With the increasing number of vehicles in use since the beginning of the century, different networks of roads were opened up: Khartoum Rabak to El Jebelein to Malakal, and another one from Omdurman to Ed Deum to Kosti to Kaka to Kadok, and from Sennar to Rabak to Kosti, and then to Kordofan and Dar Fur. The problem with these roads is that they are dusty and hard in the dry season, and muddy, wet and impassable in the rainy season.

During the early 1980s, Rabak and Kosti were linked to the national network of all weather roads. The first hard surface road came from Sennar to Kosti with a distance of 103 kilometers. The second one from Khartoum to Rabak to Kosti with a distance of 353 kilometers. The development projects of Kenana and Assalaya are linked to the all weather roads by gravel and surface treated roads.

The hard surface road to the region has enhanced the flow of goods and services, between Khartoum to White Nile to Western Sudan and the South and facilitated individual and group mobility from one region to another.

There are no national airports in the White Nile Province. What is found are a number of small air strips in Kosti, Ed Deum, Assalaya, and Kenana, to make it possible for small aircrafts to land, especially in the cotton spraying season for Ed Deum and Kosti. As for Assalaya and Kenana, they have regular trips between Khartoum and their factories' sites.

MAIN TOWNS

Most of the population still lives in rural villages, but with a growing trend of choosing to live in the urban areas, or urban growth centers. Most of the villages and nomadic camps are not permanent. Some people leave their first village to live in another one, while the nomads are always on the move, looking for grazing and water. The dominant characteristics of the settlement pattern are the big village and the small towns, but some big towns have started to emerge with a high density of population, schools, transport systems, and other social services. These towns are Ed Deum, Kosti, El Gezira Aba, Rabak, Kenana, El Jebelein, and Tendelti.

The small towns are (starting from the north): El Qutaina, Dardir, Wad El Zaki, El Kawa, El Shawal, El Marabe, Assalaya, Goda; on the western side of the White Nile bank are: Shabasha, Om Jer, El Fashoshoya, Elshor, Guoli, El Zelait, El Naiem, and Gadid.

ED DEUM.

The town of Ed Deum gained its importance as a developed trading center before any other town in the Province. It was an important port for the boats going south, taking grain and meat supplies. It was also a very significant animal market since it was in the heart of the northern nomadic region of the White Nile territories. Ed Deum became of military importance when El Mahadi declared his revolution in El Gezira Aba in 1881. At that time, a Turco-Egyptian force of 500 soldiers defended the town against the repeated attack of the Ansar.[2] At the arrival of Hicks to Ed Deum in 1883, it became a military base for the forces that wanted to go to Kordofan and Dar Fur. Hicks moved from Ed Deum, heading west with his army to meet El Mahadi, but he was defeated in Shaykan in 1883.

In the early period of Anglo-Egyptian rule, Ed Deum was made capital of the Province, but after the establishment of Jebel Awliya Dam, it was reduced to a district, which in 1939 was part of the Blue Nile Province. After independence, Ed Deum remained as a district until the new government in 1974 declared Ed Deum the Province capital town of the White Nile Province. Ed Deum played an important role in the process of spreading education in the country through its educational training center of Bakhat El Ruda. Although Ed Deum is the capital province, it ranks second in terms of population size (Amir 1980:199–200).

EL GEZIRA ABA

Gezira means "island," and Aba is a Shilluk name. El Gezira Aba is the biggest island in the White Nile. It starts from Ta'iba (northeast of Kosti) in the south until near El Shawal in the north. It is homeland for many people, nomadic as well as agriculturalists. During the nineteenth century, the area was famous for its thick and long savannah wooded forest, which attracted traditional boat builders, including the family of El Mahadi from Northern Sudan.

El Mahadi started his Jihad and revolution in El Gezira Aba. After the migration of El Mahadi and his Ansar to Kordofan, El Gezira Aba lived in decline until the mid 1940s when western tribes started gathering around El Sayed Abdel Rahaman El Mahadi in El Gezira Aba. The new migrants from Western Sudan took cotton tenancy from El Shawal north to El Jebelein and El Naeim south.

In 1970, El Gezira witnessed a bloody battle in El Jasir[3] between the new government and the traditional poorly equipped Ansar. Since that time, El Gezira Aba has undergone great economic and social changes. Under the new administration, a town council was created, new administrative building built, and most importantly, some of the schools, dressing stations, and artesian wells were spread around.

According to the third national census (1983), El Gezira Aba has a population size of 19,632 persons. Most of the town economy depends on trade and agriculture. It is the trading center for all the villages northeast of it, which belong to El Gezira rural council. The agricultural population is mostly migrants from Western Sudan, who leave El Gezira to spend the agricultural season at Gafa and Om Gidian. After harvest, they come again to their residential quarters in Aba.

Aba gained great importance when Assalaya and Kenana sugar schemes were implemented in the late 1970s and early 1980s. These two sugar projects offered a considerable number of jobs for people of Aba.

RABAK

At the beginning of the century, Rabak was a small village at the bank of the White Nile. It was flooded when Jebel Awliya Dam was established. The village was located in a new site, which is not far away from the flooded village. The place was called Qoz Abu Gimm'a, where some of Dar Muharib settled. Qoz Abu Gimm'a began to attract construction laborers when the cantilever bridge across the White Nile was in the process of establishment in 1911. When the cantilever bridge was completed, new villages emerged around Rabak to accommodate the increasing number of newcomers. The cantilever bridge made it accessible for trains, automobiles, people, and livestock to cross the river in both directions, although the traffic through the bridge was deadly slow.

Rabak town began to grow quickly after cotton ginning factories and oil seed crushing factories were established in the 1960s. In 1974, new plans to modernize the town were made. A project of healthy and reliable water supply network was completed in 1976. New social services were introduced, and a new market was built in 1982. At the same time, the bigger sugar factories in the country began operating not far from Rabak town. Assalaya sugar factory is six kilometers away, while Kenana sugar factory is 30 kilometers away. Rabak gained more strategic position when an all weather road passed through the town. Also, a modern suspension arch bridge replaced the slow steel cantilever one. Rabak began to invite workers from different parts of Sudan to work in the large-scale sugar development schemes and the light industries like Rabak cement factory, cotton ginning, and oil crushing factories.

Until the early 1970s, Rabak had only two primary schools. Now it has eight with two intermediate schools and a higher secondary school. A hospital with a 40 bed capacity will be built, and a non-all weather movie theatre is going to find its place in Rabak.

According to the third national census of 1983, Rabak has a population size of 26,786 persons, constituting different ethnic groups. The residential pattern in Rabak resembles that of El Gezira Aba, each tribe, or ethnic group, lives together in a certain part of the town, and it called that part after their tribal name, e.g. Hillt Nazza (Rabak). Other ethnic groups are allowed if they want to live in another tribal residential area, but most people found it convenient to live near their tribal kinsfolk, especially during the times of social occasions or emergencies. The different ethnic groups that are living in Rabak are: Sabaha, Nazza, Kibayshab, Danagla, Shaygiyya, Ja'aliyyin,

Rizagat, Misseriyya, Mima, Bani Halba, Fellata, and others. The town is taking a new shape as the huts and mud houses are replaced with red brick houses.

KOSTI

Kosti has a very strategic position, and it assumes a lot of significant roles that have made it the most famous town in the White Nile Province and allowed it a unique economic role in the Sudan economy as a whole.

The Kosti site was chosen by a Greek trader who used to live in Zenuba (eastern bank of the White Nile). He found that his customers who were producing dura, gum arabic, and dairy products had great difficulty in crossing the White Nile to sell their commodities at the Zenuba market. To make things easier for them, he constructed a small compound where people coming from long distances could rest and sell their products. As the new place had no name, it was called after the Greek trader's name and became Kosti in 1902.

As the small village grew economically active, the British authorities found the Kosti site acceptable to replace Zenuba as a river port for their steamers between Khartoum and Juba in Southern Sudan.

In 1911, Kosti witnessed a radical change and started to grow fast after it was made a capital district. As the steel cantilever bridge was completed, and the railway was extended from Sennar through Kosti to Western Sudan, Kosti started to play an important role from a transportation point of view. As the result of the establishment of Jebel Awliya Dam, Kosti was flooded like other towns on the bank of the White Nile. Kosti was rebuilt, but in a modern style with nice residential areas, offices, schools, and public gardens.

Starting from the 1940s, cotton was grown up and down the White Nile to be the backbone of the economy. Kosti flourished when cotton was ginned and transported from there. The existence of cotton ginning factories later on paved the way for a successful textile industry in Kosti. Another one of its successful industries is cooking oil production (from oil seeds). Kosti has one of the best grain and livestock markets in the Sudan, due to its position not far from the agricultural regions, and very near to the nomadic population of the area.

After the establishment of Kenana and Assalaya sugar schemes and after the completion of the new White Nile Bridge in 1982, the size of the Kosti population started to boom. According to the third national census, the town has a population of 91,919 people. To accommodate the increasing population, new residential extensions were made and new social services were located in the Kosti outskirts. In the last census, demographers noted that Kosti had the highest rate of growth in the country, and so it is estimated that in the year 2000 its population size will be 200,000 people, which requires an early urban plan to deal with its anticipated density (Amir 1980:188–192; Kosti Town Council Reports).

THE NEW TOWNS "SUGAR TOWNS"

The new towns in the Province are Assalaya and Kenana. These towns are less than ten years old. If one looks to these towns, they are fully developed to be urban centers. They enjoyed rapid development because they are part of the two largest-scale irrigated sugar schemes in the country.

The construction of these sugar schemes went hand in hand with the construction of the towns of Assalaya and Kenana. Each has zoned residential areas, senior, intermediate, and junior. The housing is made of concrete foundations, concrete block walls, and insulation board ceiling, with the necessary electrical installation. The higher the social status one enjoys the better residential facilities one will have. As far as the daily laborers and the nomads are concerned, they live in thatched huts (camps) or mud brick houses. This kind of residence lacks the potable supply of water and electricity and is crowded. This type of population forms the bulk of the town dwellers. More importantly, these towns were a leap forward, when medical service, water supplies, schools, mosques, playgrounds, and markets were made to serve the population. The availability of seasonal and sometimes permanent jobs drew people to make a rush migration to Assalaya and Kenana sugar scheme sites. Migrants have been coming from many provinces of the Sudan to find work in these projects. Kenana town grew into an urban center of 60,000 people in less than ten years (1976 to 1984).

POPULATION

During the past five centuries the White Nile territories were largely occupied by the Nilotic people. As northern agriculturalists and the Arab nomadic tribesmen migrated to the White Nile region, the Nilotic tribes started to retreat south. The situation was made worse by slave traders, especially during the Turco-Egyptian regime.

The main nomadic pastoralists who claimed tribal territories are, starting from the north: Kawahla, Hassaniyya, Hussunnat, Magdia, Massalamiyya, Towal, Arakin, Kurtan, Shuewahat, Dueih, Shanabla, Shankhab, Bani Garar, Dar Muharib, Nazza, Khanferiya, Kibayshab, Sabaha, Rawashda, Sebaig, Degheim, Muhammediyya, Ahamda, Selaym, Ta'aisha, and Gim'e. Other nomadic tribes that spend the rainy season in the White Nile Province are Kenana and Rufa'a al Hoi.

There are other tribes who left their territories and came to the White Nile region as families, or sections of their main tribes. These tribes are: Danagla, Ja'aliyyin, Shaygiyya, Ga'afara, Ababda, El Konuz, El Rekabiyya, El Nuba, El Fur, Mima, Dajo, Bani Hussein, Berti, Tama, Rezagat, Bani Halba, Habbaniya, and Fellata (Reid 1930:149–206;[4] Amir 1980:25–26). Most of these tribes adapted themselves to the White Nile environment. They are either dwelling in urban centers, sendentary villages, or nomadic camps. People who are living in towns are engaging in trade and commerce activities, while others are working as government officials, factory workers, etc. The sedentary villagers are peasants and small farmers. The sedentary villages provide a pool of labor for the mechanized agriculture and the national development schemes like

Kenana and Assalaya. The third category are the nomads who are still engaging in seasonal movements looking for water and pastures while at the same time trying to avoid places of agriculture.

According to the 1983 (third) national census, the White Nile Province has a population of 933,136 persons, categorized as the following:

Table 2.1

WHITE NILE PROVINCE POPULATION BY CATEGORY

Catagory	No.	Percentage
Urban	270370	29%
Rural Settled	530529	57%
Nomads	132237	14%
TOTAL	933136	100%

Source: Third National Population Census 1983.
Kosti Town Council Reports

As we near the 21st century, more nomads will be sendentarized and join the villagers, while more villagers will join town dwellers. The categories of the villagers and the nomads are experiencing the economic pressure, which results when their main cropping and grazing lands are put under development projects. This policy will lead these two groups to seek other livelihood alternatives in the foreseeable future.

HISTORY

The Nile is one of the most important rivers in the world. It makes its way thousands of miles to reach the mediterranean. The significance of the Nile was known before 4,000 years ago by the ancient Egyptian monarchs. The annual flood was welcomed by colorful festivals and sacrifices once every year to stimulate its continuity, since they knew little about its source and origin.

Where the Nile begins, inspired the imagination of many explorers, from early times until the 19th century. Despite little knowledge of the nature of the tropics, diseases, insects, or hostile tribesmen, some explorers were successful in tracing it and returning from the adventure to talk about the source of the White Nile and its people.

THE NILOTIC PEOPLE OF THE WHITE NILE REGION

The early dwellers of the White Nile region were the Shilluk and the Dinka, who belong to the Nilotic tribes of the Sudan. The place of origin of the Nilotic tribes is thought to lie to the east of the Great Lakes. From their place of origin, they emigrated in waves and series of movements, the movements were known by their tribal name (Seligman 1932:18).

Although the first waves of emigration were believed to be more than one thousand years ago, some tribes continued to emigrate until recent times. Coming all this long way, they conquered and assimilated many people. The Nilotic people have common physical features; they are tall, long headed, very dark skinned and woolly haired (Ibid 1932:13) .

The Shilluk and the Dinka are cattle keepers. Also, they raise some sheep and goats. Through time, they developed a transhumant pursuit of life. The Shilluk lived on the western bank of the White Nile, while the Dinka lived on the eastern bank. During the middle ages, the region of the Nilotes started to witness war and continuous raids. The war and raids were launched to claim cattle, women, slaves, and pasture rights. The Shilluk and the Dinka could not expand south during the middle ages because of the war-like and hostile Nuer tribe. So the Dinka and the Shilluk expanded their territories to the north, to accommodate the growing number of people and animals. As they were roaming the White Nile grassland and waterways, they encountered a northern threat "The Funj" of Sennar.

The Shilluk and the Dinka began their skirmishes against the Funj armies around the 17th century. Initially, they gained some victories, but their repeated conquest attempts were repelled by the Funj armies. The Shilluk made an alliance with the Funj Sultan Badi II (1635–1650) to protect them against the Dinka. Through that alliance the Dinka expansion to the north and west was checked (O'Fahey and Spaulding 1974:61–66).

THE ARABS IN SUDAN AND THE WHITE NILE REGION

Contact between "Bilad el Sudan,"[5] or "land of the Blacks" as it was called by medieval Arabic writers, and Arabia existed long before Islam. Arabia, with its poor grazing and water resources, witnessed small families and groups of immigrants to Bilad el Sudan. The earlier nomadic immigrants took a number of routes to reach the land of the Blacks; the first one was across the Sinai desert to Egypt, and then into Eastern Sudan, the second from Hijaz across the Red Sea into Sudan, the third from Southwestern Arabia across the strait of Bab El Mandab into Abyssinia, and then into Buttana and then Gezira (Hassan 1973:12–16).

The massive emigration by the Arab into Sudan came after the conquest of Egypt (Seventh Century). However, not quickly because the Nubians put up a stiff resistance for six centuries before a Muslim take-over of Dongola. Also, it is worth mentioning that Islamic traders and teachers were penetrating Nubia and other parts of Sudan, and thus a slow process of Islamization was taking place well in advance of large movement. In 1275, the Mamluks of Egypt launched an attack against Nubia. The military expedition was a combination of Mamluks and Arab tribesmen, who conquered the Nubians and captured Dongola. The conquest of Nubia by Mamluks and Arab tribesmen marked an era of rapid and massive emigration of the Arab of Upper Egypt into the Sudan. Now the door was wide open for Muslim Arab traders, cultivators, and nomads, especially the tribes of Rabi'a and Juhayna (Ibid 1973:100–128).

As the White Nile region had great potential, different tribes started to scramble over its territories. Between the 15th and 18th century, many tribes came from Northern Sudan and settled in the northern part of the White Nile territory. The Danagla and their families settled and worked in building boats in the present towns of Wad El Zaki, El Kawa, El Garasa, and El Gezira Aba (Amir 1980:32).

Also the Ja'aliyyin were attracted to the area after the early 16th century. Their main occupations were agriculture and trade. Sometimes they lived with the Danagla, but their main towns are Ed Deum and Shabasha. The Shaygiyya, like the former Danagla and Ja'aliyyin, came from Northern Sudan into the White Nile region. Shaygiyya were mainly adventurers, so they were employed by the Turco-Egyptian regime as armed guards and soldiers to accompany the boats and expeditions to the south. The rest of them settled in towns of El Qutaina, Wad El Zaki, El Kawa, Ed Deum, and Abu Hibera (Ibid 1980:32–33).

The nomadic pastoralists who made the White Nile their homeland came one tribe after the other, but the first to be known were the Kawahla (Awlad Kahil). Some of the Kawahla subgroups like El Hussunnat, El Magawir, El Ahamda, and El Muhammediyya migrated to southern territories of the White Nile and became semi-nomadic folks (Reid 1930:150).

The southern part of the White Nile Province west of the river bank was occupied by Baggara Arabs (cattle keepers). They were Selaym, Ahamda, and El Gim'e and on the eastern bank of the White Nile territories, the nomadic tribes were the tribes of Dar Muharib, and the seasonal visitors of the Blue Nile territories, like, Rufa'a al Hoi, and Kenana.

The increasing encroachment of the nomadic and sedentary settlers disturbed the Shilluk who used to have their northern boundaries between the mountain of El Arashukol and the present town of Ed Deum. Most historians and travelers noted that the Shilluk retreated peacefully after the area was penetrated by the nomadic tribesmen. According to Mr. Reid (ex-governor of the White Nile Province) conquest was the way to gain tribal territories. Also Wad Dayfallah, in his book El Tabagat,[6] points out that the Shilluk killed the Kawahla's Shaykh crossing the river near El Arashukol after he came from his visit to the Sultan of Sennar in the 16th century. So the accounts of Mr. Reid and Wad Dayfallah show that war and skirmishes existed at least for sometime between the Nilotes and the nomads who were drifting from north and west.

The emergence of the nomadic pastoralists in the territories of the White Nile generated a lot of competition in the region. As a result, the Shilluk and the Dinka retreated deeply into the southern fringes, and the situation was made worse when the slave-traders became active in the upper White Nile territories in the 18th and 19th centuries.

SLAVE TRADE IN THE WHITE NILE

Mohammed Ali Pasha sent his son Isma'il Pasha and the Defterdar in 1820 to 1821 to conquer Sennar, Kordofan, and the Nilotic Sudan. One of the main objectives of the conquest was to send new recruits of black Sudanese to build a new strong army for Mohammed Ali in Egypt, besides collecting gold from Sudan.

Isma'il went to the region of Fazughli to bring slaves and gold (Upper Blue Nile). His brother Ibrahim went across the Gezira to the White Nile to attack the Dinka, and the Defterdar was left with Nuba Mountain and the territory of the Shilluk (Shibeika 1971:142).

Most of them were unsuccessful in their expeditions, but still large numbers of slaves were sent to Egypt, especially after Isma'il was killed in Shendi in 1822. The Defterdar made intensive punitive campaigns against many tribes in the Sudan, and when his savage attacks were over, he ordered all prisoners of war, whether free men caught in the attacks or slaves, to be shipped to Egypt.

In 1839, Salim Qabudan[7] opened the White Nile route south, as far as Bahr El Jabal. The opening of the White Nile to the south marked the beginning of an era that brought undesirable contact between the missionaries, the slave traders, and the pagan tribes of the south. The Europeans, Egyptians, Syrians, and the Jallaba (traders from Northern Sudan) were first attracted to the ivory, but it took no time to shift to slave trade. The traders constructed the so-called "Zaribas," and sometimes it had to be guarded by the slave troops known as the "Bazingers." In most cases, the slave troops constituted half of the traders' force. The traders subordinated the tribes that lived between the Dinka and the Azande (Holt and Daly 1961:70–71).

By the early 1850s the region of Upper Nile and Bahr El Ghazal was wide open to adventurers and slave traders who were operating far beyond the control of the Turco-Egyptian authorities. As a result of this slave-trade, large segments of the southern tribes were deeply affected, their social structure, political, and economic life were destroyed. Although later in the 19th century, under the European pressures and other countries, slave trade was abolished, and it left scars that took a long time to heal.

CONFLICTS, WARS, AND COMPETITION BETWEEN THE WHITE NILE BAGGARA ARABS

With the influx of nomadic migrants into the White Nile a strong tribe called El Massalamiyya, who claimed their descent to Abu Bakr El Siddig, settled around the present area of Gadid west of Kosti; they occupied a rich place in pastures. El Massalamiyya, under the leadership of Shaykh Hamid El Sa'id, were harassing the nomadic groups that sometimes seek pastures at their region. As a result of this, the tribes of the Baggara in the region under the leadership of El Gim'e and Dar Muharib found it convenient to attack El Massalamiyya, while the army of King Adam[8] of Jebel Tagali headed to war with them.

So the strongest tribe was defeated by the Tagala'ween and the Baggara in the Battle of Om Hajar southwest of Tandalti. After the battle of Om Hajar around the beginning of the 19th century, the leader of Dar Muharib, Isma'il Wad Marymi, went to war with El Ahamda for the sake of taking over their rich land west of the White Nile. The tribe of El Ahamda was defeated, and their leader Shaykh Abu Sair was killed (Reid 1930:176–177).

The tribes of Dar Muharib, shortly after their victory over El Ahamda, were ready to go to war over killing of a cow by a Selaymi;[9] therefore, the tribe of Selaym made an alliance with El Gim'e to stand against the arrogance of Dar Muharib. Dar Muharib was defeated and crossed the White Nile to the east. After this battle, the western bank of the White Nile came under the leadership of Abu Kalam the Chief of El Gim'e tribe. But the leadership over Selaym, El Ahamda, and El Shankhab was informal, so every tribe managed its own affairs; only in the case of external threats did these tribes unite under one leadership.

During the Turco-Egyptian regime, heavy taxes were imposed on the Baggara Arabs of the White Nile; the heaviest of all was the cattle tax: "Daribat El Guto'an." The cattle tax was something new to these nomadic tribes. The leader of Dar Muharib, Isma'il Wad Marymi, refused to pay the cattle tax, so he was killed by the Turco-Egyptian authorities. As for Abu Kalam of El Gim'e, Selaym and El Ahamda, they chose to submit and pay the expensive cattle tax because they could not stand against the Turco-Egyptian regime and its fire arms.

The conflict and war continued between the White Nile Baggara Arabs for the sake of territorial domains and raids for cattle. In 1870, Selaym and El Gim'e clashed in the battle of "Dabat el Tor" in the southern part of the White Nile. They lost heavily in terms of people and cattle. The Turco-Egyptian government contained the situation and imposed more taxes and a peace treaty. Abu Kalam was taken to be imprisoned in Egypt when he failed to capture some nomads who murdered a group of Lahawe'yin in his region. He died in Egypt, and his son, Asakir Abu Kalam, was installed as a new leader for El Gim'e shortly before the Mahadi revolution in 1881 (Ibid 1930:178).

THE MAHADIST STATE AND THE WHITE NILE: AN ERA OF DRAINING THE AREA OF PEOPLE AND CATTLE

In 1881, Mohammed Ahmed el Mahadi started his revolution in El Gezira Aba. He made his first victory against the Turco-Egyptian forces in Aba. This incident turned the tribes of the White Nile and the west to become "Ansar" "El Mahadi followers" after they were convinced that he was "El Mahadi El Muntazar" or the "awaited deliverer," who would fill the world with justice and equity, after it had been filled with oppression and tyranny.

Some followers had a true Muslim faith, so they came from different parts of Sudan to see El Mahadi and swear allegiance to him. Others joined him because they were dissatisfied and filled with grievances against the Turco-Egyptian regime. El Mahadi left Aba to Jebel Qadir in Kordofan to start a new phase in the "Jihad" (Holy War) against the Turks. Many people from different tribes joined him, from and around the White Nile region, from El Gim'e area, El Mahadi was joined by Abdullahi El Ta'aishi (later known as Khalifat El Mahadi), who used to live with Ta'aisha family in Dar El Gim'e. Also El Khalifa Ali Wad Hilu joined him from the tribe of Degheim, but some of the White Nile Baggara Arabs did not join the Jihad of El Mahadi, and they preferred to look after their pastures, cattle, and sorghum (dura) fields. After the capture of El Obied in 1883, El Mahadi asked their leader Asakir Abu Kalam and his men to join him. Asakir Abu Kalam and his men moved to Kordofan and supported El Mahadi to defeat Hicks in the Battle of Shaykan in November 1883. After the Shaykan battle, Asakir Abu Kalam came to the White Nile and sent his son Omar to participate in the capture of Khartoum. Omar was killed with the army of Musa Wad Hilu in the Battle of Abu Tilayh (Reid 1930:179).

In 1885, when El Khalifa Abdullahi El Ta'aishi came to power, he called Asakir Abu Kalam to Omdurman. Then he arrested and imprisoned him on the grounds that he backed away from the Jihad against the enemies of Allah. Asakir's brother, El Faki Argoub, became in charge of El Gim'e affairs. Like his brother, he was not devoted that much to El Mahadiyya. Hostilities and hatred developed quickly between El Khalifa and El Faki Argoub. El Khalifa ordered one of his leaders in Fashoda, Yunis el Dikaym, to attack El Faki Argoub in Dar Selaym, where he was taking refuge. El Faki Argoub was taken by surprise and speared to death, and his property was made booty. All the able-bodied who belonged to El Faki Argoub's family were sent to El Khalifa, who sent them to fight with Hamdan Abu Anja in the Eastern Front in 1887 against the Abyssinians.

After Yunis el Dikaym confiscated El Gim'e and Selaym wealth and made their men captives, he crossed the White Nile into Dar Muharib to investigate their non-participation in the Jihad. Yunis el Dikaym made a truce with El Sabaha, but he demanded a fine of cattle that left the tribe broke. The rest of the tribe of Dar Muharib were defeated by the Jihadiyya (Khalifa firearmed men). Their cattle were taken away, and their captive men were sent to Dar Fur to abort the revolt of Abu Jummayza with the army of Mahmud Wad Ahmed.

Toward the end of El Khalifa regime, most of the Baggara Arabs of the White Nile were propertyless. Selaym changed their propertyless situation when General Ahmed Fadil and his army came from Kassala, crossed the White Nile into their region to strengthen the position of El Khalifa Abdullahi at Omdibaykrat. Selaym people attacked the end of Fadil's army and ran away with a considerable number of livestock and other supplies. Selaym quickly distributed the livestock among their different lineages and went deep into the southern jungles. General Ahmed Fadil had no time to follow Selaym, because General Wingate[10] was following him from behind. On the 24th of November, 1899, El Khalifa Abdullahi and his General Ahmed Fadil, and a number of his supporters were killed in Omdibaykrat by Wingate's military expedition. The battle witnessed the end of the Mahadist state.

At the beginning of the reoccupation of the White Nile by the Anglo-Egyptian regime, the Baggara Arabs suffered a heavy drain of able-bodied men, cattle and sorghum supplies, these heavy losses left these tribes very poor to the extent they were trying to make subsistence by snaring guinea fowl and spearing fish (Ibid 1930:180).

THE WHITE NILE, TERRITORIES OR A NEW PROVINCE

At the beginning of the Anglo-Egyptian regime, (1899 to 1956), the Baggara tribes of the White Nile expressed their need for separate Nazara[11] for every tribe, which means every tribe governs its own affairs. The condominium authorities refused and started to combine many tribes. That policy succeeded in generating hatred and hostilities between the tribes of the White Nile rather than bringing peace.

During the Anglo-Egyptian rule, the Sudan was divided into different provinces. The provinces never stayed the same. Every now and then, their boundaries were changed according to the administrative strategy of the condominium rule. Every province was ruled by a governor (Mudir) responsible to the Governor-General through the colonial administrative system. Every province was divided into districts Sing-Markez, each ruled by a British inspector (Mufattish), and later, in 1922, their position was changed to be district commissioners. The districts also were divided into sub-districts, and the Egyptian "Mamurs" were in charge of the sub-districts (Holt and Daly 1961:122). During the beginning of the condominium rule, the White Nile region did not stand by itself as a separate province, but parts of it were annexed to other provinces. Dar Muharib region was included in the Province of Sennar, which was established in 1899, but in 1902 the name was changed to the Gezira Province. Dar Selaym and the southern part of the White Nile region were included in Fashoda Province.

In 1904, the White Nile territories were declared to be a separate province to include the northern part of the White Nile region, Dar Muharib, Dar Selaym, Dar El Ahamda, and Dar El Gim'e. From 1904 to 1940, the White Nile Province was ruled by seven British governors (Mudirs); their capital province was Ed Deum, the center of administrative, and political power. The White Nile population suffered from heavy taxes imposed by the Condominium rule, so people tried different subsistence strategies, ranging from growing cash crops like ground nuts, to picking cotton, to tapping gum arabic.

In November 1940, the White Nile Province was combined to be part of the Blue Nile Province, and it remained so until it was declared a separate Province again in 1974 (Amir 1980:22–24).

CHAPTER TWO NOTES

1. The share of Kenana expected production is 330,000 tons. The one of Assalaya factory is 110,000 tons. The area under sugar cane cropping in Kenana is 80,000 Feddans in 1984 to 1985. The area under sugar cane cropping in Assalaya is 27,000 Feddans.

1 Feddan = 1.04 acres or .42 hectares

2. "Ansar" are El Mahadi followers.

3. The battle took place in March 1970 after Aba was bombed by jet fighters and artillery from El Tawila (west of the White Nile) and Hajar Assalaya in the east of the White Nile. In that battle more than one thousand people were killed and another thousand injured. (Note: El Hadi El Mahadi left before the battle took place. Later, he was killed near Sudan-Ethiopian borders [Kurmuk region]).

4. Reid, ex-governor of the White Nile Province, during the 1930s (Anglo-Egyptian Regime).

5. Bilad El Sudan, the name given by medieval Arabic writers to mean the "land of the Blacks," and it is the zone that south of the Sahara, settled by Beja, Abyssinians, Nubians, and the western Sudanic tribes.

6. "Tabagat Wad Dayfallah"; one of the most reliable books about the early process of Islamization in the Sudan. It was written a couple of centuries ago.

7. Salim Qabudan, a Turkish Sailor. He was the-first to open the route to the south to Bahr El Jabal during the Turco-Egyptian era (1821 to 1881).

8. King Adam of Jebel Taqali was humiliated by his neighbour Shaykh Hamid el Sa'id of El Massalamiyya tribe. He sent to King

Adam a number of blades, telling him to circumcise himself as well as his mother.

9.   Selaymi, man from Selaym tribe.

10.   Sir Reginald Wingate, headed the military expedition that followed El Khalifa Abdullahi to Omdibaykrat, where El Khalifa and some of his supporters were killed in November 1899. He succeeded Kitchener as the Governor-General of the Anglo-Egyptian regime in the Sudan from 1894 to 1916.

11.   Nazara, a tribal territorial and political district, that was ruled by a Nazir (usually the Shaykh of the tribe).

THE ECONOMIC AND SOCIAL LIFE OF THE LOCAL INHABITANTS OF DAR MUHARIB PRIOR TO THE ESTABLISHMENT OF KENANA SUGAR SCHEME

DAR MUHARIB

Dar Muharib is the name given to the White Nile Province east of the White Nile river, it includes Northern, Central, and Southern region, extending from El Shawal north to Joda south near the northern boundaries of the Upper Nile Province.

Dar Muharib ancestor was Ahmed El Muharib; he was called so because he was always quarreling with his brothers. The main tribes of Dar Muharib, and the migrant tribes and the seasonal beneficiaries of Dar Muharib are listed in Table 3.1.

Dar Muharib until 1970, with the exception of El Shawal and El Gezira Aba areas, was a nomadic region. It supported more than thirty tribes and sub-tribal sections. The nomads in this area reared camels, cattle, sheep, goats, and donkeys. The camel-keepers restricted themselves to the northern part of the province, while the cattle and sheep-keepers roamed the central, and southern parts of the White Nile Province. In the dry season, they go as far as the Upper Nile Province.

Table 3.1

The Main Tribes of Dar Muharib

The Name of Tribal Sub-Section	Main Occupation	Main Tribe	Main Group
Sabaha	Nomads	Ja'aliyyin	Ja'aliyyin
Khanferiya	Semi-Nomadic	Ja'aliyyin	Ja'aliyyin
Tomamab	Semi-Nomadic	Ja'aliyyin	Ja'aliyyin
Mesadab	Semi-Nomadic	Ja'aliyyin	Ja'aliyyin
Nurab	Semi-Nomadic	Ja'aliyyin	Ja'aliyyin
Bedeiriya	Semi-Nomadic	Ja'aliyyin	Ja'aliyyin
Nabaha	Semi-Nomadic	Ja'aliyyin	Ja'aliyyin
Nazza	Nomads	Shukeriya	Juhayna
Sebaig	Nomads	Shukeriya	Juhayna
Kibayshab	Nomads	Kababish	Juhayna

The tribes that migrated to Dar Muharib before
1–2 Centuries ago

Hussunnat	Semi-Nomadic	Kawahla	Juhayna
Muhammediyya	Semi-Nomadic	Kawahla	Juhayna
Magawir	Semi-Nomadic	Kawahla	Juhayna
Ahamda	Nomads	Kawahla	Juhayna
Rawashda	Semi-Nomadic	Rashaida	Rashaida
Massalamiyya	Semi-Nomadic	Bikeriya	Bikeriya
Ta'aisha	Nomads	Baggara	Juhayna
Selaym	Nomads	Baggara	Juhayna
Jawam'a	Semi-Nomadic	Baggara	Juhayna

Rizaygat	Nomads	Baggara	Juhayna
Bani Halba	Semi-Nomadic	Baggara	Juhayna
Fur	Peasants	Fur	Tribes of Dar Fur
Berti	Peasants	Berti	Tribes of Dar Fur
Fellata	Peasants	Fullani	Tribes of N. Nigeria

Seasonal Tribes in Dar Muharib (Main Tribes)

Wad Abu Gan'a	Nomads	Rufa	Juhayna
Abu Sorwal	Nomads	Rufa	Juhayna
Fikrab	Nomads	Rufa	Juhayna
Hazeil	Nomads	Kenana	Juhayna
Wad Bedayga	Nomads	Kenana	Juhayna

With the establishment of the Gezira scheme in 1922 and the Managil extension in 1958, followed by irrigating cotton projects on the White Nile banks, the grazing area in the north was no longer available for the camels and sheep- keepers in that part of the province. As for the northern tribes like Kawahla, Hassaniyya, Hussunnat, Massalamiyya, Towal, and Arakin, their nomadic life was destroyed by the establishment of the Jebel Awliya Dam, Gezira, Managil, and White Nile cotton pump schemes. Most of them came to be sedentarized and became tenants in these irrigated schemes. Few of them went south to resume their former mode of production, which was pastoral nomadism. Some tribes who moved south, like the Hussunnat and El Massalamiyya, have had to adapt to the new environment, which has heavier rain and rich grass, and a muddy rainy season. This kind of environment is not suitable for camel herding, so they have had to shift to cattle herding and sheep herding, and sometimes cultivating small sorghum fields in the wet season. Until 1970, the northern boundaries for Dar Muharib nomads were the southern fringes of Managil extension or sometimes Sennar-Kosti railway, while the southern boundaries were the marshes of the Upper Nile Province.

Dar Muharib region not only supported the nomads, but it supported the sedentary village cultivators (peasants) mostly from Western Sudan, and it also supported the urban population in towns like Rabak, Jebelein, and Joda. The total population of Dar Muharib area according to the third national census in 1983 is 179,245.

Table 3.2

THE DISTRIBUTION OF DAR MUHARIB POPULATION BY CATEGORY

Urban	85,788	48%
Rural Settled	35,678	20%
Nomads	57,779	32%
TOTAL	179,245	100%

Source: Rabak Council
Third Nation Census 1983

The nomads, who were approximately one third of the Dar Muharib population, were engaged either in short or long distance seasonal movements. The most important asset for the nomads of Dar Muharib is the livestock. It is not only a source of economic security but also a source of prestige and social status as well. Some of the nomads engage in agriculture, not because they like farming, but because they need to support the traditional animal sector. Producing some grain is a strategy followed by the nomads to spare part of the livestock, which is otherwise sold to obtain grain. As for the market goods, like sugar, tea, coffee beans, and soap, they also sell goats and sheep, in order to keep the cattle, selling-free to breed and multiply.

According to Dr. Bashar's animal census in 1976, the Southern White Nile Province is one of the richest areas in cattle and sheep in the Sudan. His survey included the rural councils of Tandelti, Kosti, and Rabak.

Table 3.3

ANIMAL CENSUS OF SOUTHERN PORTION OF
WHITE NILE PROVINCE OF 1976

Kind of Animal	Head	% of Provincial Total	Rate of Growth
Cattle	1,751,334	83	6.1
Sheep	1,693,593	65	2.8
Goats	376,547	45	4.1
Camels	33,108	35	3.1

Source: Kosti Veterinary Dept., Dr. Bashar Suliaman

This animal wealth in the White Nile "southern region" belongs to a number of tribes: Ahamda, Awlad Hemaid, Selaym, Awlad Hassan, Gim'e, Shankhab, Nazza, Rufa, Kenana, Hassaniyya, Hussunnat, and Ombararo.

The tribes of Dar Muharib acquire more than one third of the total number of the animals in Table 3.3, but there is no accurate number for any specific tribes. Most of the nomads do not give the government authorities the exact number of their animals for fear of taxes. Whenever there is a rumor that the veterinary service personnel are going to conduct vaccination campaigns, the nomads either disappear into the bush or come forward with very small numbers of their livestock for vaccination. Under this kind of situation it is difficult to do an accurate estimation of animal population among the nomads in the White Nile, Dar Muharib area.

The economic activities among Dar Muharib nomads depend on annual and seasonal environmental variations. The year is divided into three seasons: the hot dry season, Sayf.; cool wet season, Kharif; and cold dry season, Shita. Because there is absence of rain in Shita, in most cases it is considered part of the long dry season—November to May—while the wet season starts in June and ends in October. The amount of annual rainfall differs according to the geographical location of the area. The further one goes north, the lesser amount of precipitation, and as one goes south, the precipitation gets heavier. Also, the density of vegetation and trees is governed by the same rule: north poor, south rich.

The rain in Dar Muharib area ranges from 200mm in the north to 700mm in the south. The north is characterized by semi-desert sparse thorn scrubland with short grass, while the center and south of Dar Muharib region is characterized by the open savannah woodland with short to medium grass. The nomadic population in the area made their annual movements according to the availability of water, pastures, the land they were traveling on, and the absence of flies and insects. They made sure that they avoid land under cultivation, whether it belonged to the villagers or the owners of mechanized schemes.

DAR MUHARIB DRY SEASON MOVEMENT

The dry season starts with the beginning of November. When the pools of water hafirs start to dry up, the nomads engage in two kinds of movements. The first one is within a radius of 50 kilometers. This short movement is made by the nomads with the smallest herds. These tribes, Khanferiya, Nabaha, Massalamiyya, Kibayshab, and others, take their cattle, sheep, and goats and go into the White Nile islands and spend the whole summer in islands like El Gezira Musran (north of El Jebelein) and other islands like El Gezira Bella. With the beginning of the rainy season, most of these islands partially flooded so they join the main movement of the nomads from the south and pitch their wet season camps with them towards the area of Jebel Sagadi, Jebel Moya, Om Gidian, and El Sufeiya. Usually, the family is solely responsible for grazing and watering the livestock they own.

The users of these islands found themselves in a difficult situation when so many tribes crowded these islands. Many nomads try to get to these islands in the White Nile; it is easy to manage the herd on an island, where water is available and there is plentiful pasture, including different grasses, (El Fursh). Moreover, the nomads can shift some of the family labor to work in other areas, since fewer people can manage the livestock on these islands.

The situation grew worse for the users of the islands as pump schemes spread throughout the cotton clay lands near the White Nile banks. This blocked many of the routes to El Bahr (river). The tenants of these schemes, who are mostly from Western Sudan, began to cultivate, mainly vegetables, watermelon, and started setting fishing camps on these islands. The nomads not only came into conflict and disputes with the new settlers, but their competitiveness over grazing rights on these islands touched off quarreling and club fighting. Some of the nomads thought of the islands as a summer of continuous disputes, so some started to engage in the long distance seasonal movement, over 400 kilometers, both routes north and south. Some other nomads, who experienced loss or had a very limited number of animals, joined the peasants' summer villages, which were usually situated by the banks of the White Nile.

The main body of the nomads of Dar Muharib, mainly Nazza, Sebaig, Sabaha, joined by Selaym and Ahamda by crossing the White Nile to the east, also accompanied by tribal sub-sections of Kenana and Rufa, start their annual movement south in early November.

The important features of Dar Muharib movement are shifting camps (Farig, plural, Furgan), watering and grazing of animals, which dominate the whole dry season. The nomads usually make the decision to move south when the given available resources become scarce. Usually the Farig (camp) members make that decision when they are collectively eating food at the Khalwa (where male guests are hosted) when Shaykh el Farig (camp leader) agrees to move, the camp members and the Shaykh discuss the route of the camp, tribes, or lineages they can associate with and possible "dar" sites to pitch their camp on. The annual movement is called "da'ena." Bulls are the means of transportation in this long-distance travel.

The house in Dar Muharib is made of acacia bark, especially kitr, grass mats, shukkab, leather, and cloth. Beit (house) el Arab, or Beit el "Shukkab" is made by women, and it is shaped like a dome. It works adequately against the cold, heat, and rain. When the camp is moving, the women just roll over the mats, cloth, and bark. It is also easy to pitch, tied to the ground with a number of ropes, which makes it look like a tent. When the nomads of Dar Muharib move south, they have to avoid peasants' fields on their way and stay away from the mechanized schemes in the region. When the nomads travel through the area northeast of El Jebelein and the area of El Dali and El Mazmum, they usually try to pass quickly and keep an eye on the herds, while they are grazing in a zig-zag maneuver. In recent years, many of the nomads were up in arms with the village peasants and the mechanized scheme owners. Mainly the peasants and the scheme owners accuse the nomads of destroying their crops (usually sorghum and sesame) and polluting their hafirs. The problem is that there are numerous nomadic camps moving south one after the other, some moving slowly, others moving quickly. The peasants and the mechanized scheme guards, whenever they find crop destruction, are likely to accuse the nearest camp around. Many disputes are taken to court in El Jebelein or El Renk and other areas. So the nomads, while they are moving south, try to keep as far as possible from the cultivated fields.

If a camp is accused of crop destruction, the problem may be settled by compensation through deputation (agawid). Otherwise, the people involved will go to court. The nomads hate to go to towns' courts mainly because the procedures sometimes take long, and that disturbs their annual cycle of movement. Also, the fines may consume a considerable number of livestock.

As the nomads pass south of the mechanized schemes, heading toward Khor Doleib, many other camps of other tribes will be seen a couple of kilometers away. Dars near Khor Doleib are claimed according to early arrival. Camps or Furgan are pitched not far away from each other; although every camp is responsible for managing its own affairs concerning watering and grazing the livestock they own. In Khor Doleib, nomads stay longer than any place else since they started their movement to the south. In February, the nomads reach the dry season camps in and around the areas of Khor Ahmar, Tombak, Adar, and the northern edges of the swamp area, or the Machare Marshes. The Dar Muharib nomads and other tribes spend the rest of the dry season in the above mentioned area. In case of a bad year, usually the nomads reach as far as Sobat river and even go up the river until they reach the Sudanese Ethiopian border near the town of Nasir.

THE WET SEASON MOVEMENT

The nomads of Dar Muharib start to move north when the early rain starts "rushash." As soon as the early rain starts, the camps start to move north to avoid the tropical dampness, the flies and the insects that become active. In so many cases, camps have to wait before they move north because of lack of water in natural land depressions (rohood). Usually it is the mission of the nomadic scouts to travel north before the camps' movement to test if there is enough water, and also to look for possible camp sites when El Da'ena (the movement of herds and people) arrives.

The nomads move along with the rain. They seldom stay far behind because pools of water, running Khors, and the muddy clays will cause them a lot of trouble, especially if a cow is stuck in the mud for more than four hours. The only way to deal with it is to slaughter the cow since it can't make it on its feet to recovery. They do not move ahead of the rain because the natural depressions are empty of water, so they move along with the rain, neither after nor before it.

The migration track northward, in recent times, has become crowded with nomads. Tribes of Dar Muharib and Rufa'a al Hoi are likely to make long halts around the area of Khor Doleib, because soon the nomadic camps will make the difficult move in their way north. They may march continuously with little water supplies, and in most cases they are not allowed to approach water spots of peasant villagers, and the hafirs found inside the mechanized areas. Most nomads in the area in the rainy season while they are moving north are pushed between the mechanized schemes and the White Nile pump schemes (Ahmed 1974:30).

Dar Muharib nomads, under the pressure of inadequate water and grazing resources, drift north. In July the nomads have to make a non-stop migration to pass the areas of peasants and mechanized schemes. During the migration north, many disputes arise involving nomads, peasants, and mechanized scheme owners, mainly because of the destruction of early crops.

By August most of the nomads reach their wet season camp sites, which are usually pitched in the brown rocky sandy areas near the mountains in the region. The brown, rocky, sandy land has a reasonable elevation that facilitates water drainage. It is important that wet camp sites stay well drained and dry, for the fear of floods and parasitic diseases. Camps are pitched around the rocky area north of El Jebelein and near Om Gidian, Jebel Moya, Jebel Doud, Jebel Bute, Jebel Sagadi, El Edahim, Gala Wad el Ajouz, Goz el Gargaf, and El Sufeiya. The wet season camps so many times are knocked down by thunderstorms, and sometimes especially sheep are killed by these storms. In August and September this stormy weather is possible every three days. The nomads usually know the coming of thunderstorms when they detect the lightening in the far east. Most households have from two to three hours to prepare for the thunderstorms, checking the tent roof, poles, and ropes. Cattle, sheep, and goats are left in the open, while the calves and lambs and the like are sheltered in and around the household.

By early November, Dar Muharib, and other nomads, are heading for the annual cyclical movement. Sometimes they have to wait to leave cultivators harvesting their crops to avoid crop damaging and hence landing in court.

FAMILY SOCIAL ORGANIZATION AND RECIPROCITY AMONG THE NOMADS

Dar Muharib nomads are tent dwellers. The Pastoral unit of dwelling is Beit el Arab or Beil el Shukkab (beit means house). Every house or tent is the physical and social property of related kin, who are usually a nomadic elementary family. The Dar Muharib nomadic elementary family consists of the father, mother, and their unmarried children. Sometimes it includes the father and his wives (maximum four wives) children and elderly relatives like a grandfather or grandmother and sometimes a widow. El Beit, or the tent, is the center of domestic and economic activities of the family. It is the place where dependents are socialized and asked to be obedient to "syd el beit," the guardian of the tent or the father, who manages the family's day to day affairs and makes the decisions affecting the social and the economic well-being of the family. All people in the family are aware of their role what exactly to do in different times of the day. Younger children, 5 to 14, herd the calves, sheep, and goats. The grown up boys herd the cattle. If the father does not have a son to herd for him, he does it by himself. Girls over 14 and their mothers manage the domestic affairs of the family. This includes collecting water, firewood, wild acacia fruits, and vegetables. In the tent, they grind the grain which is a back breaking job, especially if the family size is big. They cook the food, make tents and basketry materials, milk the cows, and produce butterfat "samin or dyhin."

The tent is the place where the family keeps their few material properties. The cloth, beads, and ornaments, sugar, tea, onions, and pepper are kept in basketry containers hanging over the big nomadic bed (sa'rir el Arab) that claims two thirds of the tent size 4x3x2 meters. The milk, sour milk, water, and butterfat are kept either in skin-containers or in gourds. These are commonly used, so they place them near the tent's door, on a tree with a-y-shaped branches to protect the containers and the contents from chickens and reptiles like snakes and lizards.

Most of the belongings in the house are owned by the wife and her daughters. The husband usually has a metal box to keep his few valuable things: new cloth and cartridges. The most valuable thing for a nomad, besides his long spears, knives and strong clubs, is a rifle, which is hung opposite to the tent's door to show the social and economic status of the husband.

The wife, her husband, daughters, and younger sons sleep in the tent. The bachelors spend the night in El Khalwa (where male guests are hosted). This Khalwa usually is built of grass in shape of a square when the camp is staying in a certain area more than two weeks. If the camp is spending less than two weeks, the bachelors sleep in the open. During this time, if male guests approach the camp, they may be hosted under a big tree or a temporary shade, such as a blanket on poles.

Usually the nomads see the camp as an important part of their mother tribe. The nomadic camp in Dar Muharib can be described as a lineage (Khashum Beit) of a certain nomadic tribe, Sabaha, Nazza, Kibayshab, Ahamda, Selaym, etc. In most cases the camps take the name of the lineage, which runs through the name of the lineage founder. Iyal, Awlad or Nas, ' Abdalla, Hakima, Ibrahim, etc. are the common ways for calling a lineage or identifying a camp. Sometimes a camp can be formed by a head of an extended family (father and his wives and married sons). The nomadic camp can range from seven to 15 tents, with a varying number of people from 50 to 100. Most members are related by sharing a founding ancestor (patrilineal descent). The structure of the camp can be changed from one year to the next. Young daughters marry and leave the camp to join their husband's camp. Bachelors marry and bring new members into the camp.

To be in a migratory nomadic camp, one must have livestock. If a nomad has less than ten cattle and less than one hundred sheep and goats, there is no need for him to travel all the distance; the proper place for a propertyless nomad is the peasant village, where agriculture is his main job. Many nomads live in these villages because they lost their herds. Some nomads try to build capital in agriculture and invest in cattle, but it is a difficult move; since many of the nomads hate the laborious and boring work of agriculture, many are transformed into poor peasants.

The importance of any camp lies in the wealth of the camp and the personality of the camp leader (Shaykh el Farig). The camp leader is considered as the lineage head, who is responsible for representing his lineage or group if the tribe is to meet to solve a dispute, or congregate against other hostile tribes. The camp is considered one social unit, since all members are claiming a common paternal ancestor. The camp is considered as an economic and political unit, since their being together necessitates preserving their property and defending it against raids.

The most important feature that keeps the camp unified and its structural relations intact is the spirit of generalized reciprocity found among the Farig members. The reciprocity appears in eating habits of Dar Muharib camps. The food usually is a dura porridge served in a big wooden bowl (gadah) with soup (mulah) poured over and beside the dura porridge. All heads of households gather at El Khalwa., while their sons come carrying the food. The camp members gather in the early morning and at sunset to share their food collectively. They start eating the first food that reaches El Khalwa. When the soup is gone, they introduce the next dish, while a young boy will take the first bowl to bring more soup (Malih el Kisra). When the meal is over, tea and coffee are made available. Usually guests and elders are served at the first arrival of tea and coffee. Women and girls share food with Farig female members in a rotating manner; they gather one day in a certain woman's tent, the next day in another one. The most commonly reciprocated items, in order of importance, are:

> Raw meat
> Butterfat (samin)
> Grain
> Sugar

Milk
Tea
Cooked food
Water
Coffee beans
Sour Milk
Cooking Utensils (temporarily)

These items are reciprocated frequently between the camp tents. The concept of generalized reciprocity cements the social, political, and economic relations between household members in the tent cluster. It is one way of sharing scarce resources equally among agnatic kin to ensure the cohesive unity and spirit of giving in harsh times. The only way to receive from your kin and neighbors is to give and be generous to them. This generosity is the most valuable social element a family could obtain and the way to engage in the reciprocal spirit of the camp and the circulation of goods.

The camp is a herding unit. The cattle that belong to the tent cluster are watered and grazed by herders from the camp. During summer time when the work is laborious, (drawing water from wells), people collectively work to water the animals. If one of the tent managers of a herd is sick or exhausted, his herds are going to be taken care of by other members of the tent cluster. Men collectively guard their camp against any possible raids from other groups and gangs of animal stealers. Sometimes to discourage aggressors, firing of bullets in the air at night is required. But the annoying threat to their livestock are the hyenas, who attack the end of the herd by day, camp site by night. Whenever the camp hears the sound (laugh) of the hyenas in the bush, the male tent cluster, armed with spears and rifles, are on the alert if the hyenas are to attack the livestock in the camp site. The hyenas, every night, roam around nomadic camps; most of their prey includes chickens, lambs, sheep, donkeys, a cow, or a bull that drifts off the herd to browse in bushes around the camp.

The men in the camp are the protectors and guardians of the women in the tent cluster to ensure that the honor of the camp will remain intact. Although the domestic and elementary family affairs are the concern of the father and his wife, the camp collectively is active in the aspects that concern their economic, political, and social life.

PASTORAL MODE OF PRODUCTION AND RECENT MODIFICATION

Dar Muharib tribes are Baggara, always preoccupied with one important asset—building and acquiring a big cattle herd, accompanied by a large number of sheep and goats. A man in Dar Muharib is rich if he has "mal" (cattle). The ownership of a big herd of cattle is a vehicle to prestige, economic and political power. The cattle they herd known as the "kenana type" famous for their good milking qualities. From early childhood a person will catch the fever of building a herd when he is given a calf and a number of sheep and goats on the occasion of his circumcision. To most people this is the first step to building their future capital.

Cattle are the main interest in their life that deserves all possible attention. Every cow has a name, usually after its color. A cow may be called Hemera because of its brown or reddish color, or Ghebasha gray, or Zeraga black, or Beyada white.

Dar Muharib Baggara Arabs, to build and sustain a large herd, can put all the family labor if necessary into managing the herd. One of the most laborious jobs is herding and watering the livestock, especially in the dry season. While grazing is every day, watering occurs every other day. There are two grazing sessions in the day. The first is night-grazing (serba), which the nomads indicate is important for the welfare of the herd. In the early morning the herd comes in from night-grazing. This time of the day the cows will not be milked, the milk is left to the calves, which are freed from the enclosure of the branches and thorns zariba. As the herd approaches, the calves race for nursing.

The second grazing session starts around 10:00 a.m. The cattle are headed by two or three herders. It is the morning grazing (dahi) and will go on until 6:00 p.m. when the herds are brought back to the camp. This time, the calves will not be freed until the cows are milked. All members of the household participate in milking the cows, while others take care of the calves, sheep, and goats.

The milk is collected in skin-containers (seyin) or buckets. Some of it goes directly to family consumption, the rest is skimmed (haz el laban) by shaking it in a skin-container or a gourd, suspended to the roof by a rope. After the milk is skimmed, the butterfat is boiled and will be kept in a burma or a gourd to constitute an important element of the nomadic daily diet. The rest of the product "sour milk" is either consumed or distributed to neighbors.

The cattle raised by the nomads of Dar Muharib are the "Kenana" type, famous for their milk production. Increasing the herd is the overriding concern of the White Nile Baggara Arabs. They have a reproduction technique they have developed over time. In the summer camps, the tent cluster members gather to choose the bulls that are going to breed the herd. They are very selective in choosing the right type, especially of its milking variety. The rest of the bulls are castrated. The cattle reproductive strategy is done first to ensure top milking quality herds and prevent passing undesirable cattle types. Second, few bulls are left to serve the herd, while the majority are castrated, because this will prevent and stop bull fighting over cows, which sometimes leaves the camp awake all night, destroys the camp establishment, and sometimes injures men who try to stop the fight.

The life of Dar Muharib nomads is centered around their cattle, not only as the source of family subsistence and self-sufficiency, but also a visible sign of prestige and wealth. Their main concern is how to increase their numbers and keep them healthy. Nothing annoys a nomad like a disease among his cattle, a bitter occasion when it happens. This not only threatens his family livelihood and prestige, it also separates him from his camp until his beasts are restored to health so as not to infect his camp members' herds.

The common diseases are:

1. Rinderpest (Abu Dimay'a)

2. Fascialosis (Abu Kibayda)

3. Pleuropneumonia (Abu Genit)

4. Belherziasis (Bilharsya)

5. Foot and Mouth disease (Abu Lisan)

6. Anthrax (Homa Fahamiya)

7. Wasting from Flies (Abu Darba)

8. Blood poisoning (Abu Tonkul)

Few of the nomads have more than limited traditional ways of dealing with these diseases. They use two methods to cure their animals. The first one is using heated metal to burn the suspected infected area. The other is using incisions to cure the cattle by cutting it open to let out pus or lymph from certain animal parts. Because of these limited treatments and the traditional devices, many cattle are lost. To make up for the lost cattle, the nomads start breeding sheep, which are less subjected to disease than cattle. Sheep can easily be sold to the sedentary population in the area. So sheep-breeding has become important because first it provides the nomadic household with some market goods, and at the same time, sheep can be sold to obtain cattle.

Dar Muharib nomads, whose main interest is cattle, have often found it necessary to sell sheep or a bull to buy grain. Seeing this act as an ultimate depreciation for their livestock, many have started growing dura by themselves. For a long time, there was abundant agricultural land, but the nomads see agricultural work as strenuous and monotonous, and incompatible with their annual movement cycle. As peasants from Western Sudan started to clear the bush and claim their bilad (field), the nomads in Dar Muharib area also started to engage in clearing the bush and claiming bilad rights.

Agricultural lands are trusted to the Shaykh of the tribe or sub-tribe. The nomadic agricultural land is usually around their wet season camps. The bilad is not to be bought or sold, and the only way that the bilad can be lost, if the person is absent for a number of years. Still, if one comes back, he has full right of cultivating his bilad.

The nomads dislike the agricultural work, but as things keep changing around them, such as migrants claiming the right to own and cultivate, and the cash and market economy growing stronger with the establishment of Gezira scheme in 1922, Managil extension in 1958, and the White Nile pump schemes in 1940s. The nomads find it convenient to grow some grain to avoid selling their beloved cattle and stop paying cash to obtain grain. So the nomads practice some cultivation for the sake of protecting their livestock sector.

In the past, Dar Muharib Baggara Arabs confined themselves to a pastoralist mode of production[2] where means of production and the relations of production were very much geared to self-sufficiency, and welfare of the group in an absence of a monetized economy. Through time, with the peasant migration from Western Sudan and an increasing state intervention in the region accompanied by a rapidly advancing market economy, the nomads not only adapted their labor resources to modify their pastoral mode of production to the new changes, but they intertwined it with an agricultural one.

In the dry season, the livestock is very demanding. During this time, all the family members must help especially in the task of drawing water from wells and khor beds. So the dry season requires the family labor to concentrate on the management of the livestock sector, since there is little to do in the dura bilad. When the wet season comes, it is the peak time of agricultural activities. The management of livestock is easy in the wet season, because of the availability of water and fresh pasture lands, so the bulk of family labor shifts to the agricultural sector. They start sowing, weeding, guarding against animals and birds, and harvesting and storing the dura crop in the underground granaries. Sorghum stems are collected and stored to be used as fodder in the time of difficulty. When the harvest season (darat) is over, again the nomads start moving south, and accordingly all the family labor is shifted back into the management of the livestock sector.

PEASANT SUBSISTENCE ECONOMY

Scholars have debated over whether there are peasants in Africa. When dealing with African agricultural rural societies, many describe them as traditional agriculturalists, cultivators, and sometimes farmers. Wolf (1966) indicates that it is important to distinguish between primitive agriculturalists, peasants, and farmers. Primitive agriculturalists produce and control their labor and means of production, and the surplus is circulated between the networks of kin and relatives. Farmers, who are sometimes called "agricultural entrepreneurs," are commercially oriented, using all factors of production, land, capital, labor to generate income and profit. Peasants are rural cultivators whose surpluses are transferred to parasitic groups outside their area, or to the world market and multinational corporations.

According to Shanin (1971:30), the peasant household main feature is the total integration of the peasant family's life and its farming activity. Chayanov considers peasantization as a "specific type of economy." He notes that peasant motivations are different from those of the capitalist entrepreneurs. They aim at securing the family needs, rather than to make profit. As a result, this theory centered on the notion of the peasant trying to balance his family needs and the amount of labor required to achieve that goal (Basile Kerblay 1971:151).

According to John S. Saul and Roger Woods:

Peasants are those whose ultimate security and subsistence lies in their having certain rights in land and in labor of family members on the land, but who are involved, through rights and obligations, in a wider economic system which includes the participation of nonpeasants (1971:105).

The mode of production in Africa differs according to the given historical era. In pre-colonial Africa, for example, a considerable segment of the population controlled their own means of production and labor. During the colonial occupation, the means of production were no longer available for the rural cultivators who were forced to participate in the new cash economy, especially by having taxes imposed on them. The simple and traditional agriculturalists and nomads were transformed into peasants who struggled hard to feed their families and prevent hunger, on one hand, and put a lot of family labor effort to produce cash crops for export on the other.

The people of Dar Muharib are no exception. Migrants from Western Sudan established themselves as cultivators, but through the state intervention and merchant capital, they were turned into poor peasants or daily agricultural laborers. For the same reasons above, the nomads also are undergoing a rapid process of peasantization.

When the Baggara of the White Nile settled in their present Dar, they mainly depended on milk and meat as means of subsistence; most of them considered cultivation as the task of poor and degraded people. After the Turco-Egyptian regime and the Mahadiyya, a considerable number of animals were lost, so the nomads started cultivation as a way of subsistence and a way of regaining their herds.

The land increased in value as migrants and immigrants from Western Sudan started to clear the bush in Dar Muharib and claim land rights. In the 1940s, more newcomers from Western Sudan were attracted to work as tenants in the White Nile pump schemes. Many of these tenants grew cotton as well as sorghum. Through time, as their families became too big to be supported by a cotton field, they abandoned growing cotton to work instead as daily laborers in the cotton schemes and devoted much of the time to growing sorghum in individual fields cleared from the bush.

In Dar Muharib areas, there are certain territories which are claimed by the nomadic tribes. Most of the migrants and immigrants drifted off these lands and did their slash and burn cultivation (harig) in the unclaimed land. The newcomer can claim as much as he can manage in terms of clearing, planting, weeding, and harvesting; this process is called "kifat yadu." Most of the peasants of Dar Muharib came from Western Sudan. These tribes included Fellata, Mima, Tunjur, Fur, Berti, Bani Hussein, etc.

In Dar Muharib there are roughly 35,000 peasants of them moving seasonally to provide for their subsistence requirements. In order for the peasant family to have a normal level of subsistence, they have to shift the family labor as the annual cycles require. During the dry season, November through May, the peasants live in their dry season villages, which are at the bank of the White Nile, e.g. Khor Agwal, Sharat, Hillt Berti, Taksaboon, and the peasant population that live in El Gezira Aba and El Jebelein. In the dry season, most of them work as daily laborers picking cotton. The picking of cotton is done by the whole family to ensure some cash for the market goods. When the season of picking cotton is over, the peasants turn to vegetable growing on the "gerf" or silt-banks of the White Nile. The peasants and their families grow hot pepper, tomatoes, dill seed, lentils, onions, and watermelon. Vegetable growing is another strategy to raise cash to meet the increasing family obligations. The product is usually marketed in the nearby towns, Jebelein, Rabak, Gezira Aba, and Kosti.

Before the rainy season approaches, the heads of households construct the family hut and clean the bilad in the agricultural village, which lies to the east of the dry-season villages at the bank of the White Nile and ranges usually from 15 to 50 kilometers away. When the early rain starts in June, a scout will be sent to see if the village hafir (reservoir in the clay plains to store rainwater) has enough water for peasants and their families to move in. If there is enough water, peasants' households carry their belongings and families on donkeys to make the rainy season movement to the agricultural villages, e.g. Gafa, Om Gidian, Sufeiya, Ete'boon, El Gerfrat, etc. Once there is enough rain, the peasants' families start to plant the sorghum seed. The average family of seven people cultivate two Gadas (10 Feddans). The peasant community stays in the agricultural villages until the harvest is over. By the time of harvest, the hafir rainwater becomes muddy and contaminated with water-borne diseases. So the peasant community makes the trip again to the dry-season villages at the bank of the White Nile, where water is plenty, and the cotton schemes are near, and the chance of growing vegetables comes around again.

PEASANT FAMILIES AND THE AGRICULTURAL CYCLE

The peasants of Dar Muharib are mostly concerned with "Ma'isha," the source of living, which is intimately attached to the success of agriculture. To succeed in agriculture, one must have land, family labor, and some animals (in most cases very few to support in critical times), and above all, adequate rainfall and absence of natural hazards. In an area where peasants use the traditional agricultural technology of their ancestors, at the same time they face increasing agricultural and crop hazards, low yields, and grain failure.

After the peasants construct the families' huts and clean their bilads, the members of the households wait for enough rainwater to gather in the village hafir. Once there is enough water, sorghum can be planted, an activity in which family members participate. The father and his elder sons, use "barana" (an iron blade fixed on a long stick) or "sulluwka" (a carved wooden hoe). The father and sons start making holes in the wet soil surface. The mother and her daughters put the seeds in the holes which they then close by using their feet. In the course of a morning (dahawa) the family of seven members can plant a Feddan. As the temperature rises around 12:00 noon, the family goes home. The women will be preoccupied by preparing the food, tea, and coffee.

When the food is cooked and tea and coffee are ready, the near heads of households gather in El Khalwa for "El Ghada," the main meal in the day. Almost all of the people who engage in the farm work take a nap which ends at 3:00 in the afternoon, the time for the afternoon session (Duhiriya). At the sunset, people come from El Bilads (fields). The men go to the evening prayer (Muslims) in El Khalwa and stay for

"El Asha," the evening meal. Women milk the sheep and goats and tie up the donkeys before it is dark.

In two weeks or so, the planting of seeds will be over. As the early sown seeds sprout, a process of replanting and supplying will continue in areas, where there are seed failures.

The first two weeks are very crucial for the green shoots. The fear is not excess of rain, the real fear is the "subna" (40 consecutive days without rain), which would surely damage the sprouting crop. The heavy rain, if any, falls in July and August, which encourages the growth of other grass species. This time witnesses the weeding activity. All the family members participate in the hard laborious task. The tools used are "hashasha," or "jaraya" (a half moon iron blade fixed on a stick); a person stands up and pushes the tool under the surface of the soil to uproot and remove the weeds.

The first weeding, which is very difficult, is called "El mor" — literally "the bitter"; it requires a lot of work because any additional rain will make the task even harder. It is this time of "El mor" that the "Nafir," rotating voluntary working parties, become active among the peasants. All the agricultural village dwellers allocate their labor in a rotating cycle to help the peasants overcome the tedious job of the first weeding. The goal of the Nafir is to ensure that no bilad is going to be overwhelmed by weeds resulting in either no yields or very poor ones.

The second weeding, "junkab," does not require much heavy labor, so the Nafirs break up, and every family handles its own farm. Approaching the month of October, the sorghum will be ripening, and the family engaged in guarding the bilad from dawn to dusk to protect it from the ravages of weaver birds.[3] If the bilad is left without guardians, a peasant should not anticipate an "ardab" (2 sacks of sorghum)[4] to be harvested. So the whole family joins in scaring off the weaver birds. This is the time of the year that the family stays from dawn to dusk in the fields. Different methods are employed to prevent weaver birds from reaching the ripening sorghum heads. In one method, a person stands on an elevated platform overlooking the sorghum heads, e.g. a tree or a heap of wood. Seeing the birds coming, he/she strikes two heavy metal bars together, which will drive the birds away. The second method is to crack a whip, while the third is a scarecrow; shouting is also used to scare off the birds.

While guarding the bilads, the peasant and his family start harvesting the sorghum. Although they can cope with weaver birds, in the case of a locust invasion little can be done to protect the sorghum heads and save the crop.

Usually before harvest is over, the water in the hafir dries up, this obliges the peasant to travel for very long distances to collect water, usually from the White Nile. After the harvest is over, the peasants take their families to the dry-season villages, while the elder son or a male relative will remain behind in the bilad for approximately two weeks to guard the crop from animals' intrusions. During this time, the head of the household will come back, bringing with him a number of donkeys and empty sacks to collect the sorghum harvest. A man may make a number of trips to bring the harvest home. The harvest is stored either in a "sewayba," a traditional grain silo situated above the ground to be protected from insects, termites, and animals, or in a "mut'mura," an underground granary with the same purpose. The standing sorghum stems are also cut and collected in bundles to be used as animal fodder in the dry-season. In meeting their family subsistence needs, peasants of Dar Muharib have learned to adapt to their surroundings, ecological, and environmental, in an agricultural cycle which is limited sometimes by drought, locust, weaver birds, and sorghum diseases. The principal disease is "buda" (Striga hermonthica): the parasitic disease that attacks the sorghum cereals. To deal with the risk and uncertainty of agriculture, the peasants also engage in animal rearing, gerf cultivation, (vegetables), rope making, saddle making, designing and making wooden beds (anqarebs), gum arabic tapping, catching fish (especially the Fellata group). These are different ways of diversifying the means of subsistence if sorghum rainlands cropping fails. So peasants and their families are preoccupied throughout the year to ensure a level of self-sufficiency in a way that caters for the basic family needs.

MUTUAL ACCOMMODATION BETWEEN PEASANTS AND NOMADS

Through a history of disputes and conflicts, every nomadic tribe in Dar Muharib has come to acquire dar or territory of their own. They were mainly nomads who didn't like the agricultural work, but the perceptions of land use and ownership had changed when migrants came to the area during and after the Mahadiyya, and recently when the Sahel was devastated by desertification and drought from 1968 to 1973. The migrants and immigrants started slashing and burning to clear some of Dar Muharib land for agriculture. There was a scramble over the rainland of Dar Muharib. Once the nomads knew the pressure from outside and recognized the potential agricultural value of the clay rainlands, their tribal Shaykhs and their people made the move to control their tribal territories. Until the early 1960s there was an abundance of lands to accommodate not only the tribesmen but also migrants and immigrants. The land is not a commodity to be bought and sold. The peasants also will not pay land rent. As the land is trusted to the tribal Shaykh, the peasant who cultivates in his region, voluntarily, will give the Shaykh a sack of sorghum after harvest as recognition of the "right of the neighborhood" or as it is called "gerat el Shaykh fulan."

Paying the Shaykh rights of neighborhood precipitates an increasingly active atmosphere of social interaction, which leads to mutually beneficial relationships between the peasants and the nomads. In the wet season, there are some villages that become home for the peasants and the nomads, e.g. El Gargaf, El Sufeiya, and Nuri. The village is divided into two sections close to each other, the nomads with their tents and the peasants with their thatched huts. This multi-residential pattern facilitates the communal share of the hafir's water, sorghum bilads, and grazing rights. Also, people eat together which reciprocates scarce foodstuffs and work jointly in the Nafir parties during the agricultural cycle.

Another sign of collaboration and relations of reciprocity is the brotherly feeling the two groups have for each other. During the time of social occasions, birth, marriage, death, and emergencies, whatever kind of resources are owned by a certain person are at the disposal of the family, which needs it during that occasion.

After harvest, the peasants permit the nomads to drive their livestock in their bilads to graze the residue or the remains of production; it is also the time that the peasants' bilads are fertilized by the livestock manure.

The indigenous population strategy in Dar Muharib, for the nomads as well as for the peasants, is aimed at long lasting subsistence, not only utilizing their environment to the best of their knowledge, but interacting inter-dependently to achieve the welfare of their societies.

DEVELOPMENT TAKE-OVER

The agricultural development schemes were and are launched on the central clay lands of the Sudan, which stretch from south of Khartoum up to the Ethiopian border, and from Kassala in the east to Kordofan and Dar Fur in the west.

The large-scale irrigated schemes started with the establishment of the Gezira enterprise in the 1920s. The objective is to produce cotton for the world market as part of the policies of the British colonialists to make the Sudan an export-oriented country to provide cheap agricultural raw materials for the British industry. The succeeding policies of development have followed the same path as that of the colonialists, the so-called "backbone of the economy." which means producing more cotton. In the 1950s, the Managil extension was made an integral part of the Gezira scheme. More cotton pump schemes sponsored by the Agrarian Reform Corporation (ARC) were established on the banks of the Blue and White Nile. Other projects like Khashm el Girba were established during the 1960s and recently followed by the projects of El Suki, El Rahad, El Kenaf, and six sugar schemes. The land occupied by these schemes is approximately five million Feddans.

Agricultural development is not restricted to the large-scale irrigated projects but also includes mechanized rainfed farming. Many schemes were implemented to produce sorghum and sesame. The first of these projects was Gedaref, followed by Dali, Mazmum, Renk, Damazine, and Habila. The mechanized rainfed schemes are also situated in central clay lands of the Sudan. These schemes are managed by the Mechanized Farming Corporation (MFC), which was established by the government in 1968. The schemes include both, state farms and private ones, a total of four million Feddans under rainfed farming.

The development programs of the Sudan are geared towards crop export to increase the country's revenue of foreign currency. In the process, a reserve army of laborers is left landless and propertyless.

The goals of the development schemes, which are commodification of land and commercialization of agriculture, are in direct conflict with the rural people's self-sustaining subsistence economy. Although there is a mounting evidence that there is misplanning, mismanagement, and corruption, worse still is the insensitivity to the problems of the rural masses. Land expropriation became synonymous with rural development in Sudan. As a result, the rural population is affected drastically.

First, most of them became landless peasants. Second, their subsistence economy was destroyed, and they were forced to sell their labor to survive in a new market economy. Third, they became increasingly pessimistic and hopeless, roaming around without work, or harshly exploited by the parasitic urban propertied classes.

Dar Muharib is no exception. The development projects such as Gezira, the Managil, Dali, Mazmum, Renk, and cotton pump schemes on the banks of the White Nile put pressure on the area, but things went from bad to worse when Assalaya and Kenana sugar schemes were implemented in the heart of Dar Muharib. Here nomads and peasants alike not only became agricultural laborers but are undergoing a harsh process of proletarianization.

CHAPTER THREE NOTES

1. Iyal, Awlad, Nas: Means sons, descendants, or people who belong to a founding ancestor.

2. A mode of production refers to the basic characteristics of a certain production system, which include the means of production, land, technology, capital, etc., and the relations of production, that is, the relations between individuals—or between different classes where one controls the means of production and the other works as a producer (see Edquist and Edquist, p. 16, 1979).

3. Weaver Birds: One of the most damaging hazards to sorghum cultivation in Sudan. So many times, the difference between a good year and a bad one is scaring off the weaver birds. Most of the colonies of nesting are built on thick acacia trees on the banks of the White Nile.

4. 1 sack of sorghum = 90.9 kgs.

1. The White Nile River as it enters the Kenana Region

2. Looking west form the New White Nile Bridge is the old steel Cantilever
Bridge that connected Rabak to Kosti

3. Main irrigation canal from the White Nile

4. A Primary Canal

5. Cane Fields

6. Long-Farrow irrigation developed at Kenana Sugar Estate

7. Mechanical harvest

8. Cane Transport

9. A general view of Kenana Sugar Factory and administration

10. Kenana Sugar Factory and Refinery

11. A general View of Kenana Township

12. A type of residence for Kenana Senior Staff

13. A type of residence for Kenana temporary workers

14. A type of residence for Kenana Junior Staff

15. Kenana Camp 4

16. Kenana Camp 5

17. A peasant village

18. A nomadic village

19. Lorries connect surrounding villages to Kenana Markets

20. The market not only brings sellers and buyers together, but many came to have a meal, drink tea and coffee while chatting and exchanging news

21. A typical shop in Kenana Market that carries: lentils, fava beans, dry-salted fish, pounded okra, onions, spices, sugar, tea and coffee beans

22. A shop specializing in utensils and cooking ware

23. A fruit stand

24. A young man distributing and selling water at Kenana Market

25. A woman at Kenana Market ready to serve lunch for customers

26. "Sitt-ashai", selling tea and coffee is a popular self-employment among women not only in Kenana, but all over Sudan

27. Young boys waiting to shine customers' shoes

28. A girl from a migrant family walking for a long distance to bring firewood for heating and cooking

29. Children of migrant families have great economic value. Two kids operating a cart to transport goods between Kenana Market and the residential area for a fee..

30. Grazing lands by the silt-bank of the White Nile

31. "Kenana cattle type" known for their good milking qualities

32. As the nomads settled, they adopted wedding dances from townspeople

33. Selaym Baggara Arabs performing "Nuggara", a wedding dance

34. The Shaykh of Nuri Village welcoming our team to the guest house "Khalwa", while his granddaughter bringing a hot, spicy, and sugary tea as a sign of hospitality

35. Some key-field staff using the scheme labor and resources to invest in the animal sector for their personal gain

36. Sorghum fields around the villages are turned into cane-fields against the will of the peasants and the nomads

KENANA SCHEME AND SETTLEMENT SCHEMES IN THE SUDAN

COLONIAL AND POST-COLONIAL DEVELOPMENT PROJECTS

The early development projects in Africa were launched by the colonialists. Some of these colonial development projects were settlement schemes. Chambers (1969) noted that the purpose of these settlement schemes were either political or humanitarian. He also added that these projects, which were agricultural schemes in most cases, depended on advanced technology and had considerable resources devoted to them, land, labor, technical, and administrative expatriates, with great emphasis on capital.

The way the colonial powers invaded the African countries, the destruction of the African subsistence mode of production, land expropriation, undermining of African cottage industry, and imposing of taxes on the indigenous population created that cash need to attract the local people to work in the colonial economy. We thus see the overriding goals of the colonialists: tapping cheap raw material to fuel and feed their industries in Europe, securing new markets and consumers in the periphery, and hence, strengthen the capitalist mode of production.

The colonial design of development was geared to make the colonized countries "export-oriented." producing in most cases a single cash crop as the "backbone of the economy." What this actually meant was not the backbone of the peripheral countries, but of the core countries in Europe. In certain newly colonialized areas, vast territories were put under cropping in the late 19th and early 20th centuries. In the process not only the traditional economies were deformed and destroyed and nomads and peasants became landless, but forced wage labor was often practiced to close the gap between supply and demand in the labor market. This ensured development of the colonial mode of production in the early days of the settlement (Arrighi 1973:194).

When the colonialists left, they left behind a colonial design of development which is characterized by export-oriented economies, and in the Sudan, by large-scale irrigated projects, land expropriation, migrant labor, and poor wages.

At independence, most leaders who came to power were installed by the departing colonial power. They were not only standing up for their own interest but also for the interest of the ex-colonizers. So it is no surprise that the post-colonial programs of development in Africa were often geared to the existing policies of development. Many politicians and leaders followed their colonial predecessors' footprints.

During the late 1960s and early 1970s, the African governments began to witness serious deterioration of their national economies due to the falling prices of raw materials in the world market and poor agricultural yields of their cash cropping. As economic crisis began to mount up, more land was assigned to follow the same policy of cash cropping. The result was more poverty and misery for the population, more structural economic shakeup, and a more tightening link with the world market system. Amin underlines some of the policies of development in Africa saying:

> As we know, a so-called "liberal" political system issuing from independence, superimposed on an astonishing 'laissez-faire' economics (unlimited access to the market of the international capitalist enterprise, etc.) could only lead to the aggravation of

social and regional inequalities and recourse to shortsighted manipulations based on ethnic appeal (Amin 1974:83).

As the developing nations, especially the African nations, approach the late 1980s, severe deterioration of agricultural production is going on accompanied by collapsing economies which have little promise for an increasing 35 million Sudanese people at the brink of starvation (1985). The colonial and post-colonial programs of developing export-oriented economies proved to be pregnant with social, political, and economic catastrophes. The African nations, under these alarming situations of drought, desertification and famine, can no longer serve as peripheries. It is time to delink their economies from the export-oriented approach and concentrate on growing food. A food security approach should be adopted for a potentially starving population around the African continent.

DEVELOPMENT AND SETTLEMENT SCHEMES IN SUDAN

The Sudanese economy and its success depended greatly on irrigated agriculture. The Gezira schemes for more than two decades has represented the dominant feature of the Sudanese economy, which basically depends on the production of cotton. Chambers noted that:

A tripartite agreement was patiently negotiated between government, a commercial managing syndicate, and landowners, and by 1962 some 1,800,000 acres of near-desert had been described as 'Africa's most impressive man-made landscape.' Gezira became so much the backbone of the economy of the Sudan that it has even been considered that without it there could have been no Sudanese independence (Chambers 1969:19).

Because of the Gezira scheme historical importance, it not only brought economic change, it also brought political change and social transformation through the 1950s and 1960s. With the late 1960s and early 1970s, the Gezira scheme was witnessing economic problems, and hence the whole Sudanese economy suffered. The reason is not only the sinking prices of cotton in the world market, but also the exploitative structural dependency relation that ties the British industrial interest (Lancashire textile factories) to the Gezira economy. As the Sudanese economy was beginning to suffer serious setbacks, more land was assigned to grow cotton for export. Schemes like Gezira were extended to reach 2.1 million Feddans managed by the Sudan Gezira Board (SGB). A further 400,000 Feddans were irrigated on the Khasham el Girba scheme. Along the Blue and White Nile, 1.4 million Feddans were irrigated, also new projects like Rahad and El Suki were designed to be large-irrigated projects, with a concentration on cotton production, besides some diversification to produce wheat and oil seeds, with a total of 4 million Feddans under irrigation (ILO Report 1976). The Gezira model of development casts its shadow over the other irrigated development schemes that followed later. Because of the economic importance of Gezira in Sudan and the glory it had in the past, it remains a strong line of development that dictates the policies of developers and politicians in the Sudan.

The politicians and developers are repeatedly following the Gezira example without being fully aware of the way it served and is still serving the foreign interests that exploited not only the Gezira tenants and management, but also the government and its people.

In the recent study done by Barnett, he says of the Gezira:
It is stagnant, holds little hope of continually rising living standards for its inhabitants, and as a major component of the Sudanese economy, it exposes that economy and, thus, the society to considerable potential and actual instability (Barnett 1977:15).

The defects of the Gezira scheme, in terms of its declining, deterioration, its dim future promise for its population and the national economy, are already surfacing in other large-scale irrigated projects that followed the Gezira model.

"THE BREADBASKET" AS A STRATEGY OF DEVELOPMENT

In the 1970s, the government earmarked considerable resources and finance to start the so-called "breadbasket strategy." The aim of the breadbasket strategy is to make the Sudan the largest agricultural producer in Africa and the Middle East. This strategy generated a lot of enthusiasm and encouragement among the politicians and developers who could see the Sudan not only self-sufficient, but a net exporter of food and grain to Africa and the Arab world.

The central rainlands of Sudan is the site for the breadbasket strategy. These central clay lands of the Sudan traditionally are the homeland of the nomads and the peasants who use the rainlands for economic subsistence. They have depended on these lands for centuries as pastures and sorghum fields, besides making use of other benefits, like hunting and collecting acacia products (gum arabic) to be sold in the market. The situation began to change drastically, when the colonial government started mechanized agriculture in the Gadambiliyya area (Kassala Province) in 1944 to grow sorghum. With the success of the first mechanized experience, mechanized agriculture began to bite off the land of the nomads and peasants in the central clay plains of the Sudan. Vast territories were given to the merchants and important individuals. Towards the 1960s, the Gedaref (Kassala Province) reached an extension of 1 million Feddans. The most important characteristic of the Gedaref area farms is their size of around 1,000 Feddans (Mashro) or individual rainfed, mechanized holdings. During the same time (1950s -1960s), new mechanized schemes were opened in the Dali and Mazmum areas to reach a size of 550,000 Feddans. During the late 1960s, new mechanized schemes were cleared, which included state farms like Agadi and Garabin in the Blue Nile Province. In the 1970s, mechanized rainfed agriculture reached the White Nile Province, Kordofan, Dar Fur, and Bahr el Ghazal. The main crops to be produced in these schemes are sorghum, sesame, groundnuts, and in some areas like the Nuba Mountains, cotton was introduced. All the plans that have been started since the 1940s have neglected and disregarded the indigenous population and their subsistence. Through time, the nomads and peasants were not only pushed into poor and marginal areas, but their rural mode of subsistence was deformed and destroyed. Considerable segments of the local inhabitants either became poor agricultural laborers or drifted to shantytowns to find some sort of subsistence.

The design of the breadbasket strategy put great emphasis on cash and stable cropping production in the central clay lands of the Sudan. What is meant is "horizontal expansion," which needs vast territories to be put under cropping and to be supervised by "Public Mechanized Farming Corporation." The design of the breadbasket strategy is part of the six year plan (SYP) 1977–78 – 1982–83, the food investment strategy, and the basic program. All these programs are directed towards the rural areas to produce commercial crops and animal husbandry. The capital for these programs is provided by the Arab states. The rural areas are penetrated by foreign capital, multinational corporations, and merchant capital to modernize the traditional subsistence sector. The allocation of 4 million Feddans by the six year plan to be put under cropping only worsens the situation for the rural people.

> The strategy is characterized by the overwhelming goal of maximizing agricultural net exports, regardless of the sectoral, regional, and social imbalances created in Sudanese agriculture as a consequence. As a result of the steady replacement of small peasant and nomadic forms of food production by commercial agricultural ventures, acute deficiencies of food supply have now emerged (Oesterdiekhoff and Wohlmuth 1983:49).

By the early 1980s, the breadbasket strategy had not only failed, but it was a catastrophe for rural man, economy, and ecology. This complete failure stems from the haphazard planning carried out by the government. In planning for the breadbasket strategy, the economic rights of the nomads and peasants were ignored, and they were described not only as primitive and backward in pursuing their economic subsistence, but as incompatible with the ambitious programs of this strategy. Secondly, any country which engages in international trade must be much geared to the concept of "comparative advantage." which means calculating accurately the cost and benefit of production for export and thus also the cost of importing that which is not produced locally. The government failed to identify the real opportunity cost of production, instead they pushed the commercialization of agriculture, which landed the Sudan as a food importer instead of being an exporter.

Thirdly, the ecology and environment have been severely devastated by the strategy, especially the rainfed agricultural schemes cultivated by the "private sector." In most cases, this means wealthy merchants in nearby towns. The merchants who are investing in these schemes have as their goal the quick profit. What they are practicing in these rainfed mechanized schemes is what is known as "agricultural mining." To pursue their goal of making profit, they use the rural proletariat as cheap wage laborers to slash and burn not only the 1,000 Feddans assigned land for them, but to annex illegally the farming land around their schemes. A lot of harm is done to the environment and the economy by excess land clearing. Lands become barren without a single tree as far as the eye can see, which invites an inevitable desertification. Because of lack of supervision and inspection by the Mechanized Farming Corporation (MFC), the private investors do their ploughing regardless of the contours of the land and the system of drainage. As a result, the land begins to lose its fertility and decline as the topsoil is washed away.

The breadbasket strategy as a way of development failed because the Sudan government, irrespective of any consequences, wanted to boost commercialized agriculture to confirm its position as an export-oriented country. In the process, the rural population is wrestling with the problem of poverty and lack of food while the towns' dwellers are restless and antagonistic to the skyrocketing prices of imported foodstuff. When the restlessness and antagonism boiled over, a successful civil-strike brought down the government of Nimeiri on April 6, 1985 and with it the breadbasket strategy.

SUGAR SCHEMES IN THE SUDAN

In the past, sugar cane was grown in the Sudan solely for chewing, and sometimes to be marketed for the same purpose. Prior to the establishment of sugar refineries in Sudan, all the sugar needed by consumers was imported from abroad. Sugar proved to be a very popular commodity in Sudan, for its different uses in preparing coffee, tea, and other delicacies in Sudanese food. Some tribal communities (Baggara groups) have ritual gatherings of drinking tea with sugar. In these rural communities as well as urban areas, sugar is an essential part of their daily diet. A shortage in sugar quantities or any attempt to increase its price, creates a lot of resentment of the government. The former government (1969 - 1985), knowing the strategic importance of sugar to the people, tightly controlled the flow of sugar and increased the price, which made sugar towards the early and mid-1980s more of a luxury commodity than a basic-need one. The increase of sugar prices gave rise to black marketeering, and sugar quotas going to distant provinces vanished. Most families were touched by shortage of sugar, high prices, and long lines of people scrambling to get sugar.

The first sugar scheme and refinery that marked the present era of sugar industry was the Geneid project, established in 1962. The project lies on the eastern bank of the Blue Nile, 120km south-east of Khartoum. The size of the project is 44,500 Feddans of which 19,500 is under irrigation. Sugar cane production is handled by tenants with a 15 Feddans farm, which is subjected to a six-course system of rotation. Sugar cane is collected and crushed in the Geneid factory to produce approximately 60,000 tons of sugar per year.

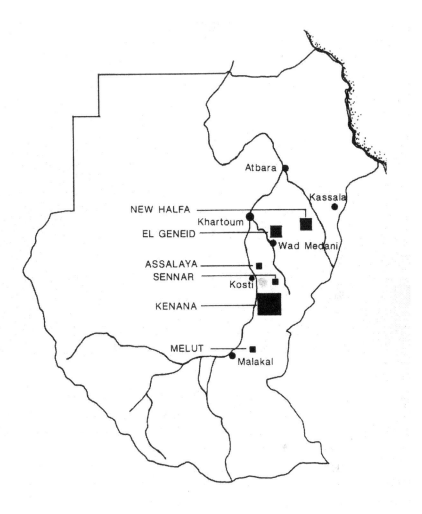

SOURCE: Sudanow, October, 1980.

Figure 4 Location of Sugar Projects in the Sudan

Table 4.1

SUGAR PRODUCTION AND CONSUMPTION IN THE SUDAN

Total Rates of the production and domestic consumption of Sugar in the Sudan between 1969–1979.

Figures released in annual report of Bank of Sudan.

Year	Geneid	New Halfa	Sennar	Total Production	Total Consumption
1969/70	18,460	56,857	–	75,317	210,342
1970/71	37,679	35,603	–	72,582	230,000
1971/72	28,475	62,905	–	91,380	241,000
1972/73	42,133	70,508	–	112,641	250,000
1973/74	45,268	73,303	–	120,571	269,754
1974/75	52,727	75,924	–	128,651	242,570
1975/76	54,155	59,794	–	113,949	274,149
1976/77	55,074	57,168	26,465	138,707	295,915
1977/78	48,336	58,214	18,177	138,209	314,981
1978/79	36,539	64,849	31,659	119,565	330,678
*All figures represented are in metric tones Source – Sudanow October 1980 *Sudan sugar consumption in 1982–1983 is: 450,000					
Sudan sugar production in 1982–1983 is	275.000				
The amount to be imported is	175,000				

Source - FAO (World Food Day) 1983.

The second sugar scheme, established in 1965, was Khashm el Girba scheme, which is sometimes known as (New Halfa). Khashm el Girba scheme lies in Kassala Province, 350km east of Khartoum. The project was a resettlement project for Halfawin displaced by the high

Aswan dam. It is irrigated from the Atabra river. Khashm el Girba dam was established on the Atabra river to ensure an adequate supply of water all the year round for cane, wheat, and vegetables. The scheme farms are handled by tenants who harvest the cane (by hand) and supply it to the refinery which has a capacity of 60,000 tons of sugar production annually. Khashm el Girba, like other sugar schemes in Sudan, has faced some difficulties ranging from expelling the Buttana nomads from their land, which resulted in a lot of crop destruction and hence crop failure, to mismanagement and technical difficulties in the sugar factory.

The third sugar scheme was North-West Sennar, started in 1972. It is about 240km south-east of Khartoum. The clay plains on which the project is executed is similar to the twin sugar schemes of Assalaya and Kenana on the White Nile. North-West Sennar Sugar Scheme started sugar production in the season of 1976–1977. The project is irrigated from the Blue Nile with its pump station situated near the village of Maiurno south of Sennar. The capacity of the factory is to crush 6,500 tons of sugar per day during the production season with an annual output of 40,000 tons of refined sugar.

In 1973, work started on the fourth sugar scheme: Hajar Assalaya. The project lies 6km from Rabak and 36km from Kenana site. Hajar Assalaya Sugar Scheme is adjacent to the southern boundaries on the Gezira scheme. Total size of the project is 31,000 Feddans and the area under cane-cropping is 27,000 Feddans irrigated from the White Nile. Before they began operating the factory, a serious difficulty arose. The heavy machinery of the factory is situated on so-called "black cotton soil," which has the feature of expanding and contracting in the different seasons of the year. When the factory went into operation for the first time, the land underneath started to crack. The factory operation had to be stopped to make the necessary revisions in construction. Only after that could the cane be crushed to mark the first season of production of 7,000 tons of sugar (in 1979 - 1980). Full production capacity is 110,000 tons of sugar annually. Hajar Assalaya, like other development projects in which land expropriation is practiced, resulted in thousands of displaced nomads and peasants in Dar Muharib area.

A fifth sugar scheme was started in the early 1970s in the Upper Nile Province: Melut Sugar Scheme. This project is not yet completed, mainly because of political instability in the region and the difficulty of transportation of heavy equipment from Port Sudan to the south.

The sixth sugar project in the Sudan is Kenana sugar scheme. The implementation of the project started in 1975, but sugar production didn't begin until the 1980 - 1981 season. The Kenana Scheme lies south of Khartoum a distance of 320km. It is 30km from Rabak and 36km from Hajar Assalaya Sugar Scheme. The total size of the Kenana Sugar Estate is 150,000 Feddans of which 80,000 Feddans are under cane-cropping. It is irrigated from the White Nile. The scheme developed the so-called long-farrow irrigation method, which sometimes reaches 2km long. This method is said to lessen the amount of labor put into irrigation. Maximum capacity of sugar production is planned to be 330,000 tons per year. The Kenana Sugar Estate is administered by the Kenana Sugar Company (KSC), composed of both public and private shareholders.

The Kenana project attracted skilled and unskilled labor, expatriates, Sudanese rural migrants, and refugees from neighboring countries. The officials and laborers who came to the area found work, whether with KSC or providing services for the people working in the project on the other hand, the indigenous population lost their land on which the project is made and failed to find jobs to sustain them while living with an increasing influx of migrants that has brought Kenana to a total population of 60,000 persons.

KENANA SUGAR SCHEME

Kenana Site Selection

The idea of establishing a giant sugar project and refinery was developed in 1971, when the Sudan was importing thousands of tons of sugar. It was decided a successful sugar project would not only satisfy the need at home but could help the economy by exporting sugar and earning hard currency. The site selection should satisfy certain requirements. These requirements are very crucial for the success of agricultural projects in general and sugar schemes in particular.

1. Climate

Elsewhere, sugar projects are located in the zones of high rainfall. This method of growing sugar cane has its disadvantages. If rainfall fluctuates, so does sugar production. A semi-arid climate with irrigation is perfectly acceptable for growing sugar cane since with irrigation control production can be predictable. Another advantage of the semi-arid climate is the near absence of in-field problems caused by rain during the harvest season. The growing of sugar cane needs a high number of hours of sunshine, especially for its maturity, and this can easily be found in a semi-arid climate.

2. Water

A reliable, constant, and adequate supply of water should be available.

3. Soils

Should have no problems such as salinity, alkalinity, or inadequate depth.

4. Land

Topographically good, with adequate regional drainage.

5. Power

An adequate and reliable source is crucial.

6. Transport

Good, all-weather road and rail should be available to link the project with the adjoining areas as well as the rest of the country.

Besides all the above points, many other details were taken into consideration when choosing Kenana location. In light of the geographical and agricultural information above, in September 1972 the former minister[1] of industry and mining allocated the following areas as possible sites for the sugar project:

a. West Bank of the Blue Nile from El Roseires to Singa.

b. East Bank of the White Nile from Malakal to Mangala.

c. East Bank of the White Nile from Malakal to Kosti.

Preliminary surveys and investigation of the above three proposed areas for the giant sugar project showed that important factors have to be reviewed carefully if the sugar scheme was to be implemented in one of these proposed sites.

a. Roseires - Singa

In this proposed site, it was found that there wasn't sufficient water available in the Blue Nile to provide for irrigation until the program of raising of the Roseires dam has been completed.

b. Malakal - Mangalla

This proposed site was rejected on the grounds that it is remote, with great difficulties of transportation and communication, approximately 1,000km away from the railway.

c. Malakal - Kosti

Since this site has three areas or possible sites within itself, two possible sites were rejected on the account of problems of transportation, power, and soil. These areas were Malakal - Renk and Renk - El Jebelein. So the favorable location of the proposed sugar scheme site lay between El Jebelein - Rabak on the east bank of White Nile opposite to the town of Kosti. This area between El Jebelein and Rabak was chosen to be the sugar project site (which became known later as Kenana Sugar Estate) because of the advantages of the area.

The Kenana[2] Sugar Estate lies between latitude 12° 51'–13° 15' and longitude 33°–33° 43'. Rabak town is 30km away north-west of Kenana site. Kosti, the largest town in the province, lies 40km west of Kenana site.

In the past, access to Kosti and Western Sudan by rail and vehicles was across the cantilever bridge erected in the 1920s with a central part that opens to allow river transport to and from the southern region. Starting from 1982 access to Kosti and Western Sudan was made easy through the concrete arched-bridge (the New White Nile Bridge), which made traffic easy and fast from both sides of the river, instead of the slow and monotonous traffic of the old cantilever bridge.

The Kenana Estate covers an area of 150,000 Feddans. The sugar cane plantation occupies 80,000 Feddans. The sugar cane fields are part of the central clay rainlands of the Sudan between the Blue and the White Nile. Within the boundaries of Kenana Sugar Estate, there is 1,350 Feddans of gravel outcrop, which has supplied material for the concrete foundation of the factory and the main township. The land in which Kenana Sugar Estate is situated belonged to the nomads and peasants of Dar Muharib, who used the area as grazing pastures and sorghum fields for centuries. Their subsistence mode of production ceased to exist when the area was converted to the new Kenana site.

1. Climate

For the greater part of the year, the climate is tropical and very hot; however, the semi-arid climate and irrigation potential is perfect for sugar production. Temperatures are highest in April and May with an absolute maximum of 45° C. , and lowest during December and January with an absolute minimum of 17° C. The mean annual rainfall is 400mm with almost all the precipitation between June and September with maximum rainfall in July and August. There is high evaporation throughout the year. Sunshine hours are high with an average of 9.4 hours/day, which is very important for sugar cane growing.

2. The White Nile

Lake Victoria is the source of the Victoria Nile, which flows through Lake Kioga into Lake Albert. As it enters, Sudan at Nimule it is called the Albert Nile. From Nimule it is known as Bahr el Jebel, and it enters the seasonal swamp "sudd" region, and it is estimated that 50–70% of the flow is lost by evaporation there. On its way north, it is joined by

Bahr el Ghazal west of Malakal. It is also joined by the Sobat River, which rises in Ethiopia. The Sobat is considered to be the most important tributary in terms of water supply (half of the total flow of the White Nile) to the river. From the areas of confluence west of Malakal until Khartoum, it is called the White Nile. When it joins the Blue Nile at Khartoum, it becomes simply the Nile as it flows through the desert to Egypt.

The highest flow of the White Nile occurs in November with an average of 1176m^3/second. The lowest flow occurs in April with an average of 515m^3/second. The highest recorded mean monthly flow of 1400m^3/second took place in November 1946, and the lowest at 392m^3/second in April 1946.

The water in the White Nile is very reliable for irrigation, and it has a good quality. So the availability of the water all year round is ensured to feed the irrigation networks of Kenana Sugar Estate.

3. Soil

The soil of the Kenana project site is called "Brown Montmorillonitic Clays." The clays are derived from basic rocks in the Ethiopian highlands, which have been deposited by the Blue Nile to form the central clay lands of the Sudan, which includes the Gezira area. West of the project area lies the dark clay soils (Grumaguertic Orthustents) deposited by the White Nile, which are sodic and saline soils and not as suitable for rainfed and irrigated agriculture as the brown clay. Soils deposited by the Blue Nile extend east to west within 20km away from the bank of the White Nile. The brown clay soils crack which facilitates the entry of both rain water and irrigation. Once enough water has been absorbed, the soils swell, the cracks close, and this prevents the water table from rising, which causes serious drainage problems.

4. Transportation

The Kenana sugar scheme and factory site is only 30km away from Rabak, which is a railhead that connects the area to Khartoum, and through Kassala to Port Sudan. Rabak is also connected to the national network of all weather roads, which also connects the area to Khartoum as well as Port Sudan. Recently, a 30km railway was extended from Rabak to Kenana site to link Kenana with Khartoum, other parts of Sudan and Port Sudan. A gravel road was extended from the site to Rabak to serve the same purpose of linking the area with the other provinces of Sudan, and traffic became even easier after the completion of the New White Nile Bridge that connects Rabak and Kosti and thus Western Sudan. In addition to rail and all weather road, there is regular river transport service from Khartoum to Kosti and from Kosti to Juba in the southern region. So the Kenana site has a good location and easy access to transport and communication.

5. Power

As Kenana needs power and electricity for different purposes, ranging from the energy to pump water to electrifying the new town, the Sennar–Kosti power line is adequate to supply the Kenana site with power.

6. Construction Materials

In the process of construction, a large amount of cement was needed. Rabak cement factory was appropriate for the purpose, with a reliable source of lime nearby at Jebel Nyefir. Kenana site is rich in the gravel, sand deposits, and granite Jebels needed in the process of construction.

KENANA IMPLEMENTATION, MULTINATIONALS, AND ARAB COMPANIES SCRAMBLE

In 1971 the idea of a giant sugar scheme in the Sudan to be managed by Lonrho[3] was mapped out by Dr. Khalil[4] and Mr. Rowland.[5] On June 9, 1972, an agreement was reached between the Sudan government and Lonrho, giving the green light for Lonrho to start the feasibility study. Another part of the agreement indicated that if the project went ahead, a jointly owned Lonrho/Sudan government company would be worked out for its implementation.

In October 1973, the Kenana feasibility study was completed by Lonrho. The study estimated the total cost of the Kenana project at L.S.

50 million ($125 million) from the project start in 1972 to its completion in 1978. The report indicated that Lonrho was evaluating the final plan to finance the project, and it stresses Lonrho's eventual involvement in the Kenana project.

In 1973, Lonrho set up a cane nursery at the site. A 9km canal was completed to draw water from the White Nile to irrigate the 2,000 Feddans cane nursery to test irrigation, agricultural methods, and grow seed cane for the Kenana Sugar Estate.

A year had passed since Lonrho had completed the feasibility study. There was no significant development in terms of Kenana project finance, which Lonrho had promised the Sudanese government. Officials in the ministry of industry (sugar project division) began to have doubts about Lonrho's financial credibility to develop the project. Things became worse when it was rumored that Lonrho was having difficulty raising adequate funds. So the whole Lonrho plan to go ahead with Kenana project was called into question. In May 1974, it was announced that after negotiation Gulf International[6] had purchased 2 million Lonrho shares, and on November 19, 1974, another 8 million shares were purchased by Shaykh Nasser Sabah el Ahmed el Sabah,[7] his brother Shaykh Hamid, and notable members of Kuwait's business and investment community. Lonrho announced that the Kenana project would involve other multinationals, European, Japanese, and Arab capital to raise the $180 million to be invested in the project with a productive capacity of 330,000 tons of refined sugar annually and to be increased in the years ahead. The Japanese partners were named as Nissho-Iwai, a company which Lonrho had earlier developed relations with. Nissho-Iwai won the $40 million contract to supply the sugar factory's bagasse—burning, 40mw power plant. This is a six boiler plant, generating 113 tons of steam to drive four turbine generators. The plant is second only to Roseires dam hydroelectric power station on the Blue Nile.[8]

On February 17, 1975, the minister of industry and mining[9] signed the final agreement for the implementation of the Kenana project. Signing of this agreement brought sudden escalation of the cost of implementing the project. In October 1973, the cost had been put at $150 million, $180 million in December 1974, and it continued to escalate to $250 million, $290 million, and then $475 million between 1975 and 1976. The cost of Kenana project implementation was believed to have skyrocketed to over 1 billion dollars when it started production in 1980–1981. The unexpected and the costly Kenana implementation is attributed to world inflation and the poor infrastructure in the Sudan. To many people this is not convincing. Only in the future may people know why the project cost so much and yet employs only 14,000 people of which 8,000 work on a seasonal basis.

The Kenana Sugar Company Ltd. registered and incorporated in February 1975. The stake of Sudan government in the company was 61%: 51% through the Ministry of Finance, to be paid by Lonrho, and 10% through the Sudan Development Corporation. The share of Lonrho Company was 12%, the Riyad-based Arab Investment Company 17%, Gulf Fisheries (which is part of Gulf International headed by Shaykh Nasser and his family) 5%, and Nissho-Iwai of Japan 5%.

Table 4.2

How the Feasibility Study Estimated
The Cost of Kenana Project

Item	£s Million	% of Total
Factory	28.33	58%
Irrigation works and Infrastructure	10.55	22%
Agricultural and land Preparation equipment	3.16	6%
Pre-production expenses	3.03	6%

Land preparation planting And seed care	1.59	3%
Other fixed assets	1.34	3%
Stores	0.99	2%
Total	48.99	100%

Table 4.3

THE ESCALATION OF COSTS

Date	Source	Cost $ Million
October 1973	Feasibility study	150
December 1974	Nissho-Iwai announcement	150
February 1975	Ministry of Industry	250
February 1975	Arab Investment Company	290
October 1976	Ministry of Industry	475

Source: Sudanow 1977.

*It is worth noting here that the cost continued escalation until it reached over 1 billion in Kenana opening season 1980–1981.

The board held its first meeting the day after the Kenana Company registration in Khartoum, and the appointment of new management staff[10] to boost the construction and development operation. After one year, the Kuwaiti Foreign Trading, Contracting and Investment Company (KFTIC) entered Kenana as a new shareholder, which led the shareholding and power structure in the Kenana Company to be revised.

As work was set to begin on the project a Kuwaiti company known as the International Contracting Company (ICC) announced that it had won the contract for the construction of the irrigation canals. The ICC is a subsidiary of the largely Kuwaiti government owned company (KFTIC), which later claimed the acquisition of considerable shares in the Kenana Company.

With the announcement by ICC tension and suspicion began to mount between shareholders. Things began to look worse when it was discovered that ICC had little experience in constructing irrigation networks and at the same time asked for $102 million to complete the job. Lonrho turned down the ICC proposal, though they are said to have walked away with a large sum of money. Lonrho gave the construction of irrigation networks to the British firm, Sir Alfred McAlpine and Son, in December 1975.

In January 1976, the first two convoys of McAlpine heavy equipment for earth-moving and excavation arrived from Port Sudan by road. In September 1976, McAlpine started digging the main canal (29km) to carry water from the White Nile to the head of the sugar estate with a capacity of 500,000 gallons of water per minute. In October 1976, the contract with McAlpine had been raised to $51.5 million to include the excavation of the Kenana sugar factory and the construction of the first three pump stations that carry the water of the White Nile to pump station 4 and then to the entire sugar estate. The Kenana pump stations would lift water gradually 42m above the river level at the rate of 34 million gallons an hour and then into Kenana cane fields. The $12 million contract for supply and installation of the four pump stations went to the Austrian firm Andritz. The contract was to be financed by the Austrian Government's Creditanstaldt Agency as an export credit.[11]

The American company, Arkel International Inc., designed the Kenana sugar factory (two phases). The refinery is designed to crush 17,000 tons of sugar cane to produce 1,700 tons of white refined sugar every day, with a total production capacity of 330,000 per year, which will be limited to the crushing season that starts in November and ends in April. The factory was supposed to begin production by November 1, 1978, but the deadline could not be met, so it started three years later.

Kenana planners wanted the refinery to be one giant factory, unlike other sugar projects around the world where sugar cane is crushed in a number of small factories within the project area. The planners argue that only one giant factory is possible in the Kenana site, because there is only one suitable area for building and operating the factory; a firm, solid gravel ridge which rises 400 m. above the dark soft clays of the Blue Nile, which swell in the wet season and crack in the dry season.

An agreement was reached in December 1975 for the Compagnie Francais d' Etude Construction Technip (which is owned by the French Government) to supply the Kenana sugar refinery.

The cost of the factory, including transportation to Port Sudan, with no site preparation or factory erection, was $170 million (FF 756 million), a 290 percent escalation cost over the $43.5 million given in the feasibility study completed in October 1973.

The $170 million was made up of $130 million (FF 578 million) to Technip to cover the cost of the items of refinery equipment, and $40 million (FF 178 million) to Nissho – Iwai to cover the cost of the factory boilers and generators.

Shortly after the agreement with Technip the project ran short of funds and finance to build the factory and other divisions of the estate. The Kuwaiti Government took the initiative and expressed its interest in investing in the Kenana project through its holding company KFTIC. The deal was signed on February 19, 1976 and is known as the "Kuwaiti Participation Agreement." This agreement gave KFTIC a 23 percent stake in Kenana, while at the same time the company earmarked $23 million as a loan to the Kenana project.

Table 4.4

The Factory Cost (in $ Million)

Iteam	Feasibility Study	Actual Cost	Percentage Increase	Contractors
Manufacturer plus ocean freight to port sudan	43.5	170.0	290%	Technip ($130 m.) Nissho-Iwai

Perparation of factory site	11.9	19.5	64%	McAlpines
Erection and commissioning	8.2	42.5	418%	Capper-Neill
Transport from Port Sudan to site	2.2	2.0	NIL	Wynns
Escalation allowance	5.0			
	70.8	234.0	230%	

Source – Sudanow August 1977

The Rate of exchange then, L.S. 1 = $2.4872

£ 1 = L.S. 0.96

£ 1 = $2.3877

Kenana Company's share structure were revised as the result of the new Kuwaiti investment. The Sudan Government now held 50%; (40% Ministry of Finance and 10% Sudan Development Corporation). KFTIC's 23% situated it as the second largest shareholder in the company. The Arab Investment Company still held 17%, while Lonrho's stake dropped from 12% to 5.5%, and Gulf and Nissho - Iwai both went down to 2.25%.

On November 25th 1976, former President Nimeiri laid the foundation stone of the project. By that time, the cost of the project had tripled. A growing dissatisfaction and frustration began to build up between the shareholders, especially Lonrho and the Kuwaiti KFTIC. The Lonrho management was widely criticized for its failure to assess the cost of the project correctly, which created a lot of financial difficulties. The KFTIC and Lonrho went into bitter disagreement when each of the companies tried to install its own managing director for the new scheme. The situation was critical since KFTIC still had to provide new finance for the project, and if their demands were not met, more financial problems would bedevil the project. On May 22, 1976, in a meeting held in Khartoum, Lonrho was terminated[12], and its management services ended. It was held that the Arab investors were blackmailed by Lonrho's management, which was held responsible for the increasing cost of the project. Lonrho was voted out, and in the same meeting, an agreement was reached by the rest of the shareholders to increase the capital of Kenana Sugar Company (KSC) by $60 million according to their shareholding stake in KSC. Also the new management agreed that KFTIC and the Arab Investment Company would provide a new loan of $32 million for the Kenana Sugar Scheme.[13]

In March 1981, former President Nimeiri and others attended the inauguration of the scheme, which marked the beginning of sugar production by the KSC. An agreement was worked out by the KSC and Sudan Government to half the production of Kenana sugar (around 150,000 tons) would be exported to earn foreign currency, while the other 150,000 tons of sugar would be sold to Sudan Government locally, but the price would be in hard currency.

KSC shareholding kept changing through the project implementation period, and so it remained after moving into its production phase. The latest change in shareholding was worked out in a meeting in Khartoum in February 1983. The latest KSC shareholders stake is: Sudan Government 32.8%, Kuwait Government 31.9%, Saudi Arabia 11.4%, Arab Investment Company (Riyad) 8.3%, Sudan Development Corporation 5.3%, Arab Authority for Agriculture and Industrial Development (AAAID) 5.2%, Nilein Bank (Khartoum) 2.0%, Sudan Commercial Bank (Khartoum) 1.1%, Unity Bank (Khartoum) 1.1%, Lonrho (London) 0.5%, Gulf International (Kuwait) 0.2% and Nissho - Iwai (Japan) 0.2%.[14]

While the multinationals and the Arab investors were scrambling over the management control of the Kenana Scheme, the Sudan Government turned a blind eye to the land and pasture rights of the peasants and the nomads in the area. So 150,000 Feddans of traditional tribal land were transformed into Kenana Sugar Estate, thus displacing over 40,000 of the indigenous population of Dar Muharib, who had been using the region for centuries in pursuing a closed subsistence economy.

THE QUESTION OF COMPENSATION AND DISPLACEMENT OF DAR MUHARIB POPULATION BY THE KENANA SUGAR COMPANY.

With the hope and expeculation of government officials that the breadbasket strategy was going to turn Sudan into the biggest food producer in Africa, they gave astonishing concessions in tax and custom exemptions, land leases, and water to the multinational corporations and the Arab companies. The goal of such huge concessions was to attract foreign capital to boost the breadbasket strategy as a way of development, and the multinationals and other companies responded. In the period from 1971 to 1985 foreign investors in Sudan got unlimited support from the Sudan Government in huge concessions and tax holidays. The scramble of foreign investors over Sudanese natural resources not only benefited them but created a new class of mainly government bureaucrats and merchants who were tapping every possible economic opportunity for themselves. So the breadbasket strategy weakened the economy, fostered social inequality, and produced more misery and deprivation for the rural peasants and nomads.

The Kenana Sugar Company is a powerful example. According to the Sugar Agreement (1972), the government agreed to lease KSC 150,000 Feddans on a yearly basis of 10 piaster/Feddan, which is almost a free lease. The time limit for the lease is 30 years, and it can be increased to another 20 years after the end of the 30 year lease. The government gave the green light to KSC to start clearing and then cultivation of the area that was chosen in the White Nile Province free of any duties, charges or any obligations to the indigenous population who subsist on the area. The government, by taking this step, not only gave away the land of the indigenous population of Dar Muharib, but they were destroying an entire rural society's life.

When the heavy earth-moving equipment started to reach Kenana site and the transformation of the land was underway in 1976, the nomads and the peasants started to pay a lot of attention to what was going on. The villages like Sufeiya, El Gargaf, Hillat Musri, Fangoga, Omdabakir, Nuri, and other nomadic camp residents started to ask a lot of questions about what is going to happen to them. Is the Kenana Scheme going to take away their sorghum fields, pastures, village sites, and camp sites?

The authorities of the scheme told them that this project is going to change their lives from a harsh poor life to a good fruitful one, where people are going to have jobs, hospitals, schools, etc. The indigenous population of the area accepted this promise with a lot of skepticism and pessimism since they can't make any correlation between losing their means of subsistence and at the same time the promise of a good fruitful life ahead. The government, to ease the tension of the local population, told them that there would be compensation for every one who cultivated any land caught within the boundaries of the Kenana project. Also, there would be compensation for every hut owned by a family. The people of Kenana region thought the compensation would be fair enough to enable them to start a new life somewhere else and pay for cost of adjustment. To their astonishment everyone who owned a Feddan of land was compensated 75 piasters, and everyone who owned a hut was compensated ten piasters. This compensation is not on a year to year base. It is once and for all. A family of seven persons, owning three huts and ten Feddans, has been compensated approximately L.S. 8 ($20) once and for all for their sorghum fields, huts, and tent sites. The local population knew that they were in a dawn of bitterly frustrating changes, changes happening as they see their means of subsistence slipping away into so-called "integrated rural development." A delegation of Shaykhs wanted to meet with the KSC administration when they saw their tribal life was on the line. The KSC promised the Shaykhs priority of job opportunities, a canal to be extended outside the irrigated area to be used by livestock owners, and small plots of land for the local population to grow whatever they saw fit. The Dar Muharib Shaykhs were happy for the promises, and they were glad to tell their people that they "got a deal." But time has proved that the promises were false and were made to reduce immediate tensions and get rid of angry frustrated former users of the land.

As the construction was going on, the inhabitants of old Sufeiya were asked to leave, because the site of the village was the place of pump station 2 (P.S. 2). The inhabitants of Hillat Musri were asked to leave, because their village is within the boundaries of Kenana town site. Other villagers and nomads moved to Campo Khamsa (Camp 5), directly south of the sugar factory and adjacent to the heavy equipment workshop.

The Scheme began to attract an influx of migrants as the implementation was underway. The expatriates and the government officials were living in prefabricated houses and newly constructed dwelling units. The migrants, refugees, and the local inhabitants were living in Camp 5. Suddenly, Camp 5 began to snowball out of proportion as waves of migrants and casual laborers came, mainly from Western and Southern Sudan. In addition, some drought stricken villagers scrambled to make it to Kenana (Camp 5). Endless rows of compact metal shops (known as Camp 5 market) began to supply goods, food, and services for people in and around the area. Peasants began to put some of their products in the market: grain, ropes, firewood, and the nomads brought animals and milk products.

Camp 5, which was built of thatched huts, wind-screens, boards, and tins, accommodated people from all over Sudan with different economic and cultural backgrounds, which made it a hot bed of crimes and ethnic tensions. The local inhabitants now not only suffering from the loss of their properties, also had to fight being dominated by outside people. The cases of ethnic tensions and individual frictions were accompanied by a high rate of theft of KSC properties (mainly vehicles, machinery and fuel). The KSC administration began to be alarmed by the high theft rate. However, they were more alarmed by the fire hazards of Camp 5, which was not far away from the refinery. Therefore, the KSC administration, after a meeting with the local government authorities, started to arrange for a new location for Camp 5. The agreement between KSC and the local authorities pinpoints the importance of providing clean potable water, schools, dressing station, etc., for the inhabitants of Camp 5, who were also going to be relocated based on whether they were new migrants or local inhabitants.

In early 1981, the dwellers of Camp 5 began to be relocated. The local inhabitants of the area, the nomads, and the peasants were told to choose between three congregated villages: Abu Togaba (about 5km south of the factory), Nuri, and Fangoga, which are far from the Kenana site. Most people preferred to live in Abu Togaba because of its closeness to Kenana site. All the new migrants and refugees of former Camp 5 were relocated in present Camp 4 and Camp 5 about 5km west of the factory. Most people who now live in these two camps are either casual workers or families migrated to the area to engage in making and selling tea, food, and local beer (Marissa), and hang around to see if there are new opportunities from KSC to employ people.

With the implementation of the Kenana Sugar Scheme, the situation has continued to worsen for the nomads and peasants, who are the original users of the land. They are not only victimized by their land and property loss, but most of the promises made to them by KSC have proved to be false, including the priority of working opportunities (which went to the new migrants and immigrants). Since then, great numbers of local Kenana dwellers have migrated to other regions. However, some prefer to stay and face a fierce struggle for survival.

KENANA PRODUCTION COST

The Kenana sugar scheme estimation of production cost is far greater than other African sugar producers. The World Bank estimates that the Kenana production cost is 50 to 100 percent higher than the cost of other African sugar producers (Wohlmuth 1983:210). The production cost is not only higher than other African producers; it is also higher than production costs of other Sudanese sugar schemes. The estimated production costs of L.S. 95 to 115 per ton in Kenana are higher than the national average production costs in the Sudanese sugar industry (which includes sugar schemes of Kashm El Girba (New Halfa), Sennar, Hajar Assalaya, and El Geneid, which has experienced difficulties in sugar productivity since the 1960s.

The high production costs in Kenana is far greater than the world market sugar prices. A fact which jeopardizes Kenana sugar competitiveness in the world market. Kenana production cost is not near South American sugar producers who can sell between 6 and 10 cent a pound, and the Asian and African producers who sell between 8.2 and 10 cents. It is estimated that in order to cover the Kenana scheme costs, a price of U.S. $450 per metric ton will be essential for ten to fifteen years after the beginning of production to break even. Another source estimates that Kenana will break even at approximately U.S. $473 per ton, including debt and loan repayments, and about U.S. $283 after debt and loan repayments (Ibid 1983:211).

Kenana scheme is heavily dependent on foreign loans, capital, and other forms of foreign exchange transactions even after it began to produce. In the second production season, U.S. $50 million were needed to start production. This policy of injecting continuous foreign capital into Kenana Scheme could lead to serious debt in the future.

Kenana was like other development projects launched to boost agricultural production within the context of the breadbasket strategy, but the Kenana Scheme had first priority. In Port Sudan, it had unlimited harbour services, and an area assigned especially for Kenana equipment. It also had priority of transportation over land and rail, which contributed to delays of establishment of other projects like building all weather roads, new educational institutes (University of Gezira and Juba), development of mineral projects, the Jonglei project, pipeline projects, and sugar schemes at Assalaya (1974), Sennar (1974), Mangala (1975), and Melut (1975). The priority given by the government to Kenana Scheme did not help to reduce the Kenana project costs. However, it made other infrastructure and developmental projects suffer increasing cost of delays, which postponed the contribution of these projects to the Sudanese economy.

The land, which was populated by wildlife and acacia trees, was slashed and burned to be ploughed for cane growing. Environmentally, the area is affected by its loss of wild life, and it exposes the area to desert encroachment through dust and sandstorms. The other devastating effect is to the traditional users of the land, who now have no land, no jobs and no role to play in the new market economy.

CHAPTER FOUR NOTES

1.   Mr. Musa Awad Belal.

2.   The name Kenana is the name of a nomadic tribe that emigrated from Arabia to Sudan during medieval times. They live in the Blue Nile Province, but some segments of the tribe spend the wet season in Dar Muharib area. Kenana tribe is famous for their cattle quality that is known as the "Kenana type," a good milking type. Also Kenana tribe was famous during the Mahaddiyya. They and Degheim making the famous combat division known as the "green flag" under the leadership of Ali wad Hilu.

A Kenana tribesman informant told me that the name Kenana was given to the scheme because, in the ruins of El Jebel (present residential area for the senior staff) a name of Ali el Kenani was written long time ago, when it was found recently, the area called after his tribe, Kenana.

3.   A multinational British company, its interests range from trading and mining to sugar plantations. Most of its economic deals are executed in Africa. This company is widely criticized for its exploitation of African countries. The company has a bad record in Britain. The former Britain conservative prime minister attacked Lonrho with the phrase, "The unacceptable face of capitalism."

4.   A famous Sudanese businessman.

5.   Then Lonrho's chief executive who was known to have excellent relations with the former President Nimeiri.

6.   A Kuwaiti company.

7.   A Kuwaiti businessman and a member of the Kuwaiti ruling family.

8.   See Sudanow August 1977.

9.   Then Mr. Bedaraldine Suliaman.

10.   Then chairman of Kenana company was former Major-General Mohammed Idris Abdalla.

Lonrho management appointed Mr. Rene Leclezio, who worked with Lonrho sugar enterprise in South Africa, as managing director.

Sudan's government appointed Mr. Mohammed El Beshir El Wagie Chairman of the government controlled sugar corporation, Mr. Salah Abu El Naga of Bank of Sudan, Mr. Ibrahim Salih Mohammed of Ministry of Finance, and Mr. Ishag El Rasheid of the Attorney-General's chambers as directors in the Kenana Sugar Company. Dr. Khalil and Mr. Rowland also had seats on the board, representing Lonrho and Gulf International. Also, Nissho - Iwai, Sudan Development Corporation, and Arab Investment Company, have one seat each.

11.   See Sudanow August 1977.

12.   After Lonrho termination from KSC, Mr. Rowland (Chief Executive) sent a message to Nimeiri asking him to use his power in favor of Lonrho to come back into KSC management. Later, he knew from a minister that the government can do nothing in that area and told him his company is no longer needed in KSC management.

13.   See Sudanow August 1977.

14.   See Sudanow April 1983.

CHAPTER FIVE

KENANA ORGANIZATION OF THE SYSTEM OF PRODUCTION

LAND PREPARATION

Most of the land preparation activities are done by machines. When the transformation of the land started at Kenana site in 1976, the first stage was bush clearing. In this first stage a caterpillar D8K Tractor and Root Rake were used to uproot the bushes and pile them into heaps. The piles were then burned. The land was then ploughed using a disc harrow and a caterpillar D8K. Thirdly, land plaining was carried out. Land plaining is important because the surface of the land must have no ups and downs during the time of irrigation. After survey and layout was completed, the land was ridged using Mouldboard ridger to turn the land into farrows, which is the last stage in land preparation before cane planting and irrigation.

In this manner, 80,000 Feddans were brought under cane cropping. The area is divided into five agricultural divisions. Every agricultural division has a total size of 16,000 Feddans. The division is broken into small units to be used as cane fields. Such small areas planted in a complex pattern. Those first planted to cane would be harvested approximately 12 months after the seed cane is planted. After the harvest, usually the same area is irrigated again for a new crop. The cane is harvested for the second time after 2 years (called the first ratoon). Usually, an area will serve the refinery for three consecutive years before it is uprooted or ploughed out in case there is cane disease. The land then goes through the previous stages of land preparation: discing, land plaining, survey, layout, and ridging, before it is planted again.

SEED CANE AND PLANTING

Seed cane for the Kenana Scheme is grown at the estate cane nursery. The seed cane is examined carefully by agronomists for any possibility of fungus. The seed cane is cut by hand when it is 9 months old. It is stacked into bundles and transported to the fields by cane trailers. The daily laborers place the seed cane into the long farrows. It is fertilized and covered by a tractor and irrigated.

Recently, a great deal of effort has been expended by Kenana agronomists to investigate new commercial varieties of cane that have great resistance to the smut disease and less propensity to flower[1] prior to harvest.

IRRIGATION

Water from the White Nile is carried to the fields by four pump stations and a main canal 29km long. The four pump stations have a combined lift of 42m above the river level to reach the cane fields at the head of the estate.

The water is pumped from the White Nile by pump station 1 into the main canal and then lifted further by the rest of the pump stations, to be distributed into the primary canals that follow the contours of the land. At the off-take at the main canal there is a system of controls to regulate and adjust the supply of water in the primary canals according to need.

Water from the primary canals is fed to field canals, which run along the cane field edges. Workers feed water into individual farrows by syphons. The irrigation system used at Kenana is the long farrow type. The length of field farrows ranges from 1,500 to 2,000m long. This irrigation method is believed to reduce labor and facilitate machine operation in fields. A drainage system provides runoff from both irrigation and rain. The drain water accumulates at El Mazlagan and Khor Kleikis. This has produced a big surface of stagnant water that never reaches the White Nile. It now constitutes a health hazard to the nearby villages.

There is an irrigation manager who is in charge of the functioning of the irrigation system. His assistants and the irrigation controllers are the link between him and the canal checkers, gatemen, watchmen, and irrigation workers.

During the production season (November–April) the flow of water is very good. This is mainly due to the availability of electricity generated by the sugar factory using baggase as fuel. However, the peak time for irrigation is April - June, a time when the Kenana Scheme depends on the national supply of electricity to run the estate. The national supply of electricity is very erratic. It is common to have a number of power outages every day, sometimes lasting for many hours. It is during this time that cane fields suffer frequently from an inadequate supply of water, which affects the cane yields at the time of harvest.

FERTILIZERS AND WEED CONTROL

Fertilizers (potash and urea) are used heavily to maintain fertility. Herbicides are used to control weeds. Hand weeding is used to fight Cynodon Dactylon[2] (Najila), which is emerging as a threat to the cane fields. Sugar cane in Kenana, as in the Sudan generally is afflicted by the smut disease (Ustilago Scitaminea). Agronomists at Kenana are not only trying to prevent the smut disease but are developing new cane varieties with high resistance to it.

HARVEST, CANE TRANSPORT AND SUGAR PRODUCTIVITY

The start of the harvest season (November - April) marks the beginning of the production period in Kenana. The production season sometimes can be prolonged to May or June, which gives Kenana 210 crop days.

There are two methods of harvesting cane at Kenana; the first is the mechanical harvest, which constituted 60 percent of the work in

1983–84. The remaining 40 percent of the harvest was carried out by hand cutters.

Three different makes of cane harvesters are used: Claas, Massey Ferguson, and Toft. The first is manufactured in Germany, and the second and the third are manufactured in Australia. The Claas and M.F. harvesters belong to KSC, while the Toft is rented to KSC by the Australians. A payment of $2 is made per harvested ton of cane. When the rented machines have brought enough money to cover the original price, they will become the property of the Kenana Scheme. The Claas and Toft machines are good in the field and are not susceptible to problems, but the M.F. machines often cause trouble. The M.F. harvesters frequently catch fire. In the production season of 81–82 – 82–83 five were burned, and one completely lost. Engineers and mechanics suspect that the soft cane trash that sticks to the different parts of the machine while it is operating is heated up and spreads fire to the whole machine. To counter this difficulty there is an assistant to clean away the cane trash. They also have a fire engine standing by to cool off the heated machine and wash away the suspected material.

Every machine is operated by a driver and his assistant. Every four to six harvesters have a foreman who reports to a supervisor, who is under the authority of a superintendant. The superintendant is the link between the people working in the field and management. Authority at this higher level goes from the assistant manager to the Mechanical Harvest Manager to the Cane Crop Coordinator (C.C.C.).[3] He has regular meetings with other heads of departments: agriculture, administration, etc., to monitor the process of sugar production.

Harvest is a 24 hours task. Work is divided into three work shifts: morning, afternoon, and night. During the harvest there are different mobile service units following the location of different harvesters all over the estate to supply them with fuel, oil, and grease. They provide cleaning, change flat tires, and supply new spare parts. The mobile service Unit I visited has five Australians, who are experts on M.F. harvesters, one Panamanian, a Sudanese engineer, a supervisor, five foreman, a head mechanic, three mechanics, three assistant mechanics, four greasers, an electrician, a welder, and a technical clerk, which bring the total number of mobile service staff unit to 27 persons. The continuous presence is necessary to fix the harvesters, order new supplies, or receive technical information from the agricultural workshop at Pump Station 4.

Hand cutting constituted 40 percent of total amount harvested in the 83–84 season. The KSC administration is intending to increase the percentage of manual harvest to over 50 percent in the coming few years. The main reason for this is that hand cutting is far less costly than mechanical harvest. In the first and second years, mechanical operations were the dominant mode of cane harvest. The KSC has learned from the comparisons that if they have to depend on machines to carry out the harvest the cost will continue to rise. Fuel consumption, spare parts, cost of maintenance, and time lost to machine breakdown at harvest sites are all costly, especially in foreign exchange. So the KSC administration increased the numbers of cane-cutters (Kata-Kau) from 1,500 in the season of 82–83 to 3,000 in 83–84 season. The savings were substantial. In 83–84, the mechanical harvesting costs were about $3.00 per Feddan while hand cutting was about $2.00 per Feddan. Nevertheless, it is intended to keep the harvesters working side by side with the manual labor, in case there is a strike of cane-cutters like the one that took place in the production season of 81–82.

There are important reasons in addition to cost savings for the KSC administration to put great emphasis on hand cutting rather than mechanization. Among these are:

1. Provides chances for employment, 3,000 jobs for rural low-income group in the season of 83–84.

2. Saves time, since machines breakdown at harvest sites.

3. Hand cutting is efficient if it is compared to mechanization. The hand cut is made at the very lowest part of the cane plant, where it is believed that sucrose is concentrated, which enhances the possibility of good yields during cane processing.

ORGANIZATION OF HAND CUTTING

Every 40 cane-cutters are under the supervision of a headman. A senior headman oversees every six headmen and thus 240 cutters. Above the senior headmen the responsibility lies with a supervisor, who is under a superintendant. The Hand Cutting Manager oversees all hand operations, and like the Mechanical Harvest Manager, he reports to the Cane Crop Coordinator (C.C.C.) and thence to to the General Manager of Sugar Production (G.M.S.P.).

The cane-cutters are migrants from Southern and Western Sudan. They are preferred to local nomads and peasants who are not acquainted with such rigidly organized and hard physical work. The cane harvesters are transported from their camps early in the morning to the cane fields. Headmen check if there is any absence or sick report. Then everyone is assigned to his task (Magtoiya), which is an area of cane 45 meters by six farrows. That means an area of 270 square meters. Before going into the cane fields, the workers are trained to achieve certain working processes:

1. Cut cane plant as low as possible.

2. After cutting, place the cane in organized rows with the flowering end of the cane in one direction.

3. Top off the flowering end of the cane.

4. Arrange the cane properly to facilitate the working of the continuous loader.

After every worker makes sure that his machete is sharpened, the work starts. The completion of the 270 square meters is the minimum required daily work. If the worker finishes this minimum, he will be paid L.S. 4. However, the average cane harvest by the cane-cutters is two tasks per day. This will earn a cutter L.S. 8 plus a bonus of L.S. 2 as incentive, which will give him a total of L.S. 10 per day or L.S. 300 per month, the highest pay for daily workers in the country.

When a substantial area has been harvested by hand cutting, the continuous loader takes over. It gathers the cane, cuts it into small pieces, and feeds it into the truck/trailer unit. When the trailer has its maximum capacity, it leaves the cane fields for the factory.

CANE TRANSPORT

Cane transport has a department of its own. The staff and workers in this department totalled 1,383 persons of which 500 were truck drivers in the 83–84 season. The work in this department is as carefully organized as the other departments. In every area or part of the Scheme, there is a cane transport section that organizes the work between the field and the factory, or specifically between the field tower and the factory tower. The communications between the two towers are made by Duty Despatch Clerks who use an HF radio[5] to communicate. The cane transport is organized through the "cane despatch record."

After a truck is loaded with cane, the Duty Despatch Clerk calls the factory tower that a truck is on its way to the factory so that the time of arrival at the factory may be registered. After the crop is unloaded in the factory cane yards and the truck is ready to leave for fields, the Factory Tower Despatcher will call the Duty Despatch Clerk in the fields and tell him that a truck is on its way to the fields. This elaborate system of communication ensures a continuous 24 hours flow of cane to the factory. It is also a continuous check on the truck drivers who work a non-stop, eight-hour shift. Many of them try to race to or from the factory and sometimes have traffic accidents,[6] especially in the early morning hours when drivers feel tired and sleepy. But truck drivers seem never to stop racing with each other because the earlier one gets to the factory, the better incentive he is liable to get.

The Kenana factory consists of cane yards, power houses, a mill house, boilers, evaporators, clarifiers, a refinery, and a long conveyor to the bagging shed and the two warehouses. These warehouses have a storage capacity of 35,000 tons of sugar each. There are molasses storage tanks, which are located near the warehouses. The factory has two separate lines of production for processing cane and producing refined white sugar. In the crushing season, the factory can mill 17,000 tons of sugar cane per day to be converted into 1,700 tons of processed sugar. The annual capacity is 330,000 tons of white sugar.

FACTORY MANPOWER AND PRODUCTIVITY

The factory manpower is diverse. It includes expatriates, Sudanese officials, skilled and unskilled workers. The management of the factory affairs and production operations has been carried out by the American company Arkel International Inc. Since the inception of the project, the most striking feature of the operation has been the high turnover of labor, especially when the production season is over.

Table 5.1					
FACTORY MANPOWER BY TRADE					
NOVEMBER 1983					
Serial No.	Section	Staff	Permanent	Temporary	Total
1	Civil Maint.	9	55	61	125
2	Mill House	18	45	118	181
3	Raw House	32	24	59	115
4	Refinery	17	26	33	76
5	Boiler	24	48	49	121
6	Electrical	21	21	19	61
7	Power House	6	8	6	20
8	Maintenance	15	80	26	121

9	Water treatment (W.T.M.)	12	4	9	25
10	Laboratory & weight Bridage of Cane (Lab & W/B)	28	8	39	75
11	Instrumentation	13	7	2	22
12	Workshop	20	37	7	64
13	Sugar Ware- house (S.W.)	3	27	135	165
14	Stores	40	39	54	133
15	Safety	23	78	125	226
16	Administration Office	13	6	10	29
17	Time keeping & labor coordination (T.L.C.)	31	5	11	47
18	Design office	9	4	–	13
19	Factory transport	2	28	2	32
	Total	336	550	765	1651

Source: Kenana factory, time keeping and labor coordination office.
*The factory includes 289 expatriates.

In the crushing season of 1983–84, the total number of factory workers was 1,651. Of this number, 765 work as temporary laborers. All these were laid-off after the end of the production season. This constitutes 46 percent of the factory workforce. The permanent staff in the factory work all year round, in the crushing season they are fully engaged in their original assignments, but during the "dead season" most of the workforce is shifted to factory equipment maintenance, while the temporary laborers are asked to leave. Some of the laborers stay around looking for temporary work, others engage in providing service to people working in the Scheme, while the majority return to their places of origin to participate in the village economy.

The Kenana Sugar Factory is designed to be one giant refinery (two production lines). It is one of the biggest sugar factories in the world and is thus completely dependent on large-scale technology. Large sugar factories are not popular even in developed countries because of the possibility of being stopped during production as a result of a breakdown in a small part, which brings all the process of production in the factory to a standstill. So sugar schemes in the developed world are designed so that the cane is crushed in small units scattered around the project to lessen the risk involved in operating one giant factory. There would be advantages if Kenana had been designed as several small crushing units scattered around the scheme. First, these units are more labor intensive rather than capital intensive, and hence the dependence on foreign capital and technology is less likely to be. Second, small units can be easily managed, mechanical difficulty can be spotted and tackled, and even if the unit shuts down, the cane can be transferred to another unit, and so production is only slightly affected. Third, the existence of small crushing units in the vicinity of the scheme may increase spin-off job opportunities and social services to a larger part of the low-income population in the surrounding areas. The Kenana factory now has some mechanical difficulties[7] during the crushing season, although these difficulties are not serious, since its operation started in 1980–81. However, as time goes on, machine depreciation and replacement will become one of the main problems facing the project.

Whenever there is industrial development, the by-products of that industry tend to be an important component of the process of production. Kenana administration has taken no practical steps to utilize the two important by-products of the project: bagasse and molasses. An enormous amount of bagasse is used as fuel to feed the power system of the factory, but bagasse can be made into useful products to be used in the area itself (like paper, furniture, and building material).

Table 5.2

CROP DETAILS FOR THE FIRST THREE PRODUCTION
SEASONS

	1980–1981	1981–1982	1982–1983
Cane ground	1,239,536	1,741,550	2,220,616
Sugar produced MT	110,417	164,404	229,536
Crop days	185	177	154

As for the molasses, it is stored in tanks at the site waiting to be transported by tankers for over a thousand miles to Port Sudan and then stored there again until a foreign buyer can be found. Since the cost of transportation is very high, and the problem is aggravated by the lack of sufficient molasses storage tanks at the Port, often it is sold at a loss. No significant hard currency is being earned in return. The molasses can be very useful inside the Sudan, in the chemical industries, but even more important element of diet for starving people in Eastern and Western Sudan. Instead, Kenana administration has created a very limited use of molasses in a syrup and jam "sample industry." It is sometimes misused and haphazardly managed when it is applied in the streets of Kenana Township in the place of asphalt.

KENANA WORK FORCE

During the 1983–1984 production season, the work force of Kenana was 14,589. The work force is predominantly male. The female work force numbered only 87 during the same production season. Most of the female work force are either secretaries or typists, although there are a few occupying high positions in the Kenana sugar company. The Kenana work force is based on a sharply defined hierarchy with workers at Grade 1 at the bottom and senior staff ranging from Grade 10 to 14 at the top. A Grade 1 worker usually is an unskilled laborer doing manual work like cane cutting or irrigation. The head of the senior staff is the Managing Director, who is the ultimate authority on the Scheme, to whom all heads of different departments and divisions regularly report. There are regular meetings between the M.D. and the key officials of Kenana to tackle the different matters concerning the process of production. Although the working force is categorized as senior and junior staff, the daily laborers stand as a group by themselves, separate from the junior staff. So the Kenana work force is divided into three different groups: senior staff, junior staff, and the daily laborers. According to this categorization, people are weighted in the Kenana scale of grades. The higher the person's grade, the better the salary and housing. For senior grades there is an easy access to other facilities such as medical care. The lower the person's grade the poorer the access to accommodations and other facilities. There is increasingly a lack of job security in the lower grades. The sharply defined system of job classification, which produces senior staff, junior staff, and the daily laborers, is the same system which is keeping these groups apart in all other matters. They interact only if the place of work demands it; otherwise, every group has a separate social life, lifestyle, and its own separate social clubs.

One of the most important characteristics of Kenana work force is that both labor and job opportunities are seasonal. Over 8,000 (see the table 5.4) laborers recruited at the beginning of the production season work for 6 months and then are laid-off at the beginning of the dead season. A closer look at the above table shows that in the production season of 1980–81 the actual temporary laborers were 8,673, of which 6,135 worked in agriculture and manual harvest. At the end of the production season, 68 percent of the Kenana work force, which constituted the temporary laborers, was laid-off. This high percentage of labor turnover continued through the succeeding production seasons. It is a dominant feature of large-scale agricultural industry and generates major social dislocations in the work force.

Table 5.3

KENANA WORKFORCE AND THE SYSTEM OF GRADES

Grade	Type of occupation	Training/ Education	Other Observation
1	Casual worker daily paid, seasonal	Illiterate or primary education	Seasonal jobs
2	Driver with small license, mechanic	Learning by doing	Seasonal jobs
3	Semi-skilled laborer, mechanic in the workshop	Learning by doing	Seasonal jobs
4	Technicians, plumbers, carpenters, blacksmith, tinsmith	Primary Vocational training	Seasonal jobs
5	Clerks, technicians, personnel officer	Secondary education	Seasonal jobs
6	Supervisor, purchasing officers, technicians in the workshop	Higher secondary school, or industrial institute	Seasonal jobs
7	Agricultural inspectors, engineers	Graduate of the University of Kartoum or equivalent institution	Students who graduated from the University of Kartoum or other universities start their term of employment with G7. After working some time, the Graduate will be given increment and be promoted to G8.

8	Superintendants, engineers	Higher Vocational training and education	Most field staff who are in this grade come promoted, especially the university graduates. People arrive at this grade through promotion
9	Chief engineers, or administrators	Higher vocational trainging or education	
10	Assistant managers in different divisions	Higher education or vocational training	
11	Assistant managers in different divisions	Higher education or vocational training	
12	Managers, and head of department and high administrative posts	Higher education or vocational training	This staff in these grades, make daily reports directly to the managing director
13	Managers, and head of department and high administrative posts	Higher education or vocational training	This staff in these grades, make daily reports directly to the managing director
14	Managing Director		An authority on the Scheme

Table 5.4

KENANA SUGAR COMPANY LIMITED

Staff and labor returns, April 25 1981

Department/ Division	Sudanese		Other		Expatriate	Sub- total	Total	Prev. month
	Permanent	Tempo- rary	Perma- nent	Tempo- rary				
Management officers	3				6	9	9	10
Administration	464	39	2		12	517	517	524
Finance	247	260			16	523	523	375
Internal audit	4	1			2	7	7	7
Insurance & Risk					1	1	1	3
Medical								
a. curative	34	14			2	50		
b. preventive	66	137				203		
Total medical							253	245
Personel	60	13				73	73	71
Training	12				4	16	16	17
Agriculture								
a. agriculture	423	4612	1		4	5040		
b. agronomy	40	134			1	175		
c. land prep.	142	182			1	325		
d. harvesting	293	1523			3	1819		
Total agriculture							7359	6615
Engineering & Construction	541	237			5	783	783	788
Factory	466	1271			410	2147	2147	2126
Transport & maintenance								
a. workshop	302	200			167	669		
b. transport	69	20				89		
Total T&M							758	764
Khartoum	209	12			5	226	226	223
Port Sudan	47	18	2		1	68	68	64
Total	3422	8673	5	–	640	12,740	12,740	11,832

Source: Kenana Statistical Office

CHAPTER FIVE NOTES

1. If the cane variety has great propensity to flower, it gives poor yields during harvest, since some important cane stem contents go to flower formation.

2. It is rumored that the introduction of Cynodon Dactylon into Kenana scheme resulted from an expatriate's idea of spraying the seed along the side of the irrigation canals. This was intended to prevent water erosion, which sometimes destroys the canal. But shortly after that practice was begun, the tough weed found its place in cane fields through irrigation and started to grow out of control.

3. The post of Cane Crop Coordinator is held by an American expatriate.

4. The post of General Manager of Sugar Production also held by an expatriate.

5. Kenana Sugar Estate uses round-the-clock HF radio/telex communications in the site, also between the site, Khartoum and Port Sudan. This system of communication makes monitoring of work easy, and it provides a good reach out to Khartoum and Port Sudan, especially at times of emergency, e.g., breakdowns during the production season.

6. During my stay in Kenana, two truck drivers were killed when their trucks made a head-on collision, December 2nd, 1983.

7. November 24, 1983, the factory stopped for 24 hours. The cause was technical difficulty, so a spare part had to be flown from London.

STATISTICAL PROFILE AND SOCIOLOGICAL CHARACTERISTICS OF THE KENANA POPULATION IN 1984–1985

KENANA POPULATION

Prior to the inception of the Kenana scheme, the region was populated by nomads and peasants. These two indigenous groups shared the same environment, the natural resources, and an Islamic culture. Although they were pursuing a different mode of subsistence—one based on nomadism, and the other based on peasantization—they nevertheless had an extended system of cooperation and mutual help, which was expressed in the system of voluntary exchange of working parties during labor peak times.

The structural population dynamics in the region began changing rapidly when the Kenana area was pinpointed as one of the most promising sites for a sugar estate and a unique development location in the Sudan (1973).

Land transformation, construction, and new establishment began to emerge as the new site attracted daily laborers, officials, technicians, and contract expatriates. In a period of less than ten years, the Kenana site became an urban center accommodating a population of 60,000. Most of this sharp increase has occurred through migration and emigration during the last ten years. The Kenana population can be divided into five groups, these groups are:

1. The official (field staff).

2. The seasonal workers.

3. The small businessmen, and other people working in the service sector.

4. The nomads.

5. The peasants.

All these groups share one development site, but they differ tremendously. The greatest difference lies between the migrants who came to the scheme and the traditional users of the land. These groups have deeply different social origins, ethnic indentities, and levels of education, economic and cultural backgrounds. Within this diverse community it is the field staff that manages the scene and dominates the other groups by virtue of their leading role in running the Kenana Sugar Estate.

THE OFFICIALS (FIELD STAFF)

The officials or the field staff are responsible for managing the Kenana Sugar Scheme. Unlike the seasonal laborers, they are permanently employed with KSC, and they enjoy a better standard of living than any other group in the region. Kenana field staff is categorized into senior staff and junior staff. The senior staff are the people with university or post university education, vocational training, or the equivalent. They occupy positions between grade 10 and 14, which are at the top of the sharply defined system of job heirarchization in Kenana. The qualifications of the junior staff are secondary or higher secondary education, vocational training, or the equivalent. The junior staff are the majority of the official, working in the clerical jobs, workshops, and machine operations. They occupy positions ranging from grade 4 to 9.

The senior staff can be divided into the expatriates and the senior Sudanese staff. Since the establishment of the scheme, the expatriates have occupied very important positions in the estate. Although some significant positions like Managing Director (M.D.) and Agricultural Manager were Sudanized, key jobs like General Manager of Sugar Production (G.M.S.P.) and Cane-Crop Coordination (C.C.C.) and other senior management, engineering, and chemistry jobs are still in the hands of expatriates.

EXPATRIATES

The presence of expatriates in Kenana began with the first step of its implementation when the multinational corporations provided heavy equipment to transform the land and build the irrigation networks. The expatriates role continued in assembling the sugar factory and supervising its operation of producing sugar. This long process demanded a considerable number of foreign experts in the different scientific and engineering professions. The following table shows the nationalities of expatriates who worked with KSC in 1981.

The number of expatriates who worked with KSC in the production season of 83–84 was down to 619. This is attributed to the Sudanization of some jobs held by expatriates in the beginning of the scheme.

Expatriates have been recruited to the Kenana work force in two ways. Recruitment by individual contract may arise by the Kenana technical committee discussing the kind of qualifications needed to fill a certain job. When this has been established, they notify their office in London. In response, expatriates forward their applications. In the second case, multinationals send their employees to fill certain jobs. This includes consultants and highly specialized people as well as the so-called contract laborers who work in the factory and the agricultural workshop.

The recruitment of expatriates is deeply influenced by the multinational corporations who select their own staff to go and work abroad. Staff who work directly for various multinationals have their company interests in mind and insist on their home policies and rules of management. In the process, their management style becomes very authoritarian and non-compromising. Jobs like General Manager of Sugar Production (G.M.S.P.) or Cane-Crop Coordination (C.C.C.) or Operations Manager concentrate a lot of power and control. Such power may be exercised over a wide range of other expatriates, senior Sudanese staff, and the junior staff. There is substantial risk of arbitrary management and even strong subordination of lower level employees may not avert sacking as a primary sanction for such authoritarian management.

Table 6.1

Kenana Project Expatriates

Kenana Suger Company Limited

Monthley Returns as of 25 April 1981

Nationality	Kartoum	Site
British	I	79
Greek	I	
Ecudorian		2
Italian	I	
U.S.A	I	17
Portuguese		32
Egyptians		17
Salavadoreans		11
Panamanians		33
Guatemalans		19
Philippinoes	I	21
New Zealanders		2
Indians	2	269

Pakistanis		134
Bangladesh		1
French	1	10
Japanese		1
Argentinians		1
Ertrians		8
Canadians		3
Mexicans		1
Kenyans		2
Cubans		1
Zimbabweans		1
Koreans		84
Mauritians		8
colombians		1
Grand Total	8	757

Source: Kenana statistical office (site).

Kenana factory has the greatest concentration of expatriates in the site. Arkel International Inc. manages the factory operations. The work relation between the factory expatriates and their Sudanese counterparts is tense and suspicious, and sometimes, it can display an explosive pattern. For instance, the factory management fired 46 Sudanese engineers in 1982 when they tried to gain some trade union rights. Since that time, the factory management and the Sudanese engineers have had a hard time coping with each other. An engineer remarked that the Sudanese engineers have no sense of job security, and this situation is exacerbated by management neglecting their technical abilities as when an expatriate doubles them in the same job. The informant added that this situation led to depression and frustration in some Sudanese engineers, who have resigned from their jobs. Many argue that the aim of the present factory management is to discourage Sudanese technical personnel from replacing the expatriates through a process of Sudanization.

The expatriates and contractors enjoy excellent terms of service. They have very high salaries in comparison with their Sudanese counterparts.[1] They live in modern western designed, prefabricated houses. These houses have from one to four bedrooms and are equipped with the necessities and means of comfort. They are given a car and free gas. As for the contract laborers, they live in the bachelors center, where everyone has a room of his own.

Expatriates are allowed to use Kenana supermarket, which is restricted to the senior staff. They are given substantial subsidies in buying their groceries from Kenana produce farm shop.[2] They have more extensive medical service, and in the case of an emergency, an expatriate can be evacuated by air to Khartoum and if necessary abroad.

The expatriate staff also has the use of the Kenana Senior Staff Club (KSSC), which includes an international restaurant, a swimming pool, other indoor sports, disco, and a bar.

The concentration of privilege together with management power gives the expatriates a central role at Kenana. The Sudanese are pushed into marginal positions of participation, which has led to tensions and personal frictions in the place of work.

SUDANESE SENIOR STAFF

The senior Sudanese staff must have university and post university education or training to acquire their present jobs in Kenana. The senior Sudanese staff can be subdivided into elder and younger employees. The elder staff fall into the age group of 40–56, while the younger staff fall into the age group of 26–35. Although these two groups may be similar in job status and seniority, they have different social and economic origins, attitudes towards work, and manipulation of managerial power. The older senior staff, although they are very few in number, hold key jobs on the scheme, which include the Managing Director, Administration

Manager, Agricultural Manager, and the Central Workshop Manager. This group of the staff came from well-established families. Most of them came from urban centers such as Khartoum and Gezira. Only very few came from the White Nile Province. This group had already attained job experience somewhere else before their recruitment in Kenana.

One segment of these older men have their specialization in sugar technology, agriculture, engineering, irrigation, production, and labor organization and were recruited from pioneer sugar schemes in the Sudan like Geneid and Khashm el Girba schemes. The second segment of the elder senior staff works in administration, accounting, finance and electronics. These are government bureaucrats and technocrats recruited from Khartoum. These two groups, despite their job differences, are well integrated together on and off work. This group has a very close relationship with the managing director of the scheme. They are not only experienced and have a high occupational calibre, but they are also very influential and exercise considerable managerial control. This group works side by side with the expatriates on equal footing. Both of them are experienced and well-equipped for the senior jobs. By virtue of their work, the expatriates and elder senior staff have a continuous face to face relationship, at the place of work, where they have appreciation and mutual respect for each other. Outside the work place, personal contacts and social relationships are very limited.

The older senior staff enjoy good working conditions, including salaries, increments, bonuses, etc. They live in the senior staff residential area known as Coseley and T 2, also occupied by expatriates, which is separate from the residence of the junior staff. Everyone has access to a car (Suzuki) and free gas for use during working hours, in accordance with the nature of the employee's job, as well as for recreational purposes.

The older senior staff are confident and relaxed in their jobs and working relationship. The younger senior staff, on the contrary, are restless and discontented with things around them. The younger senior staff are primarily graduates of the University of Khartoum, (faculty of agriculture, engineering or others). Some of these graduates have had scholarships abroad, completing higher degrees in sugar technology, engineering, and agronomy. The bulk of the young senior staff were born in rural areas of the Sudan, began their education there, and then through competition were chosen to go to the University of Khartoum to pursue a higher education. This group comes from families that depend on farming or small business as a source of livelihood. The younger senior staff work as engineers, field-inspectors, agronomists, and in various other technical and administrative jobs.

Some of these employees are in their first jobs. Generally speaking, those with Sudanese supervisors have found the working relations satisfying and encouraging, but many responsible to an expatriate find working relations are tainted with suspicion and misunderstanding. A factory superintendent engineer sums up the situation as follows:

1. The factory is dominated by expatriates. A Sudanese superintendent in the factory should be in full control of his section, but that job is duplicated by an expatriate to enable tight control of the factory by the foreign engineering management.

2. The factory management is adopting the policy of evaluating Sudanese by expatriates, which is one way to keep tabs on the Sudanese technical cadre.

3. The expatriates have close contact between themselves. This close contact produces a certain formulation of policies known to them, but not to the Sudanese side. This keeps the Sudanese staff out of decision making and sharing of management affairs.

4. There is an engineering blackout because expatriates go ahead and construct an engineering project without the knowledge or the participation of their Sudanese counterparts.

The young senior staff are eager to bear responsibilities and get well-acquainted with the new technology. They want to prove their technical skills, but they feel that deliberate underestimation by expatriates is based on the assumption that the Sudanese staff would not absorb technology. This has angered and frustrated them. Some of them have already left as the result of this situation, while others are trying to wait it out.

THE JUNIOR STAFF

The junior staff is constituted of clerks, accountants, technicians, heavy equipment drivers, mechanics, supervisors, and administrative personnel. This group is composed of employees with diverse educational attainments, ranging from primarily school to college. People seeking employment in this category register their names at the Kenana labor office. School graduates who are waiting for a possible job often stay with relatives or friends from the same region. They make daily visits to the labor office to see if new announcements of job opportunities have appeared. When a notice of a vacancy reaches the labor office, they nominate not less than 30 contenders. These nominated contenders will be asked to come for an interview. As for the recruitment of higher grades: graduates and engineers, it is through application forms. Promising applicants are then interviewed at the main administration building and final decisions are made.

The junior staff comprises the largest group of officials included in the surveys conducted during this research. Most are young 88.4 percent of the informants fall in the age group 26–35. The survey shows that over half are married (55.2 percent) and brought their wives with them from their place of origin. The survey also shows 43.7 percent of the junior staff came originally from Khartoum and Gezira Province, while a further 37.5 percent came from the White Nile Province, leaving less than 20 percent originating in all other regions of the nation. It is significant that about four-fifths of the junior staff in the survey came from this riverine region: Khartoum, Gezira, and the White Nile Province. This is mainly due to a large concentration of population in this triangle, and somewhat greater educational services than are available to other parts of the Sudan. Since only a few students who complete high school are able to enter a university, the majority began looking for work. Since jobs are scarce, the school graduates accept the first job offered to them and sometimes depend on the aid of an influential relative working in a development scheme to find them a job.

Some junior staff at Kenana began with seasonal work. If successful, they may begin climbing into higher official grades and become semi-permanent or permanent staff. A member of Kenana junior staff is expected to show that he is very keen in doing his job, and completely respectful and obedient to his superiors. The junior staff generally regard acquiring a job with KSC as a positive step in the ladder of social mobility, but at the same time, they feel there is heavy pressure on them. In the workplace, they are expected to do their job with accuracy and adequate performance, and they feel pressure, which results from the authoritarianism of the KSC bureaucracy. In their personal lives, they have severe financial problems in balancing their personal needs, and their extended family demands on the salaries they earn. The majority of this group have extended families in their place of origin that they must support. Not only is money sent home, but sometimes the parents, brothers, sisters, or other relatives looking for work come to live with them in a house that has one room. Some of them use the kitchen as a guest room. Others build a hut to accommodate their relatives. Although some of the junior staff have adjusted to their increasing obligations where they can hardly break even, others have left Kenana. Many have gone to the Gulf States and Saudi Arabia when they felt occupational insecurity, indebtedness and were overwhelmed by their financial difficulties.

THE SEASONAL WORKERS

RECRUITMENT OF SEASONAL WORKERS AND THEIR PLACE OF ORIGIN

The production process in Kenana depends to a great extent on the seasonal daily workers. The daily work includes irrigation, agriculture, factory, and most important, harvest work. Although there are seasonal daily workers in many different departments and divisions of KSC, the cane-cutters are the most important to shed light on.

The demand for seasonal workers to participate in the process of harvest was understood to be substantial during the planning of the scheme. However, the demand increased in volume when it was found that cane-cutters are far cheaper than mechanized harvesting. Cane-cutters with sharp machete can do a fairly good job, especially if compared to harvesters, which have an increasing tendency to catch fire or breakdown. This results in a lot of time lost in the harvest site. Furthermore, the cost of running and maintaining the harvesters is expensive in terms of fuel and spare parts imported from abroad for hard currency.

The first effort of KSC to attract cane-cutters was made in 1980, when two agricultural supervisors were sent from Kosti to Nyala and Waw. Their main job was to recruit daily laborers in general and cane-cutters in particular. Local authorities in the two areas agreed to help in this recruiting task. People who showed interest were given an advance payment of L.S. 10, free meals, and a free ticket by train to Rabak and then to Kenana. Due to this recruitment initiated by the KSC, the bulk of the cane-cutters (Kata-Kau) in the estate continue to come from Western or Southern Sudan. The importance of this recruitment strategy for KSC was that it worked as a safety valve against labor shortage. It was also an advantage for poor rural laborers who could not afford to pay the cost of transportation looking around for work. This policy of recruiting seasonal workers from the place of origin was abandoned after the first production season. As a result, since that season, workers have come not only from the west and the south, but from all over. The KSC now has a very wide range of choice. In mid October of every year, massive numbers of people come to Kenana from throughout the country to be interviewed and tested for the hard job of cane-cutting. Field staff on the behalf of the department of harvest and officials from the personnel division conduct the interview and the test according to which cane-cutters are chosen. Large numbers of migrants gather for the interview in p.s. 2 and village 2 (centers of cane-cutters recruitment in Kenana), but few of them will be chosen. The first criteria for screening the laborers is their physical appearance: the underaged, the old, and the weak are excluded. The apparently able-bodied are subject to physical stress tests, such as climbing a high place while carrying a heavy load. Those who pass this test will be recruited. If a man has a certificate showing he has previous experience with the job of hand cutting, he will not be required to take such physical tests.

After the cane-cutter is chosen, he is asked to sign or fingerprint a contract, which specifies work will end with the end of the production season. A medical checkup is also required before the laborer starts work. If a worker shows any medical problem, he will be replaced.

If we look into the following table showing distribution of cane-cutters (Omal el Hasad) by province, we will find, according to the survey we conducted in the production season 83–84, that 52.4 percent of the number of cane-cutters surveyed came from Northern and Southern Dar Fur, followed by cane-cutters from Southern Sudan with a percentage of 22.6. The bulk of western cane-cutters are Fur (Awlad el Fur), followed by Massalit, Bani Hussein, Gimir, and Tama, while the majority of southern cane-cutters are Dinka, followed by Shilluk, Nuer, Baria, and Azande. In the White Nile Province itself the majority are Hussunnat and Muhammediyya (Branchs of Kawahla), who live in El Muhammediyya and Omdabakir in Kenana region, (the only nomadic group in the Kenana area who work as cane-cutters). The few cane-cutters from Kordofan belong to the Baggara groups of that region.

Table 6.2

Provincial origins of cane-cutters

As represented in 5% sample survey

Name of province/or Provinces	No. of Cane-cutters	Percentage of Total No. surveyed
White Nile province	37	10.3%
Northern and Southern Kordofan	12	3.3%
Northern and Southern Dar Fur	188	52.4%
Upper Nile province	32	8.9%
Equitoria	13	3.6%
Bahr el Ghazal	36	10.1%

Gezira & Khartoum province	31	8.6%
Northern region Nile and Northern province	9	2.5%
Eastern region, Red Sea and Kassala province	1	.3%
Total	359	100%

Eighty percent of the surveyed cane-cutters fall into the category of 26–35 years of age. These young migrants are moving between their village community and the large-scale irrigated scheme of Kenana. Migrants from Western Sudan are leaving their villages, which have experienced drought, desertification, conflicts, and the sporadic presence of famine. Under these economic, political , and environmental pressures, migrants leave Western Sudan, not only to find work and subsistence security for themselves, but also for families which have been left behind on the brink of starvation. When the production season is over, they buy grain, but return some of the cash in hand, to be spent on the family's other needs, including storing seed in hope that rain will come.

Migrants from Southern Sudan also engage in this seasonal labor migration because of economic necessity. However, political instability is also an important factor in Upper Nile Province, which drives able-bodied men north to look for work and sometimes to settle. Nevertheless, the majority go back with the primary purpose of buying cattle with money, which they are able to save.

As for the nomads of Kenana region, who took cane-cutting jobs, it is their first encounter with a physically hard task as a means of subsistence. The destruction of their traditional herding economy has forced a great number of nomads to accept the fact that they must work as cane-cutters. However, the majority of them are disqualified on the basis that migrants from the west and the south can do a better job. This aggravates the misery and poverty experienced since they lost their means of production.

Some migrants to Kenana intend one-way or permanent migration. The migrants who are aiming at permanent employment at Kenana have to be skilled workers or have higher education. Without qualifications there is only seasonal labor available. Thus, most are engaged in what is known as "circular" migration, which is repeated back and forth movement from rural areas to big plantations, development schemes, or urban centers. One important feature of this seasonal labor migration in Africa is that it takes place in countries that have a long dry season. The circulation of seasonal labor is between small rural communities and large-scale market enterprises. The seasonal laborers moving betweeen two different poles are trying to make ends meet in a system where self-sufficiency is no longer possible because of the penetration of the market economy.

Kenana seasonal labor is closely geared to movement between villages and the Scheme. The production season in Kenana starts in late October and ends in April or May. The seasonal laborers, especially the cane-cutters, return to their place of origin immediately after harvest is over. When they arrive at their villages, they participate with other family members in preparing land for the wet season that starts in late June. They work with the family through the agricultural cycle, sowing seed, weeding, guarding the fields against animals, and scaring off birds. As crops ripen in late October and early November, the KSC recruitment for cane-cutters starts. They leave their villages before taking part in the harvest which will be carried out by the rest of the family.

The annual circulation of seasonal labor between the rural areas and the riverine region in the Sudan started with the inception of schemes like Gezira, Managil, and the private cotton pump schemes during the 1940s. Laborers and their families come to pick cotton, earn some cash, and go back at the end of the picking season. The rate of seasonal labor migration increased with the expansion of mechanized agriculture in the late 1960s. Migrants came from very distant regions to work as wage laborers during the harvest. The establishment of sugar scheme like North-West Sennar, Assalaya, and Kenana have diverted a considerable number of seasonal laborers from cotton picking or mechanized schemes. The result is severe labor shortage in these two sectors and an increasing number of daily laborers remaining around sugar schemes. These seasonal laborers have a preference for working in sugar schemes, because the rate of payment per day is higher. The sugar schemes are also adjacent to big towns, and there is easy access to transportation.

THE WORK AND PAYMENT OF THE CANE-CUTTERS (KATA-KAU)

The cane-cutters in Kenana are locally known as "El Kata-Kau."[3] The number of cane-cutters increased from 1,500 in the season of 82–83 to 3,000 in the season of 83–84. They harvested about 40 percent of Kenana cane crop in 83–84, while the rest was done by machines. In the production season ahead, the number of El Kata-Kau will be increased to achieve about 50 percent of the total harvest. More manual labor is being added to reduce the high cost of mechnical harvest, which has proven to be expensive if it is compared to hand cutting. The high cost of mechanization stems from the fact that the harvesters are susceptible to fire damage and technical difficulties. The cost of production at Kenana is already above the average production cost of other African (as well as the Sudanese) sugar schemes. So increasing the manual harvest is an attempt to curb excessive production costs.

The cane-cutters live in p.s. 2 Camp, Shandi Foug, 2 A Camp, Camp 4, Camp 5, Omdabakir, and El Muhammediyya. A typical working day for the cane-cutters starts at 4 o'clock in the morning. To carry out our observations, we accompanied a field inspector to Camp 4. We found 200 cane-cutters gathering around women who sell coffee and tea. While they drank the coffee and tea, they chatted and laughed, looking into the darkness to see if the trucks that take them to work were in sight. In Camp 5, we found 500 men waiting for the same trucks. As we approached them, we could see they were covered by blankets and bed sheets to protect themselves against the cold. At 4:30 in the morning, the trucks arrived. For identification of different trucks going to different areas, there are flags to help the big congregation recognize their own working groups. Horns were blown to notify the nearby workers that everything is ready before the departure to the cane fields.

When the cane-cutters arrived in the harvest site around 5:00 a.m., every headman checked the presence of the forty men under his charge. Sick reports and absences are forwarded to the supervisor and then to the field inspector.

At 5:30 a.m., after every worker makes sure that his cane machete is sharpened, they went into the cane fields. The task every worker is given is called "magtoiya," which is 45 m. x 6 farrows of cane. The work continued for 3 hours, after that trucks that carry the breakfast, tea, and the potable water arrived. Everyone had a sandwich of fava beans or lentils and a cup of tea. The work resumed again after the breakfast break. When a considerable area had been harvested, the continuous loader took over, collecting the harvested cane, and feeding the crop into the trailer/truck units. When the trucks are filled with cane, they leave the harvest site for the factory, where the cane crop is unloaded in cane yards ready to be processed.

The average cane-cutter works two "magtoiyas" per day, which gives him a daily wage of L.S. 10 or L.S. 300 per month. If a cane-cutter manages to do more than two maqtoiyas, he will be given the so-called "double bonus," or two times the wage he obtained for two magtoiyas. Since manual harvesting is physically hard and tedious, the KSC administration has developed a system of incentives that rewards the worker for a variety of achievements. If the cane-cutter works for five consecutive days, with an average of a maqtoiya and a half per day, he is given a khaki working uniform. If a cane-cutter works consecutively for seven days, he receives a sharpener. If he works every day for a month, he is given L.S. 10 as incentive. Also, he earns double his rate of payment for work on Fridays. At the end of the harvesting season, the workers with the highest tonnage of cane receive additional incentives, which include radios, bicycles, blankets, and clothes.

When cutters are working in the fields, they are closely observed by headmen and supervisors to identify low rates of performance. Under certain circumstances, a cane-cutter can be discharged immediately. These circumstances include the following:

1. If he is absent for three consecutive days without a sick report or permission.

2. If he refuses to work or discourages other workers from doing their job.

3. If he quarrels with field staff or other workers.

4. If he urges workers to strike.

5. If he participates in a strike.

There are no tenants on the Kenana Scheme. The system of tenancy used elsewhere requires that the occupants should be accommodated by the administration as permanent or semi-permanent participants in the organization of production. The KSC administration has not wanted that possibility and the continuing obligations to tenants which might disrupt the maximization of profits.

The relations between the administration and direct employees (e.g. cane-cutters) is one of control and subordination. There is much power and authority concentrated in the hands of the field staff. The seasonal laborers are expected to show their abilities, respect and obedience to their superiors; otherwise, they can easily be sacked and replaced by others who conform to the rules. Such a system works easily where jobs are scarce and subsistence agriculture is becoming less possible each year.

The cane-cutters have different tribal affiliations and demonstrate strong commitment to their own ethnic group. During the work they team up together, and while they are beside each other, they chant tribal songs to encourage the work and beat the monotonous rhythm of the harsh job of cutting cane. Because each ethnic group attempts to live together, they take the same truck between their camp and the cane fields. When the work ends at 11:00 a.m., they return together to camp, gather at a place where they socialize together, eat in small groups and attend the "afternoon beer" in a collective tribal gathering.

RESIDENCE AND ACCOMMODATION OF TRIBAL KIN IN THE CANE-CUTTERS' CAMPS

Camp 2A (village 2) and Camp p.s. 2 contain about two thirds of the cane-cutters surveyed. The rest lived in Camp 4, Camp 5, Shandi Foug, Omdabakir, and El Muhammediyya. The latter group live with their wives and children. If a worker is married, KSC will give him a hut as a family residential area in Camp 4, 5, or Shandi Foug. As for the cane-cutters of Omdabakir and El Muhammediyya, workers use their own huts or nomadic tents, since they are old established villages in the region. The workers without families who live in village 2 and p.s. 2 Camp are housed four men to a hut. Usually people live in the same hut are from the same tribe.

Of the cane-cutters surveyed, 58.2 percent were married, and 41.8 percent were single (a tiny .6 percent of these were divorced). While a considerable number of the cane-cutters are married, only 20 percent of the married workers brought their wives with them. Such men usually came to work more than one season. This group lives in Camps 4, 5, or Shandi Foug with their families. The rest, who journey to Kenana alone, live in village 2 and p.s. 2 Camp. The Kenana sugar scheme attracts an increasing number of migrants, and as might be expected, most are unskilled. The growing migration is a response to workers who return after a six month production season bringing with them a bicycle, a radio, market goods, and money that can be used in bridewealth or to buy livestock. This impresses their villages in general and stimulates youth to come to Kenana the next season to obtain the same things. While only a limited number get the seasonal jobs, the rest stay with their employed kin or village mates or drift to the nearby villages looking for work. An employed head of a household may build a hut to shelter or accommodate his kinfolk, who are looking for work. A group of bachelors may build a windscreen for the same purpose. If a man finds no work with KSC or any other job, he may join his tribal fellows who were more fortunate and go to work with them in the cane fields. A worker who is helped by a relative can earn more by achieving more magtoiyas of cane. At the end of the month, the regular worker gives his relative a share which, in our survey, amounted to about 25 percent of the total monthly payment he receives from KSC.

SOCIAL LIFE IN THE NEW SETTING

Migrants leave their modes of life behind when they come to Kenana. Nevertheless, they do not form a new, multiethnic group, but only associate with their tribal fellows. Thus, the working members of the tribe, and sometimes their families, constitute a safety net for newcomers. When a new migrant arrives, the first thing he asks about is the Farig (camp) of his tribe (e.g. Farig El Fur, El Zaghawa or Farig El Zandi. etc.). With the increasing rate of migration of tribally related people, these Farigs grow bigger in size. Since migrants no longer seek work only in the crowded area of cane-cutting, many are now working as servants, tea makers, coffee makers, or waiters in restaurants.

During mid-day, people who may be found in the tribal Farigs are the women and children of the seasonal workers. The women and children collect water and while collecting water from the drain water runoff, they catch fish. This is done by two people submerging a piece of cloth in the shallow water and bringing it and the catch to the surface. Catching fish this way is one means of supplementing the family diet, which depends on dura porridge, okra, and dried salted fish. Chewing cane[4] is a popular habit after meals in the cane-cutters' camps and also gives some variety to the diet.

When the cane-cutters return from work at midday, they stop by the canals to wash because they are covered with the dried sticky cane juice and the black dusty ash that results from burning the cane fields before harvest. After the midday meal, most men take a nap. Later, cane-cutters start to gather for the afternoon beer. The beer is brewed by wives of the migrants. Made from sorghum, it is called "marissa." When the people gather for the beer, they form small ethnic gatherings, where they chat and exchange the latest news of social events in the homeland, which may be brought by a recent migrant. These ethnic gatherings congregate and disperse peacefully, but the presence of strangers and members of other groups is discouraged. Strangers approaching such a tribal gathering are not viewed as interested in participating in the beer party but are thought to be tracking down women. So these people are requested to leave to avoid touching-off a tribal conflict. Although cane-cutting is a harsh job, it is very sought after because an average worker may earn L.S. 1,800 for the season of six months. With this amount a worker cannot only subsist and obtain small items but can save up to L.S. 1,000 a season. This can generate a number of choices, especially in remote rural areas. When cane-cutters obtain their first monthly payment, they deposit it all with a trusted small merchant in the market of Camp 5 (Sug Khamsa) or Sug el Zink. These merchants are usually those who have a substantial shop made of iron sheets and a variety of the most demanded goods. Cane-cutters who live in one hut eat together, so they buy all their food items from this merchant. At the end of the month, they share the cost of living equally and subtract it from the deposited money. At the end of the season, everyone takes what remains of his money and prepares to go home. We interviewed the cane-cutters about what they do with the saved money. Most had definite plans. For instance, a young man from Dar Fur remarked that he planned to get married and said the cost would be L.S. 500; another said when he goes back to Dar Fur he is going to open a small shop in the village. Others noted that they wanted to buy grain and store it in the village for future emergencies.

As for cane-cutters from the south, they said it is difficult to marry if you work only one season in Kenana. They indicated that bridewealth is very high and recently has become a combination of livestock and cash as well. One young man from the Dinka tribe remarked that, last season, he bought two cows and three sheep, but he noted that he still had a long way to go to gather an appropriate bridewealth which consisted of 10 cows, 20 sheep, 25 goats, and L.S. 300.

Another informant from the Shilluk indicated that he had worked with Kenana Scheme since the first season, and now he has a shop built of iron sheets at his village in the Upper Nile Province. He said the managing of the shop is left to his brother while he is away. At the end of the season, he planned to invest all his money in buying the most demanded market goods: grain, sugar, tea, cigarettes, oil, soap, and sweets. He said when he goes back, he will release his brother to participate in managing the livestock of their family, and he will resume work in his shop until the new season in Kenana approaches.

About 80 percent of the cane-cutters expressed their intention of going back to their place of origin. The remaining 20 percent planned to stay to look for work in the non-agricultural sector in Kenana, but they all agree they will come back to cut cane next season.

In response to a question as to how the cane-cutters lives have changed due to their seasonal work with KSC, the distribution of answers was as follows:

1.	My income has risen	34%
2.	My standard of living has improved	27%
3.	I have found work	11%
4.	I have settled in Kenana	10%
5.	No change	18%
		100%

It appears that over 80 percent believe their economic, social, or work status has changed because of the seasonal work at Kenana. The circulation of labor has become a dominant factor in the Kenana region. Migrants move from their villages on the expectation of satisfying their economic needs within the context of a job and a cash income which will improve their standard of living.

As recent as the production season of 2007–2008, the manual harvest and the hand-cutters employment has been completely abandoned for a full mechanized harvest, because of the avalabiltiy of local supplies of oil and gas. Thousands of cane-cutters and manual laborers were dismissed.

SMALL BUSINESSMAEN, AND OTHER MIGRANTS WORKING IN THE SERVICE SECTOR

The establishment of Kenana scheme as a large-scale enterprise created Kenana Township for the accommodation of the new staff. Temporary thatched huts were built to house the seasonal laborers. The number of people coming to look for work increased rapidly, which required establishment of an adequate system of service. KSC administration arranged a number of institutions to cater for its regular staff, especially the senior staff. The growing needs of the seasonal labor depended largely on the arrival of small businessmen and other migrants. These services included selling market goods, food, other necessities, and entertainment. The survey shows that half (50.9 percent) of the informants working in the service sector came originally from Western Sudan (Kordofan and Dar Fur). About a quarter came from the White Nile Province. A further 11.7 percent came from Gezira and Khartoum Province, while 9.8 percent originated in Southern Sudan. The rest (2.2 percent) emigrated from the neighboring countries of Ethiopia, Eritrea, Chad, and Uganda.

This group who provides services for the people who work on the scheme live in Camps 4, 5, and Shandi Foug among the seasonal laborers. In these camps, people usually make their own houses and sometimes build their own metal shops or thatched local buildings to be used as restaurants, cafes, and places of entertainment where local beer and liquor is served.

SERVICES PROVIDED BY WOMEN IN KENANA SITE

As men are the working majority in the Kenana agricultural sector; women are their counterparts, working in the non-agricultural sector. Women who provide services and entertainment for the field staff and the temporary workers come mainly from Western Sudan and the White Nile Province. The migration of women from Western Sudan is driven by misery, poverty, and conflicts which are exacerbated by the Sahelian drought of the last ten years. There has been rapid disintegration of family ties among the poor of Western Sudan as men have left hoping to find work in the east. In this situation when the father is absent, the mother must take the responsibilities of the head of the household. Yet if the father as a head of the household could not support his family, there is little reason to expect the mother will be able to do so. Women know it is a losing battle, if they and their children stay behind. Although many women and their children have difficulty raising money to pay for the cost of transportation to the east (Dar Sabah), they sell anything in their houses that can be exchanged for money: a sheep, a goat, a donkey, chickens, eggs, or the things a woman makes to be sold, such as local mats (Birish), basketry, and pottery. Once a woman has accumulated the cost of the journey to the east, she and her children travel by lorries or train hoping to find something to do near a scheme like Kenana. Once she is at such a site, she does what she thinks best to make a living. As for the women in the survey listed as coming from the White Nile Province, most are originally also from Western Sudan, where women are allowed to work and participate in the family's economy, either as hired laborers or by selling goods that they produce. Women from other Provinces of Sudan have also been driven by economic necessity, while those who emigrated from the neighbouring countries have mostly fled civil war.

There are also poor families among the nomads and peasants who have been the traditional residents of the Kenana region. Many are in urgent need and might be assisted by their women folk, but they say that it is very unsafe and dishonorable for indigenous women to come into contact or intermingle with new settlers and unpredictable strangers. Although these women worked in the traditional economy, they are now restrained from participating in the new economic activities which have emerged. On the other hand, a migrant woman can engage in a number of occupations. The most important of these are selling prepared foods such as porridge (kisra) and sauce or coffee and tea. Often these foods and beverages are sold together. The sale of vegetables and other uncooked produce or of clothing and fabrics is also practiced. Women also brew and sell local beer (marissa) and liquor (aragi), and engage in prostitution, to which the sale of alcoholic beverages is linked.

Two case studies will help to illuminate the circumstances of women migrants, who have come to Kenana.

NAFEISA MUSA

Nafeisa is 27, and her sister is 25. Neither one of them married. They migrated from Northern Kordofan in the early days of the scheme. After working two years, they were joined by two younger brothers, 12 and 9 of age. Nafeisa and her sister Haleema first took the job of baking and cooking for a number of junior staff. They continued in this for two years, then in 1978 they started their own restaurant in Sug El Zink (Kenana Market). They rented a shop and bought local mats and stools for customers. Their business grew rapidly and has become a popular place for men to come from work to eat breakfast or lunch and have coffee and tea. To handle an increasing number of regular customers, plus drop ins, Nafeisa has employed 4 women to bake and cook for her. She and her sister continue to manage their business and take care of selling the coffee and the tea. Their prices are 50 p.t. for breakfast or lunch, 15 p.t. for coffee, and 10 p.t. for tea.

The members of the junior staff, who have regular salaries, are allowed to take their meals on credit and pay their bills at the end of the month. To keep track of the customers who are served, she keeps a book. Since Nafeisa does not know how to read and write, every customer is asked to register under his name the cost of his meal and if he drank tea or coffee. Casual customers pay at the time they finish a meal. The monthly net income from the restaurant is between L.S. 500 and L.S. 700 after she pays the rent, the wages of the women baking and cooking for her, and the cost of the meat, vegetables, cooking spices, sugar, tea, coffee beans, and sorghum flour. The success of the restaurant has enabled Nafeisa to open a bank account. She is also moving into investments. She bought a house in Kosti (for around L.S. 30,000 to L.S. 40,000) and a Toyota pick up for L.S. 6,000. The economic success of Nafeisa and her sister Haleema has made them well known figures among the men and women of Kenana. Some other women who also prepare and serve food become very envious and filled with hatred towards this woman who has attracted a wide base of customers. She was attacked and clubbed by other women near her house in Camp 5, causing a head injury. She had to travel to Khartoum for medical treatment, but after a couple of weeks, she returned to resume her flourishing business.

HAWAYYA ALI

Hawayya is 23 years of age. She was married to a man in a rural village for two years. However, the marital relationship between her and her husband went from bad to worse. Her husband suspected her of infidelity, beat her, and threatened to kill her. Because of her husband's brutality and her excessive fear, she ran away to Kenana. She met a woman from her region who manages a house where beer is brewed and girls are available to entertain men. Bit el Shaykh owns the establishment which consists of four thatched huts and a sunshade. All are inside a square windscreen, which demarcates Bit el Shaykh's house from houses nearby. During the day Hawayya goes to Camp 5 market to sell tea and coffee; it is a place to meet potential customers, especially men who earn regular wages. She invites them to come by after sunset for beer and entertainment. The owner of the house depends mainly on these prostitutes to market her beer and liquor. The price of the beer and liquor goes directly to Bit el Shaykh, as well as half of the money earned by the girls. The hut rent and the expenses of food are separate.

PETTY TRADERS

Before the inception of the Kenana scheme, there were petty traders in the villages and nomadic camps throughout the White Nile Province; this group came from Sahelian origins, mainly the Fellata group, who live now in Rabak and Kosti. This group of petty traders is locally known as "El Sawama." They travel by foot or by donkey, carrying light goods and fabrics to be sold in the villages and nomadic camps. These goods include clothes, fabrics, cooking utensils, china, tea and coffee cups, womens' ornaments, and herbal medicine. Before the scheme, there was a low level of demand in the villages and nomadic camps because people were not fully engaged in the market economy. The petty traders covered long distances to visit as many villages and camps as possible to make up for the low level of demand in the places they visited. The operations of petty traders changed drastically when Kenana was established. They greatly reduced their mobility and began carrying a wide range of goods and materials to meet not only the demand of the local people, but also the need of employees of Kenana Scheme.

THE EXPERIENCE OF MOHAMMED SALIH ILLUSTRATES THESE CHANGES

Mohammed Salih and his family live in Khor Agwal, but his parents migrated with their families from Dar Fur when they were young. His father died when Mohammed was young. So he helped his mother cultivate sorghum in their bilad in the wet season. In the dry season, he worked for wages in the nearby town of Rabak. In the early 1960s, he accumulated L.S. 50 and began working as petty trader after the harvest. He travelled on foot from one village to another in the Kenana region to display his goods and materials. Mohammed recalls that in those days there was little cash circulation in the region. He estimated that during a whole day he might not sell 50 p.t. worth of goods. Things changed for Mohammed Salih when, in 1972, he and his mother harvested 70 sacks of dura. He sold 60 sacks to give him a capital of L.S. 600, a fairly good capital for a petty trader at that time. He met a friend who told him that he was going to the town of Melit in Northern Dar Fur where cheap clothes, fabrics, watches, radios, blankets, shoes, etc. come from Libya across the border. Mohammed Salih says that after he came back from Melit with new goods of high value like watches, radios, and cassette recorders, his business took off. He now goes back every two months when his imported items are sold out. He estimates that every trip he makes to Melit yields a net profit ranging between L.S. 200 and L.S. 300.

With the establishment of Kenana, Mohammed began displaying his imported market goods in the Kenana open market with other traders who try to be present at Kenana from the 30th to the 7th of every new month because this is the period when KSC salaries are paid out. Mohammed Salih says that if a person is lucky and his merchandise is good, especially the imported items, he can sell about L.S. 300 worth in that one week of each month. He added that his busy week is usually followed by a slack time. That is the reason petty traders leave for Rabak and Kosti, where markets are larger and the chance of selling goods is not dictated by the rhythm of the month.

Recently Kenana security forces stationed at the main entrance and exits of the scheme have banned the entrance of petty traders to Kenana on the grounds that stolen goods can be bought and sold in Kenana Market. According to Mohammed Salih this policy is ineffective because petty traders avoid taking any means of transport which bring them into contact with the police and security forces at these stations. Instead they take routes which are out of sight of the police and security forces. When a petty trader reaches Kenana Market no one annoys him.

SMALL MERCHANTS (OWNERS OF PETMANENT METAL SHOPS)

When planning of Kenana Market started at the beginning of the project, merchants, businessmen, and prestigious individuals of Rabak and Kosti made applications to obtain shop plots. The Kenana Town Council which was in charge of assigning shop plots, turned down the already-established businessmen and gave an opportunity to applicants who had no business before but did have some money to start a small business. In Kenana Market, Sug el Zink, and the camp 5 Market, approximately 3000 shop plots were assigned to applicants who were mainly newcomers to the Kenana area. The small merchants constructed their shops of metal sheets to discourage thieves and lessen the chance of destruction by fire. These shops are built in rows next to each other, inside each shop there are goods displayed on wooden shelves, and a long table with a scale on it stands at the shop entrance. Sacks of goods and tins of cooking oil are scattered around the shop .As the inside of the metal shop is very small, the merchants make a temporary sun shade of metal or empty sacks to accommodate more displayed goods and more customers. Most of the small merchants originally invested between L.S. 2000 and L.S. 5000 in these shops.

The small merchants display a variety of market goods, with the exception of sugar, the most demanded commodity. Strangely enough, the sugar factory is only 1km away from Kenana Market, still there is no sugar for public display at these shops. After the sugar is produced at Kenana, it is shipped by train and trucks to other parts of Sudan, especially Khartoum. In Khartoum, quotas are assigned for different provinces of Sudan, but the bulk of the sugar supply never officially leaves Khartoum. It is said there are many channels for smuggling and black marketeering of sugar. Some of the small merchants in Kenana obtain sugar (usually in a black market situation). So they sell it by the same method. If a small merchant has sugar, it is always concealed under the table covered with piles of sacks. The original price of one pound (rottale) of sugar is 27 p.t. (1984), but the merchants sell it for 60 p.t. If supply is short and demand is high, the same amount is sold for 150 p.t. Merchants are very cautious when it comes to selling sugar. A merchant caught selling sugar in the black market can be assessed a large fine, imprisoned, and most probably will be evicted from the market. So any person who is not well known or trusted by the merchant is suspected of being a potential security man in civilian clothes comes to sneak and spies on him. Although small merchants can make windfall profits from selling sugar, the risks are great. Furthermore, such small merchants have to be trusted by bigger merchants in Rabak and Kosti before they can obtain black market sugar.

Table 6.3

Prices of Sugar 1984–1985

Amount of sugar	Original price	Black market price in urban center	Black market price in rural areas
1 lb. (rottale)	27 p.t.	60 p.t.	150 p.t.
1 sack 50 kg	L.S. 35	L.S. 70	L.S. 100

In the Kenana region, the people who are exploited by this black market are the poor people like the nomads, the peasants, and the self-employed migrants. These people have no other choice but to buy sugar and other commodities from the Market. People who are employed with KSC get a subsidized 10kg of sugar every month, along with other subsidized commodities sold at the Kenana consumer cooperative.

There are two ways that a small merchant can get goods for retail sale. First, they may be bought from the wholesale merchants at Kosti; however, many Kenana merchants are skeptical about prices of these wholesalers. Instead, they prefer to buy what they need from the Mangala. The Mangala are merchants from the Gezira and Managil area. They pack their lorries with market goods and travel long distances to sell them. In other words, they are "wholesalers on the move." The Mangala buy a variety of commodities from Port Sudan, Khartoum, and Wad Medani, including sugar, tea, coffee beans, cooking oil, tomato sauce, soap, rice, powdered milk, clothes, fabrics, razors, batteries, torches, and household utensils and bring them right to the front door of the small merchants' shops. Although there is a lot of bargaining before the transaction is made, the Mangala always sell only when they are sure they will get the profit they have in mind. In this situation, the small merchants are intermediaries between rich merchants and poor consumers and must calculate their position carefully when adding their own profit before the commodity is displayed for the customer.

El Haj Khalifa is a good example of a small merchant. From the Fur tribe, he came to the river valley ten years ago. He worked as a hired laborer in different areas including the Gezira Scheme, Geneid, and other mechanized private schemes. When Kenana started, he opened his shop stocked with merchandise worth L.S. 4000. The shop includes goods like sugar, tea, coffee beans, powdered milk, soap, cooking oil, fabrics, spices, dried meat, dried salted fish, and grain. He says that Camp 5 Market is very profitable if the merchant knows how to attract customers. He feels that to attract customers you have to be friendly, compromising, understanding, and also generous in distributing coffee and tea.

His main customers are the sugar cane-cutters who buy a lot of grain, sorghum, flour, and dried salted fish. During the production season, he sells L.S. 150 worth of goods per day. During the off-season, his sales decline to L.S. 50 per day because most of his customers return to their places of origin in the rural areas. He depends on the Mangala to provide him with the goods he wants. Grain comes from El Renk area, and the dried salted fish comes from fishermen at the village of El Hedaib on the banks of the White Nile between El Jebelein and Rabak. Although he is happy with his new business, he remarks that his shop and other small merchants' shops are not safe and secured from thieves during the night. Last year, a thief broke through the roof of his metal shop and stole L.S. 500 worth of imported cigarettes. After that, he hired a man as a night guard to discourage thieves from coming around his shop. He pays the guard L.S. 15 a month. A guard can look after 2 to 5 metal shops and collect L.S. 15 from each of the merchants involved, thus earning up to L.S. 75 per month.

El Haj complained that the lack of security is not only in the Camp 5 Market but also in the Camp 5 residential area. He and his wife discovered that their eight sheep had been stolen during the night while they slept in Camp 5 residential area. After two days, he concluded that his sheep had been slaughtered, because he found their hides, which had been thrown away. He feels that the security forces and police patrols are always concentrated around KSC property and their staff residential area. In Camps 4 and 5, people have to be on the lookout for their own property and belongings.

OTHER SERVICES IN THE MARKET PLACE

Although restaurants and shops have flourished, other forms of commerce were also introduced in Kenana Market to satisfy the increasing needs of an increasing population. A great number of men and women sell vegetables, including onion, green and red peppers, egg plants, potatoes, okra, tomatoes, and spices. The vegetables come from peasant villages along the banks of the White Nile. Fruits come from Sennar, Singa, and Wad Medani. Vegetables are marketed by the pile (kom) or by weight. An average pile of vegetables is 50 p.t., while a kilogram of vegetables is 80 p.t. Fruits like mangoes and oranges are sold at L.S. 3 a dozen. Vegetables sellers reach the peak of their selling time between 8 a.m. and 11 a.m. Not only Kenana population, but nearby villagers and nomadic camp dwellers come to buy vegetables, meat, and bread, and to sell their traditional products.

GOODS AND SERVICES AVAILABLE AT KENANA MARKET

1. Saddle and rope making

2. Basketry and mats

3. Pottery

4. Leather works

5. Tailors

6. Herbal medicine practitioner

7. Fortune teller

8. Bicycle repair

9. Radio and cassette-recorder repair

10. Blacksmith

11. Goldsmith

12. Beds and mattresses

13. Shoe shining

14. Milk and butterfat

15. Animal fodder

16. Barbers

17. Porters

18. Meat, fruits and vegetables

The services listed are now available. Many additional people are ready to go into the market to provide some kind of service as demand emerges in an economy becoming more dependent on cash transactions.

THE NOMADS

THE KENANA SUGAR SCHEME AND THE DILEMMA OF THE NOMADS

According to the Sugar Agreement (1972), the government agreed to lease Kenana Sugar Company 150,000 Feddans at 10 piasters per Feddan per year. This is a purely nominal rent, but the government went further by setting the time limit for the lease at 30 years and granting an option for another 20 years when the first 30 years expires. The government gave all these concessions to KSC and, at the same time, totally ignored the rights of the traditional users of the land, the nomads and the peasants of Dar Muharib in the White Nile Province. The government gave the KSC the right to transform the land and establish the scheme without any obligations whatsoever to the indigenous population of Dar Muharib.

The nomads were severely hit by the fact that they could no longer use their pastures, nor cultivate sorghum in their fields, or even live where they used to live. Suddenly, the nomads were told by KSC authorities that they could no longer use the land. Instead, they were promised compensation for the fields and huts they lost. They were told a canal would be extended outside the irrigated area to carry water for their animals, and they would be given plots of land to grow whatever they wanted. These promises were never kept, and during the autumn of 1978, 40 thousand of the indigenous population of Dar Muharib were displaced.[5] The nomadic population faced a severe crisis. They had lost their land and now had to attempt to save their animals. This was made even more difficult by regulations the KSC adopted to protect the cane crop from plant diseases and the irrigation water from pollution. The regulations forbade keeping large animals around the scheme or cultivating adjacent to it. The pressure mounted as the scheme began operating in 1980, and the region was flooded with an influx of migrants from the different provinces of Sudan and the neighboring countries. The nomads began to deplete their animal resources by selling them to buy sorghum. Their current status as landless people is a nightmarish dilemma. With this influx of migrants came beer and liquor, narcotics, prostitution, and crime. These are social problems that the nomads had never been exposed to before. They felt completely alienated and disoriented. The nomads began to leave the area, moving to the southeast (Blue Nile Province, or to the boundaries of the White Nile Province and north of the Upper Nile Province). Moving to these territories has triggered conflict because the land is already occupied by private scheme owners, peasants, and nomads.

The out-migration of Kenana nomads has been determined mainly on the size of the family herds. Families owning more than 500 cattle plus sheep and goats were the first to leave the area. They were followed by families whose holdings were modest, around 100 cattle and perhaps 200 sheep and goats. The wave of out-migration continued down to households owning no more than 25 cattle and a few sheep and goats. The people who had less than 25 cattle and those no longer having any livestock were left behind. With so few animals they simply could not make a risky and uncertain out-migration from Kenana. The poor nomadic people who have no choice but to stay, they are around 12,000, or about 30 percent of the nomadic population of Kenana before the scheme. The out-migrants experienced enormous difficulties, ranging from conflict over trespassing, to accusations of damaging crops, to occupying land already claimed by others. The bulk of the nomads who left Kenana region have been pushed into poor marginal land, which cannot support them or their animals. A few of them who have appropriate kinship bonds and marriage ties have been accommodated within the original tribes of the Blue Nile Province, Kenana, and Rufa'a al Hoi.

SOCIO-ECONOMIC LIFE IN THE NOMADIC CONGREGATED VILLAGES

The Kenana Sugar Company administration assigned three villages to Kenana nomads who stayed behind but recognized no obligation to build any housing or community facilities in these villages. The three villages are Fangoga, Nuri, and Abu Togaba. The nomads chose to settle in Abu Togaba because it is close to Kenana township. The other two villages are still occupied by the original dwellers. A considerable number of nomads also settled in Omdabakir and El Muhammediyya. Of the total nomadic population still living in Kenana region, 78.7 percent live in the village of Abu Togaba. The rest are scattered among the other villages surrounding the Kenana Scheme.

Abu Togaba, which now has about 10,000 former nomads settled in it, is divided into tribal residential clusters. These residential clusters, numbering eleven, are occupied by members of the Sabaha, Nazza, Sebaig, Khanferiya, Rawashda, Massalamiyya, Kenana, Ahamda, Kibayshab, Gawama'a, and Fur. The community has a varied appearance because the settlers, who had to build their own housing, chose varied types. A considerable number of them built the typical nomadic house made of bark, mats, and cloth, while the majority built thatched houses with mud walls. A few of them built houses with sun-baked bricks. There is little in the houses of these poor people besides the traditional beds, mats, and cooking utensils.

Every tribal residential cluster has a Khalwa to entertain their guests, and also they have their own animal enclosure. Some of the households tie their animals to posts just behind their residence. The ownership of livestock is very important in Abu Togaba, not only because it is the traditional mode of livelihood of these pastoral nomads, but also because livestock is still the main source of subsistence for many of the displaced nomads. These people have little chance of finding jobs with the Kenana Sugar Scheme, as we noted earlier in discussing cane-cutting. Yet many families no longer own any animals at all.

Prior to the Kenana Scheme, the nomads were largely self-sufficient. They engaged in a number of forms of traditional exchange of animals and grain involving complex forms of reciprocity. These depended on values of products and social statuses internal to the nomadic society. The situation changed immediately after the inception of the Kenana Scheme, when making a living or doing any business required market transactions. When the land and the pastures were stripped away from the nomads, it meant a forced participation in a new market economy. However, they lost the resources and did not have the experience in market exchange to deal with this situation. So the nomads of Kenana have been forced into the labor market to support their families.

NOMADS' EMPLOYMENT WITH KSC

According to our survey among the nomads, about 95 percent are illiterate or received only informal education. Less than 5 percent attained some kind of formal education. These are usually the sons of the Shaykhs, and other rich nomads in the region who could afford to send their children for schooling in Kosti, Rabak, or El Jebelein. Most of the former nomads' sons employed with Kenana work as mechanics, drivers, guards, and seasonal laborers.

The following table shows employment among the nomads' sons of Abu Togaba village. We find that of the 383 men employed with KSC only 12 have permanent jobs. About 96 percent of those with jobs are working on a seasonal basis, and they will be laid off when the dead season approaches. When they are laid off, there is no guarantee that they will be employed again in the next production season. Despite this seasonal employment of some residents of Abu Togaba, the rate of unemployment is over 90 percent among men who are ready to work. A son working in the Kenana Scheme, even on a seasonal basis, is considered to be a safety net for his family. He becomes responsible for his parents, younger sisters, and brothers, because there is little chance of wage employment for any of them.

Table 6.4

Nomads' Sons employed with KSC 1983–1984, Abu Togaba Village

Type of Work	Tribe					
	Rawashda	Nazza	Massalmiyya	Kibayshab	Khanferiya	Kenana
Factory workers	15	10	4	30	–	3
Agriculture & irrigation workers	2	5	1	15	–	2
Clerks	–	2	–	–	–	–
Accountants	–	–	–	–	1	–
Drivers	12	–	2	35	3	4
Mechanics (workshops)	8	8	–	–	–	–
Safety and security workers	–	1	–	1	–	–
Fire fighters	–	1	–	–	2	–
Guards	5	12	–	2	–	2
Radio communicaters	1	–	–	–	–	–
Grandmet (food service)*	–	12	–	2		
Total	43	51	7	85	6	11

*grandmet is a British company that contracted to supply food to Kenana. The contract was terminated December 1983.

Table 6.4 (continued)

Type of Work	Tribe					
	Fur	Bani Halba	Gwama'a	Sebaig	Sabaha	Total
Factory workers	2	3	10	3	20	100
Agriculture & irrigation workers	13	6	12	–	10	66
Clerks	–	1	–	–	–	3

Accountants	I	–	–	–	–	2
Drivers	3	2	12	I	10	84
Mechanics (workshops)	5	I	5	–	30	57
Safety and security workers	–	–	–	–	–	3
Fire fighters	–	–	I	–	–	3
Guards	4	I	10	2	5	43
Radio communicaters	–	–	–	–	–	I
Grandmet (food service)*	–	–	7	–	–	21
Total	28	14	57	6	75	383

Although there has been a catastrophic change in the traditional life of the nomads, the position of the father as the authority is still strong, even if he is not employed. If a nomad has a son working for a wage, the son usually gives the bulk of his salary to the father, who is expected to use it according to his family's needs. The son has to support his father, and hence his family, because he is next in line if the father is unable to work or dies. As long as the father is alive, he enjoys unique authority among his family no matter what his economic circumstances.

NOMADS AS CANE-CUTTERS

Only a few former nomads have been able to gain employment as cane-cutters. These men come from the villages of Omdabakir and El Muhammediyya. In an interview with the cane-cutters of these two villages, they explained that they have difficulty in convincing the officials that they can do the job as well as any migrant. Nevertheless, after several attempts, some of them get the job. They say that they are willing to take forms of work with which they have no acquaintance because it is the only way for them to make a living now that their land and animals are gone. Their cane-cutter migrant colleagues jokingly refer to them as "El Arab who became Kata-kau". Cane cutting needs a lot of physical tolerance and patience.

The nomads are adapting to the job, but still their number is very limited in comparison with migrants from the west and the south.

Table 6.5

CANE-CUTTERS IN TWO NOMADIC VILLAGES

Name of Village	Number of Families	Total population	Number of cane-cutters
El Muhammediyya	80	449	35
Omdabakir	99	559	46
Total	179	1008	81

A CASE STUDY

At the harvest site, I found Mohammed and his 18- year-old son Hassan from Omdabakir village. The two work together. I asked the father whether his son works with him in cane-cutting regularly. He answered, "Yes, I need his continuous help to achieve as much as we can, and so have more money." I asked him whether he gives his son a portion of the wage received. He replied, "Not in cash, because we are using this money to buy grain, sugar, tea, coffee beans, clothes, and save up what we can to buy a sheep or a goat after a while. So the wage belongs to all the family members, and there is no individual preferential treatment because we cannot afford that." He also added that if things kept deteriorating without sign of change, the family planned to leave Omdabakir for the Blue Nile Province like the 600 people who already have gone there from his village.

LIVESTOCK IN THE NEW SETTING

As we have seen, livestock remains very important to the former nomads who continue to reside around the sugar scheme. A family who still owns some cattle, sheep, and goats can market dairy products. A gallon of milk sells for L.S. 2.5 in the Kenana Market. A bottle of butterfat will bring L.S. 3. Furthermore, the family consumes these products themselves. If there is an urgent need for cash, the family can sell an animal, usually sheep or goat, at "El Zariba." the animal market of Kenana.

Table 6.6

Livestock holdings in Abu Togaba

Type	Number
Cattle	675
Sheep	1180
Goats	645
Camels	26
Donkeys	103

Although animals are the only economic assets remaining to the nomads, they have also been a source of conflict with the administration of the KSC. When the scheme opened there was a need for protection and order. Accordingly, police and security forces were established with radio communications, vehicles, and arms. A police station was built in Kenana town, and a number of police posts were located on the perimeter of the scheme. The Scheme boundary is patrolled by horseback to keep animals out of the cane crop. This has generated conflicts, since the KSC sees livestock as a threat to the cane and the nomads see little alternative to finding grazing near the Scheme.

This has become an explosive issue because the police and the security forces have resorted to violence and intimidation to scare off the nomads and their animals that approach the cane fields. Mohammed Adam, an informant from Abu Togaba, related that while he was herding his cattle near the cane fields, a police officer riding a horse came rushing at him. The police officer started whipping him. After he was repeatedly whipped, Mohammed was asked to go with the police officer to the police station at Kenana. Mohammed Adam knew that if he went and was accused of trespassing, he might stay for a number of days in prison, be given an expensive fine, or face physical abuse and intimidation. Wishing to avoid this, he argued there was no need to go to the police station. Instead, he suggested it was better to make a compromise. After a short discussion, the police officer agreed to accept L.S. 75 for not taking Mohammed Adam to the police station.

The police have also been concerned with the old livestock routes passing near the boundaries of the Scheme. For example, they intercepted a nomadic family taking an old route from the Blue Nile Province to Kenana. The family, consisting of a man and wife, two older daughters, and three young children, were going to pitch their camp near Jebel Kodi in the vicinity of Abu Togaba. The police surprised them by beating and scattering their animals. He then began to beat the man in front of his family. He did not resist because he knew that he would suffer later at the police station. When the beating was over, the police warned him not to bring his animals anywhere around the cane fields. The man and his family had a difficult time rounding up their dispersed livestock. The nomad kept his family in the bush and went alone to Kenana Market to sell a sheep and buy market goods. He told me that, it was the first time he had ever taken such bitter humiliation in front of his family. He felt that an incident like this was a serious challenge to his position as a father who is supposed to be the guardian of his family and a defender against aggressors. He also said that he intended to flee the region as soon as possible and join Kenana and Rufa'a al Hoi tribes in "Bahr Azrag," the Blue Nile.

To control animals that wander in the vicinity of the cane fields, big enclosures were made in Kenana and at the agricultural villages around the scheme to lock up animals until their owners show up to claim them. If a man identifies his lost animals, he has to pay a fine before the authorities set them free. The fine is L.S. 1 for a cow or a camel, 35 p.t. for goats and sheep, and 25 p.t. for donkeys. As the incidents of physical abuse, punishment, and legal and illegal fines continued, the livestock owners started to tie up their animals to wooden posts near their residential area after sunset.

NEW SUBSISTENCE STRATEGIES

TAKEN BY THE NOMADS

In the absence of adequate compensation for the land and lack of compatible job opportunities for the nomads, they were faced with mounting pressure to find a way to adapt themselves to the new situation. Few are lucky enough to find jobs with the KSC for the rest, so other strategies must be found.

THE FIRST STRATEGY

Some nomadic families keep a few animals in their village, but a family cannot keep a large herd in the village because of the difficulty of managing them in a place where cane fields are only 1km away. The few animals kept by the family are milked every day, and the milk, butterfat, and sour milk are taken to the town of Kenana to be sold there. If a family can produce dairy products, they can be sold easily in a densely populated area. The problem with this strategy is the difficulty of finding pastures and water without being intercepted by Kenana police and security forces. Most owners use the drain water of Khor Kleikiz to water their animals and browse the bushes along the banks of the White Nile, but they must also buy fodder for their animals, because pastures are insufficient to support the livestock.

SECOND STRATEGY

Some nomads sell handicrafts, including mats, basketry, leatherwork, water-skins, ropes, and woodland scents products. The job of doing handicrafts is carried out by women as part of their household work. Preparing handicrafts for the market is an endeavor to replace the economic activities women carried out prior to the inception of the Kenana Scheme. The nomads are very reluctant to allow their women to engage directly in market activities. Only "old" women (over 50 years of age) and very young girls (under 16 years of age) are allowed to market family products and buy market goods. Some nomadic families under great pressure have let their young girls go to work in the field staff houses as washerwomen or baby-sitters. This occurs only under tremendous pressure of poverty and economic necessity.

THIRD STRATEGY

Some able-bodied men who cannot find work within the Kenana area leave to work in private mechanized schemes, which extend from east of El Jebelein to the Damazine region. Men usually go to work there at harvest time. They stay there until the harvest season is over, and they return home bringing grain and some money. This does not last long, and again they must migrate elsewhere to seek employment to support their families.

FOURTH STRATEGY

A considerable number of Kenana nomads engage in gathering green grass and firewood and put them in Kenana Market. They go to the banks of the White Nile, to the edge of irrigation water drainage ditches and inside cane fields,[6] to cut the green grass, put it into sacks and bring it to the Kenana Market, where it is bought by livestock owners and animal keepers. A bundle of green grass is sold for 50 p.t.

The other group, which collects firewood, may either sell it right away or turn it into charcoal, one of the most demanded sources of energy in Kenana. Most of the nomads prefer selling charcoal, since it fetches L.S. 7 per sack. The making and selling of charcoal is forbidden, and the makers are tracked down by the authorities from the Department of Forestry. They make surprise sweeps in the bush, where the nomads process the firewood into charcoal (Kamayin). The Forestry Department argues that this practice of cutting of the bushes and trees harms the environment and upsets the ecology, but at the same time, people who are pushed to fight for their survival will take the risk because they are so uncertain about their worsening economic situation.

FIFTH STRATEGY: SHARECROPPING

Some men go outside the Kenana Scheme boundaries seeking a plot of land to cultivate. Some people have tribal affiliations in villages like Nuri, Ahmar Iyn, El Babanousa, Wag Wag, Abu Shara, El Sherifiyya, Om Kewaka, Wad Hassabu, Iyal Yousif, Iyal Es'a, Hillt Om Sunt, and Abu Edakheira. Since these villages lie outside the boundaries of the Kenana Scheme, ownership of the land is still intact. There have been rumors that these lands of peasant villagers may be annexed to the Kenana Scheme, but there is no confirmation of that allegation. An affiliated person from Kenana can be given a plot of land to cultivate on a temporary basis. Some owners of the land are kind enough not to take any portion of the harvest; others take one third. A person from Abu Togaba, cultivating in one of these villages, must gain the acceptance of the village Shaykh and his supporters and must abide by the oral agreement between himself on oneside and the Shaykh and his village men on the other. Not all displaced nomads have the chance of being accommodated by a village agricultural communities.

For some of them cultivation means extending into marginal and fragile lands, where there is little success in terms of production. But the subsistence need is strong enough to make nomads try any alternative even if it is remote.

THE PEASANTS

THE PEASANT VILLAGE OF NURI

The site of Nuri village first was chosen in the 1930s as a nomadic wet season camp. The place is perfect because it lies in the foot of the mountain of Jebel Nuri in an elevated area, which is well drained. One of the great advantages of the Nuri site is that it is near a number of natural land depressions that serve as giant water pools in the wet season. Usually the water in these natural depressions outlast the water resources of the nearby villages. The village is not far from Khor Kleikiz, which drains the rainy season water from the southeastern region into the White Nile. In the wet season, a considerable number of Dar Muharib nomadic tribes camp around Khor Kleikiz because of the availability of water and grazing areas in autumn and early winter.

Agricultural lands around Nuri village began to be cleared to establish claims to land rights. A number of tribal groups claimed ownership of agricultural lands. These tribes now live permanently in Nuri. They include Sebaig, Nazza, and Berti. Other temporary peasant families come to spend the agricultural season and then move on to their dry-season villages along the banks of the White Nile. The peasants in the village have always had concerns about water resources. In the past, at the tail end of the wet-season when there was no water in the Hafir, they made a long journey to the White Nile to fetch water. This process is called El Raw'ya. Every household sent a person with water-skins and tins on donkeys or camels to go to the White Nile and bring water. The journey takes six hours round trip and was done every day until the rain began. As the number of village dwellers increased from a few hundred to over two thousand, two Hafirs were built to ensure enough water through the dry season. To prevent water contamination by animals, the first Hafir is protected by thorn bushes, while the second is protected by barbed wire. The villagers are told to water their animals at home and not to bring them near the Hafirs. There is a guard for each Hafir to keep away animals and also women who might do their laundry close to the Hafir.

The pattern of residence in the village is dictated by tribal affiliation and kinship ties. Resident tribes of Sebaig, Nazza, Berti, and recently Dinka and Nuer, share the village, but each tribe has a defined cluster of homesteads (referred to as Hillt Sebaig, Berti, or El Dinka, etc.). There is little difference in the structure of the houses. All the people in the village use straw and mud to construct their huts. However, the village school, dressing station and flour mill are built of red bricks.

The peasants mainly cultivate sorghum (dura), but some also keep a small number of livestock for milk, and to be used as a ready source of cash during emergencies and economic hardship. There is considerable economic difference in the village. The longer people have lived there as permanent residents and the bigger the sorghum fields they have, the better off they are and the higher they are on the economic and social ladder of the village. At the middle of this economic and social ladder are the peasants who stay in the village during the agricultural season and engage in the dry season migratory cycle after harvest. At the bottom of the village, economic and social strata are migrants and newcomers who work as agricultural laborers in the fields owned by other villagers and by nonresident merchants from nearby towns.

PEASANT FAMILIES' LABOR STRATEGIES

Prior to 1976, peasants in Nuri village had an average of two Gadas (10 Feddans) of sorghum fields. At that time, there was plenty of land, but they did not have access to sufficient labor to work larger fields. Family labor was the primary workforce, and all members of the family participated except infants, mothers recovering from birth, new brides, and very old people who were unable to work. An exception and a most important characteristic of that period was the existence of the "Nafir" or voluntary working parties. People worked in rotation to supplement family labor during agricultural peak times (first weeding and harvest). In the dry season, some people did gum arabic tapping or livestock managing, while others left the village to cultivate vegetables at the "gerf" of the White Nile. The core of the peasants' families' strategy was the self-sufficiency and welfare of the family in the village. Even though the family was the economic unit, in bad years a spirit of cooperation existed between the peasants to ensure that no family starved. If it happened that certain families were very low on sorghum supplies, help came from relatives as well as other villagers.

The cohesiveness and mutual help in the village was kept alive in this way and was the theme of village relations. Village products could be exchanged in light of urgent need in a kind of generalized reciprocity, which thrived in the absence of market economy and cash transactions.

The Kenana Scheme had a far-reaching impact on Nuri. The southeastern boundary of the cane fields is nearby, and Kenana town is only 50km away. Rumors spread that the scheme might claim more land than was originally thought. Immediately, residents of Nuri began to clear and claim more land. Some increased their holdings from 10 to 50 Feddans. Others, such as the Shaykh and two other families, claimed up to 500 Feddans to the east and southeast of Nuri. This very rapid increase in the size of the agricultural holdings of some families has had many consequences. It exaggerated existing wealth differences and created a labor demand which had not existed previously. People like the Shaykh and two of his relatives started to employ migrant laborers who originally had come to work at the Kenana Sugar Scheme but could not get work. As the number of unemployed migrants increased at Kenana, competition for employment became severe. This forced wages way down below the subsistence level and encouraged many people in Nuri to employ cheap, outside labor.

In Nuri village, these migrant laborers made huts and temporary straw dwellings at the south end of the residential areas. They came to work to earn wages, but the daily wage in the village is only one tenth of that paid to Kenana Scheme daily laborers. The unemployed or laid-off migrants who turn to work in Nuri village face the drudgery of field labor at an extremely low wage, but this is inescapable if one is forced to seek employment off the Kenana Scheme.

Table 6.7

Agricultural Activities and Wages in Nuri Village

Agricultural Activity	Wages per Gada (5 Feddans)
Planting	L.S. 1

First Weeding	L.S. 40
Secound wedding	L.S. 20
Harvest (cutting, collecting, piling and threshing)	L.S. 25

Labor recruitment is through negotiation followed by verbal agreement (Mughawala) between the migrant and the owner of the field. It is a system of task completion, with payment after the work is done. The calculation of pay does not seem to be based in any way on the effort exerted by the migrant to accomplish the task. To increase the number of work hours per laborer, the owners of the sorghum fields ask migrants to stay at the field site and not return to the village before the completion of the task, unless seriously sick or there is an emergency. This is particularly required during the harvest period for sorghum. This crop involves a great deal of work in terms of cutting the sorghum heads, collecting them, putting them in piles, threshing, and packing, besides guarding against crop losses by weaver birds and animals.

Table 6.8

Field size, Labor and production in Nuri Village 1983–1984

Respondents in sample	Average field size	Kind of labor	Avg. sorghum production per feddan
23	10 feddans	Family	3 sacks
9	100 feddans	Hired	2.5 sacks
3	500 faddans	Hired	2.5 sacks

As can be seen in the table above, 65.7 percent of the informants in the sample survey still depend on family labor to cultivate their fields. These families maintain the peasant outlook and still try to balance their subsistence needs and availability of capable, manual family labor.

The rest of the informants (34.3 percent) are on the road to becoming cash farmers or entrepreneurs. They are now using hired labor and tractorization to increase their scale of production. Then they sell the output into the market which suggests the maximization of profits is the motive of this segment of Nuri village.

NURI IS A CHANGING VILLAGE

There are two patterns of agricultural development that have shaken the lives of the peasants of Nuri and destroyed the communal economic relations of village solidarity. These have set on the path to capitalist transformation of this rural community. In the early 1970s, the Mechanized Farming Corporation (MFC) began allocating sizable holdings in the central clay plains of the Sudan. The recipients were wealthier merchants and private investors from the towns. Areas where allocations were made included places in the White Nile Province, such as El Rawat and El Jebelein. The average size of farms assigned by MFC was 1,000 Feddans. The aim was to induce investors to provide the capital to buy machinery (tractor, harvester) and hire agricultural laborers for maximum production. The policy goal was agricultural development based on entrepreneurship. It was argued that there was surplus rural labor, and furthermore they would be a "demonstration effect" on rural people. The picture of the town merchant every year becoming wealthier and wealthier because they have sizable farms, a tractor, and could employ laborers; inspired and awakened the awareness of some of the more enlightened villagers like the Shaykh and others, that there is an alternative to poor peasants' subsistence life. The Shaykh of Nuri and a few of his relatives have certainly responded. They have large fields because the village land and its vicinity is trusted to the Shaykh. They also had resources of livestock, which could be turned into cash to buy tractors and hire wage labor.

The second force inducing change in Nuri was the massive migration of people seeking work at Kenana. Far more men were available than were needed in the Sugar Scheme. When they reached Nuri, it was the right time for the Shaykh and his relatives to employ them as agricultural laborers. Since the establishment of Kenana Scheme, the population has increased rapidly, which makes marketing of grain a very profitable business in Kenana Market. The Shaykh and his relatives began not only to harvest sorghum, but to harvest a considerable profit in the Kenana Market. As a result, the Shaykh and his relatives have bought tractors[7] of their own to enhance sorghum production. The capitalist transformation of Nuri village has gone in a way that must closely fit the plans first set in motion in the 1960s.

It must be pointed out that income disparity is not the only change in Nuri. Community facilities have improved. A flour mill replaced the hardship of sorghum grinding. In 1979, a school was founded. The school now has three primary classes and accepts both boys and girls. The school employs two male and two female teachers. There are 169 students: 145 boys and 24 girls. Although the teachers enjoy appreciation and respect in the village, nevertheless the villagers have some skepticism about females working as teachers. The two female teachers are qualified and can handle teaching well, but it seems men in the village have a preconceived idea about the role of women as subordinates. The presence of female teachers in the village for the first time undermined the belief that women are only for housekeeping and domestic affairs. As time passes, the men tend to accept and respect them more, especially as there are girl students in the school. These girls, it is argued, can learn women's affairs better from female teachers than from their male counterparts.

Another important change was the establishment of a dressing station in 1979. However, the dressing station is hampered by the lack of medical supplies. The medical assistant says that there is a shortage of medical supplies even in the towns and big hospitals. This is due to financial difficulties and the shortage of hard currency that prevents the Department of Health in Khartoum from importing medicine and equipment from abroad. As a solution to the shortage of medical supplies in Nuri village, the medical officer buys basic needed medicine from

Khartoum or Kosti pharmacies and then sells it back[8] to the people of the village.

These fundamental changes in Nuri mean far more than the growth of its size and economic diversity. Its flour mill, school, and dressing station are regional attractions.

Its improved water supply is vital to its health and growth, and its shops attract money and trade. It is now a growth center for a periphery of villages around it (Abu Khor, Omsungoor, Hillt el Dawi, Wag Wag and Ahmer lyn), whose populations use all these facilities. We also remember what it has lost in the old social order.

CHAPTER SIX NOTES

1. The salaries of expatriates are paid in U.S. dollars. A contract laborer is about $2,000 per month, while his Sudanese counterpart doing the same job has a salary of about L.S. 90. It is rumored that a top figure among the expatriates, monthly salary between 20 and 21 thousand U.S. dollars (but I don't have enough information to deny or confirm such a figure).

2. Kenana administration set up produce farms in which they grow vegetables, fatten sheep, cows, and raise poultry. There is also a fish farm to meet the increasing demand of employees. There are subsidies for employees, but people who are not working with KSC are not allowed to buy their groceries from the Kenana Farm Shop.

3. El Kata- Kau is onomatopoetic. It is the sound produced when a number of cane-cutters are working beside each other.

4. Cane-cutters are allowed to take a bundle of cane whenever they want, as long as they do not sell it.

5. Displaced tribes of Dar Muharib were the Sabaha, Nazza, Kibayshab, Hussunnat, Massalmiyya, Rawashda, Sebaig, Khanferiya, Muhammediyya, Kenana, Ahamda, Selaym, Gawama'a, and Bani Halba.

6. Kenana Scheme administration allows people going inside the fields to cut the green grass and the sugar cane leaves as long as they do not hurt or damage the cane crop.

7. The price of a new tractor is L.S. 21,000; a used one is L.S. 7,000 (1983/1984).

8.   Some medical assistants in the remote dressing stations can easily get carried away, not only selling back some basic medical supplies they bring from towns, but sometimes they sell the Department of Health's own medical supplies, which are supposed to be free to the rural public. Some medical officers make considerable money out of this business. As a result, many of them will delay or refuse to be transferred to a town where they are constantly checked by other medical personnel.

CHAPTER SEVEN

SOCIAL SERVICES IN THE KENANA SCHEME

A part of the original agreement between Lonrho and the Sudan Government was that social services and infrastructure should be included in the Kenana feasibility study. The study concentrated on the material aspects of the project with the overriding goal of maximizing sugar production. The services planned and the system of social infrastructure that was built are largely confined to the Kenana township and the factory settlement to serve the expatriates and Kenana field staff. These facilities and services exclude the largest segment of the population in the area made up of migrant labor, the nomads, and the peasants.

The Kenana Sugar Project was designed to be a production scheme. The main departments on the Estate are considered vehicles to reach that primary goal. These departments are agriculture, cane-harvest and transport, production, administration, finance, personnel, the department of engineering and maintenance. Social services are under the control and supervision of the department of administration and public relations. Here it is treated as one of many divisions within the same department. This gives it a limited role, and it fails to reach the wide spectrum of the Kenana population.

The provision of social services infrastructure could play a significant role in the process of social change and transformation if it were made available to all people living in the region; employees and indigenous population as well. However, as long as there is limitation of these services to a certain selected segment of the society, integrated rural development is doomed to failure.

EDUCATION IN KENANA TOWN AND THE SCHEME AGRICULTURAL VILLAGES

After the Kenana project was established and workers started to bring their families to Kenana, the need for schools was apparent. In 1979 the first primary school, with six classes, opened on the site to accommodate boys as well as girls who were mainly the sons and daughters of Kenana Scheme employees. The establishment of the first primary school (Kenana Southern Primary School) was followed by the Eastern, Western, Village 2, and Camp 5 Primary Schools, to assimilate the rapidly increasing number of Kenana Scheme employees' children. As the Scheme administration established a wide base of primary schools within the area of the factory settlement population (Kenana town, or El Sufeiya), the need for the secondary education became urgent. As a result, general and higher secondary schools were founded to accept the sons and daughters of Kenana employees. The average cost of building a school in Kenana town was L.S. 230,000, which made them extremely expensive schools in comparison to the average government school that cost from L.S. 15,000 to 30,000. The Kenana schools were built of permanent building materials. They were well equipped in terms of furniture, textbooks, exercise books, pencils, and other supplies. Kenana teachers are recruited from the towns of the White Nile Province. Those chosen are subject to Kenana employment conditions so that a Kenana teacher enjoys a far better salary and standard of living than his/her counterparts working in the public schools in other parts of the Sudan. The contract of the Kenana teachers lasts for two years and is renewable for more years.

Although the Kenana schools were started only in 1979, today they are considered primary and secondary educational models not only for the White Nile Province, but for all the Sudan. This is because these schools are fully equipped, well managed, and run by qualified teachers. The problem with these schools is that they are restricted to Kenana employees' families, which excludes the indigenous population, who are desperately in need of modern educational opportunity.

Table 7.1

Schools, Teachers, Pupils in Kenana Scheme, 1983–1984

Name of school	Type	Number of classes	Teachers		Pupils		Total
			Male	Female	Boys	Girls	
Kenana Eastern School	Primary	6	2	2	208	185	393
Kenana Western School	Primary	5	5	2	220	131	351
Village 2 School	Primary	1	1		5	41	46
Kenana General Secondary	Junior	3	7		177	63	240
Kenana Higher Secondary	Senior	2	6		52	38	90
Total	5	17	25	4	632	438	1120

EDUCATION IN THE LOCAL INHABITANTS' VILLAGES OF KENANA

The southeastern part of the White Nile Province that extends from Rabak to the boundaries of the Blue Nile Province did not have a single primary school until 1976. The villages and nomadic camps of Dar Muharib that belong to the Rabak and El Jebelein rural councils had only the Quranic schools (Khlawi) of El Shaykh Musa El Khanferi. At the present, the Quranic teaching is held in the khlawi El Shaykh El Mahi in Abu Edakheira (northeast of El Jebelein).

If we focus our attention on the villages around the Kenana Scheme that extend from Omdabakir to Nuri, we find that the rate of illiteracy is over ninety percent. There are numerous reasons for this, which include:

1. Lack of primary schools in the region.

2. Schools are located in towns, which are remote and inaccessible to children in the villages and camps.

3. The demanding agropastoralist mode of production that requires participation of all family members, including school-age children, in the different economic activities around the year.

4. The long -isolation and encapsulation of the region, which reflects its neglect by the executive authorities.

5. Lack of awareness of education and its benefits, which resulted in an absence of enthusiasm to send children to school in El Hadaib or El Jebelein.

6. Shortage of school places, which leaves the majority of school-age children outside the system of education, even if they desire schooling.

Before 1976, schooling was available only to people who could afford to send their children away to towns, pay for their needs while they were away, and not need them to participate in the family labor while they were in school. The only people who could do that were the Shaykhs and the rich families. The bulk of Dar Muharib people could not afford to send their children away for education.

As the wheels of production started to turn, Kenana region was alive with people who came from different economic, educational, and cultural backgrounds. A closed, isolated society suddenly was wide open to technological innovation and rapid change. The indigenous Kenana population knew they were witnessing a massive technological, economic, social, and cultural change. This suggested to them that whatever they encountered in the new development site—of well-paid jobs, modern houses, cars, leisure and recreational facilities—could only be attained through education. The indigenous Kenana people recognized that it was too late for them to have a piece of the pie, but not too late for their children one day to be Kenana Scheme field staff and enjoy the privileges of employees.

The local population grasped the fact that education was the main avenue for success in pursuing a well-paid career in a developing society. As a result, education became an urgent social demand. Many school-age children were allowed to go to school. Nomads with sizeable livestock herds began to hire herders and hence release their children to go to school. The inhabitants of remote villages and camps began to send their children (boys) to live with a relative or a tribal member in a village with a school, or at least near a school. In spite of the willingness and enthusiasm of the indigenous Kenana people to send their children to school, they were dismayed by the scarcity of primary school educational opportunities in their region. This was true of Sudan in general and of the Kenana Township and region in particular.

In the early 1980s, five schools were established in the Kenana villages to be managed under the auspices of Rabak rural council. These schools were poorly equipped and lacked the basic school materials like benches, desks, textbooks, exercise books, and pencils. The number of pupils enrolled in these village schools in 1983–84 constituted only twenty-two percent of the total number of pupils seeking enrollment. For example, when the primary school of Camp 5 opened its doors for registration for the first year class, five hundred pupils showed up. Although the school's capacity was only eighty seats, 110 new pupils were admitted because of the large turnout. This gives us an idea of the teacher-to-pupil ratio, which negatively affected the teachers as well as the pupils.

In Kenana region today, we find two different school systems. The first one, in Kenana town, is well-constructed, well-managed, and adequately equipped. The second one, in Kenana villages, is facing enormous problems, which requires the attention of the Rabak rural council and the Kenana town council, and KSC administration too, to boost the level of education in these schools. The main problems facing the schools of Kenana villages are the following:

1. Poor construction. Built of straw and mud. When the rainy season approaches, they are vulnerable to thunderstorms.

2. Lack of teachers.

3. Teachers in these schools lack adequate staff housing, and there is a severe shortage of other basic services.

4. Inadequate facilities, especially benches, desks, text books, etc.

5. As the money economy starts dominating the area, many pupils quit school and go to work as messengers in the Kenana Scheme or sellers in the Kenana Market. This sets the pattern for many pupils to leave school.

6. Lack of adequate funds to build and maintain the basic school facilities.

Table 7.2

Schools, Teachers and Pupils in Kenana Villages, 1983–1984

Name of school	Type	Number of classes	Teachers		Pupils		Total
			Male	Female	Boys	Girls	
Fangoga School	Primary	3	4	–	114	40	154
Camp 5 School (Madenit El Hijra)	Primary	4	2	6	147	91	238
El Gargaf School	Primary	6	5	2	252	76	328
Abu Togaba School	Primary	6	4	5	189	115	304
Nuri School	Primary	3	2	2	145	24	169
Total	5	22	18	15	847	346	1193

MEDICAL SERVICES IN THE KENANA SCHEME

The factory settled population (Kenana town) is served by the main hospital in Kenana site. The Kenana hospital is very modern, with a capacity of 20 beds. It is adequate in terms of its new medical equipment and availability of drugs, medicines, and medical staff.

Table 7.3

Kenana Medical Staff 1983–1984

Type of Job	Male	Female	Total
Medical Officer	5	–	5
Dentist	–	1	1
Medical assistants	6	–	6
Lab technicians	1	–	1
Lab assistants	2	–	2
Theatre attendants	2	–	2
Nurses*	15	3	18
Midwife nurse	–	1	1
Cards clearks	15	2	17
Sanitary workers	3	–	3
Guards	2	–	2
Total	52	7	59

*There is a foreign nurse who handles the sick expatriates' cards.

Besides the Kenana hospital, there are five clinics and dispensaries in the Scheme agricultural villages. Each is manned by a medical assistant or a nurse. In the area of curative medicine, the Kenana hospital handles the cases of the most common diseases in the area, which include, in rank order:

1. Malaria

2. Bilharzia

3. Work injuries/burns

4. Dysenteries and gastro-enteritis

5. Obstetric problems

6. Measles

7. Whooping cough

8. Ophthalmic infections

The Kenana health services are only provided for the Estate employees and their dependents. When any Kenana employee or any member of his family seeks medical treatment, the head of the household must present his employment card to make sure that the person is currently employed with Kenana Scheme.

Equating provision of medical services with a Kenana employment card hurts the indigenous population of the area, who are in desperate need of adequate health service. Even serious illness and emergencies among the local non-employed people are denied admittance to Kenana hospital. The local people must use public transportation to get to Rabak or Kosti. This may be too late in emergencies. With the new construction of Kenana hospital extension by a Bulgarian company (70 hospital bed capacity), the hope is that the local people will stand a chance to use the facility. If the dwellers in the Kenana area, whether employed or not, are not treated on equal footing, eradication of infectious diseases is a long way off for the region.

In the area of environmental health and preventive medicine, residue and solid wastes of the factory are collected and dumped in the southern region of the factory. The most serious of the factory waste is watery toxic hazards. Liquid toxic wastes cross Kenana town in open ditches and are released in land depressions between Camp 5 and the village of Abu Togaba. These land depressions are breeding grounds for flies, mosquitoes, and other insects that endanger the population with the breakout of epidemic diseases unless the Kenana environmental health section steps up its preventive campaign. This applies not only to flies and mosquitoes but also to infected snails, which carry bilharzia (schistosomiasis) and are found in the irrigation canals and the drain water.

HEALTH SERVICES IN KENANA VILLAGES

Prior to 1976, there was no health service in the region. There were some dispensaries available in Rabak and El Jebelein at that time, but because of the lack of effective transportation and the difficulties of reaching these areas in the wet season, the local inhabitants depended extensively on traditional methods. These included herbal medicine, Muslim Saints as traditional healers (Fakirs), and local practitioners who treated broken and dislocated bones. These practitioners used methods of incision with razors and heated metal in treating lymph and other disorders. Since the traditional healers and herbal medicine have their limitations, the Kenana area was a fertile environment for the parasitic and water-borne diseases, like bilharzia, malaria, and diarrhoeal diseases, which take a heavy toll on the population's general health.

In 1977, two dressing stations were established in the Kenana region, one in the village of Sharat and the other in Taksaboon. In 1980, dressing stations were established in the villages of Fangoga, Abu Togaba, and Nuri. These dressing stations lack adequate medical supplies, and sometimes they have shut down, either because there is no medicine, or there is no medical assistant or nurse. These dressing stations are the only source of medical treatment for the local population in Kenana. During the wet season when the nomads pitch their camps in the vicinity of Kenana, the demand for health services is high. At this time, there is either a shortage of medical supplies or none available at all. This forces sick people to seek medical treatment in the town's private clinics and pharmacies, where the cost of medical examination and treatment is far above what the local people can afford.

As curative medical care is very limited, so also is preventive medicine. The stagnant drain water that results from irrigation of cane fields does not reach the White Nile. It makes a sizeable water pool southwest of the village of Abu Togaba, which has a continuous supply from Khor Kleikiz. There is another big water pool southwest of El Muhammediyya village from the drain water of El Mazlagan. These large water pools near these villages are on land once used as pastures and vegetable gardens. Since environmental sanitation and personal hygiene are poor among the villagers, this stagnant water poses a health hazard and perpetuates the rate of infection in these villages.

In order to stop the progress of these diseases, the health authorities in the region should provide curative medicine and at the same time put great emphasis on the environmental health issues. They should control the snails and the mosquitoes, educate the villagers about primary sanitation methods (like building and using pit latrines), and above all urge the concerned authorities to construct a system of clean potable water supplies[1].

POTABLE WATER

The supply of clean water is a problem that has faced the indigenous people of Kenana for a very long time. People adapted to the situation by depending completely on the White Nile during the dry season. Every village or camp has a unit called El Raw'ya[2]. which is made up of individuals representing households in that residential compound. Each morning every family saddles a donkey or a camel and sends one of its members to join El Raw'ya, which leaves for the White Nile. The members of El Raw'ya must leave in a group, because when they fill their water-skins and tins, they need each other's help to lift up the filled containers and balance them on donkeys' backs. The daily journey to collect water takes six hours. When El Raw'ya returns to the settlement, the water is handled carefully. The priority of uses is drinking, cooking, spiritual Muslim washing before prayers (Waduo), and watering chickens and small or sick animals. The average family consumption of water is two tins or two water-skins per day, which is equivalent to eight gallons of water.

When the dry season is over and the residents in Dar Muharib see the gathering rain clouds, there is a sigh of relief from the villagers and the camp dwellers, because water can be collected from the nearest land depression or water hole (Rahad or Hafir) instead of by long daily journeys. The first day that the land depressions and water holes are filled they become the focus of attention, a place not only for collecting water, but a site to meet different people, chat, and exchange news. The water in these Hafirs or Rahood is muddy, giving it a dark brown color, and it may look dirty to a foreigner, but the nomads and peasants enjoy having water in their back yards. Some households use the water as it is; a few others apply herbal treatments to settle the mud. When the dry season sets in, people again saddle their donkeys and prepare for the work of bringing water from the White Nile. This traditional pattern of collecting water is still practiced by the segment of the population, which does not have access to local water supplies.

Modern water treatment began in the region with a small plant during the Project construction phase. This water was distributed to people who were working at the Kenana Scheme. In 1978, the Sufeiya or Kenana township water treatment plant was completed and began to distribute water to the settled factory population in the Kenana agricultural Villages 2, 3, 4, and Pump Station 4. The produce farm small water treatment plants were built to provide the residents in these areas with clean water. The supply of water for the plant of Sufeiya comes through a pipe from pump station 3 with a capacity of 200m^3 per hour. In simplified terms, the water treatment process is as follows:

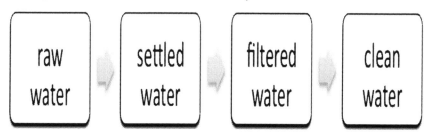

Water treatment needs an injection of different chemicals at different points of its processing. The water treatment staff keeps a daily chemical log showing the commonly-used types every day. The most commonly-used chemicals are alum, lime, calcium, poly, and soda ash.

Table 7.4

TOTAL CHEMICAL CONSUMPTION
BY THE PLANT IN JANUARY 1984

Chemical	Alum	Lime	Poly	Calcium *Hypo	Cl2 Gas	Soda Ash
Amount in kg	7228	1632	40	302	540	260

*Hypo is short for Hyposulfite.

The total water production in the Sufeiya plant is $196,137m^3$ monthly (a cubic meter is 222 gallons), with a daily average of $6,327m^3$. The Kenana treated water is labelled as one of the best in the country. There is an adequate supply of water for the core settlement in Kenana town, where water is distributed to the houses of field staff through pipes and taps. There are also some public taps in and around Kenana community facilities. For the labor camps of the cane-cutters, the water is carried by water tankers and stored in tanks situated in these camps. For the Kenana employees who are living outside the core settlement, water is delivered by tankers. The peak of water consumption is in the dry season. When the weather is extremely hot, the need for water is greater than the Sufeiya treatment plant can deliver. The capacity of the plant well is $320m^3$, and the water tower's capacity is $500m^3$. This amount is consumed rapidly, which dictates a continuous process of water treatment to satisfy the increasing need for potable water for the Kenana community.

The migrant population, who live in Camps 4 and 5, and the nomads who are settled in Abu Togaba village, who are not employed with the Kenana Sugar Estate, suffer from the lack of clean drinking water. The water tankers daily distribute $302m^3$ (five percent of the daily amount produced by the water plant) to Kenana employees' houses in the above-mentioned areas. Camp 5 and the village of Abu Togaba have water towers, but the water in them is not treated to be drinkable. The water supply in these towers comes through an exposed canal. Animals have access to these small canals, and some people wash their clothes and themselves in them. The water in the towers in Abu Togaba and Camp 5 is not good for drinking. When I was in Abu Togaba village (quarter of El Gawama'a tribe), as a sign of hospitality water was offered to me. The water has a nasty smell and a sour taste. The people use this water for washing, but prefer not to drink it, if they can borrow a bowl of clean water from an employed relative or neighbor. When they can't find clean water, they must drink from this polluted water.

In 1983, fourteen pupils from the school of El Gargaf contracted bilharzia as a result of drinking this polluted water. I asked the staff of Kenana water treatment plant why the supply of water in Abu Togaba and Camp 5 was so unclean and so unhealthy that it poses a risk to the people living in these places. They replied that these water towers do not belong to them, but belong to the rural council of Rabak.

The KSC administration allots L.S. 100,000 annually to the development of community facilities in the nearby villages. The most urgently needed facility in these villages is a network for the delivery of clean, safe water. This is not only for the welfare of the people who are not employed with Kenana, but also for the laid-off workers during off-season when the water tankers discontinue their delivery of potable water to them.

HOUSING

The traditional house in Dar Muharib is made of acacia bark, grass mats, leather and cloth and is known as Beit el Shukkab. The house is made by women, and it is designed like a tent with poles tied to the ground. Beit el Shukkab is made of light material so that all the components of the house can just be rolled up and carried by bulls during the seasonal movements of the nomads. This type of nomadic house is still found in villages where some of the pastoralists settled down. A second type of housing which is widely used by local inhabitants is the thatched hut made of straw. Sometimes, for further improvement, mud walls are added. The last type of traditional housing is the square room made out of sun-baked bricks. In the present traditional communities of Kenana, we find all of these types of local housing existing side by side.

When the KSC administration relocated the indigenous population to new village sites, no efforts were made to build any type of housing for the people who were being displaced. The indigenous population made their own residences after the KSC relocation. This resulted in a repeated picture of villages and camps appearing as they did centuries ago, but existing in the present. While nearby, the Kenana factory settlement enjoys a new pattern of housing, with well laid-out residential areas with running water, electricity, and TV services.

In 1976, when the project was under development, prefabricated houses and mobile homes were installed for the expatriates and the top management staff at the engineering site. Temporary residential units and huts were built for the Sudanese junior staff and workers. At this time, Capper Neill International Inc. constructed a camp for its working team. Other multinational corporations also constructed camps to accommodate the work force that was assembled.

In 1979, the Kenana administration started to construct the Scheme employees' residential areas which, included the Coseley,[3] T2,[4] El Alamiyya,[5] Abdalla Elkhidir.[6] By October of 1983, the Kenana housing units accommodated 2,728 employees of whom 1,800 were married with families. Many more small units and thatched huts were constructed to house the workers and the seasonal laborers.

The higher the qualifications of an employee, the better his chance of occupying a comfortable housing unit. The senior staff and the top management are accommodated in the Coseley and Type 2 housing, which is designed and equipped to suit modern life. This category of Kenana Scheme employees does not have difficulties concerning housing. Social problems like crowded houses are absent among this group, because they have few dependents living with them. The junior staff, the workers, and the seasonal laborers all confront housing problems. Junior staff usually accommodated in type 4 housing units (T4). This is a one bedroom house, yet the junior staff have the highest number of dependents, with an average of 7 persons in every house. Since there is only one bedroom, these houses fall short of accommodating all the family members and more distant relatives who come to look for work. The kitchen is sometimes used as an additional bedroom, and sometimes a hut is built in the family courtyard for the same reason.

The sites and housing types provided for workers and seasonal laborers are inadequate. In the autumn of 1983, approximately half of the residents of Camps 4 and 5 fled to nearby high areas because of the devastating effects of a flood. In these camps, some reconstruction and provision of small canals is required to drain the water away and prevent floods.

RECREATION FACILITIES

The establishment of recreation facilities is an integral part of the process of development, especially in the rural areas where people lack almost all the essential sorts of services. The Kenana administration established recreation facilities within the residential areas of the core population and the factory settlement community.

The best of these recreational facilities is the Kenana Senior Staff Club (KSSC). This club is well-equipped with all the necessary equipment, games, and services to entertain the senior staff. It offers a dining room, a bar, a video club, committee rooms, a swimming pool, tennis courts, families section, and a children's playground. The club premises and the recreational services are available only to the senior staff and their families

A more modest recreational centre is the Junior Staff Club, which provides dining facilities, a library, an assembly room, an exhibition room, and an open theatre, which most of the time is used to show TV programs and video cassettes. The Junior Staff Club also includes a basketball court, families section, a children's playground, and a football (soccer) ground adjacent to the club.

The third recreational club is the workers club, which includes the same kinds of services and premises as the Junior Staff Club.

The recreational facilities on the Kenana Estate are restricted to the core settlement of the Scheme. These social and cultural clubs are mainly confined to the Kenana Scheme employees. The large segment of new settlers, unemployed migrants, and others must find other outlets to pass time and entertain themselves. In Camps 4 and 5, they often engage in visiting prostitutes, abuse of liquor, and hashish.

If the Kenana Scheme administration allotted enough finances to build and supervise more social clubs in the core settlement area, and also distributed some of these clubs in the local villages in the vicinity of the Kenana Estate, this would have a positive effect on the process of change and social transformation.

ROADS

In any development scheme, an adequate all-weather network of roads is essential to link the development site to other parts of the country. This also facilitates transportation within the Scheme, which is very crucial in the process of production. Of course, this means other social services can be delivered, and all sorts of people and machines can move easily.

The nature of the clay soil in the Kenana region results in changes from dry season dusty roads to impassable, deteriorating, rutted, wet clay surfaces in the rainy season. To construct all-weather roads, grading, compacting, and gravel surface treatment is required.

The most important road in Kenana is the one that links the factory, administration complex and the Sufeiya township to the town of Rabak, which is the link to the national, all-weather road network, and Sudan railways. This road is 30km long. The first 18km of road from Rabak are sandy and lateritic soil. This part of the road was treated with grading, recompacting and construction of a system of drains. The following 10km were treated with gravel to prevent softening and rutting during the wet season. The last 2km of this road, which goes into the factory and the administration complex, were treated with gravel and asphalt. Roads in the core settlement area are treated with native deposits of gravel.

Kenana Estate roads and farm roads were built from the materials excavated when the main irrigation canals were constructed. The Estate roads were raised and compacted and supplied with a drainage system to serve as access roads to the irrigated areas and agricultural villages.

RAILWAY

The Kenana Sugar Scheme is connected to the Sudan railway system by a 30km spur track that runs from Rabak to the Kenana Sugar Factory. The track laying was carried out by Sudan railway authorities. The railway that links the Kenana Sugar Factory and Rabak is considered a privately-operated line, constructed mainly for the purpose of bringing in machinery and taking away sugar.

AIR STRIP

An airstrip was built 2km south of the factory. The airstrip is 1km long, with a gravel surface, all-weather runway for small aircraft. The orientation of the runway is north to south. The runway was built according to International Civil Aviation Organization (ICAO) specifications. The air strip is used by Kenana light aircraft that commute regularly between Kenana and Khartoum for the purpose of carrying senior staff, mail, important messages, and help in emergencies.

SECURITY AND LAW ENFORCEMENT IN KENANA

The establishment of development scheme requires some measures for the protection and guarding of the scheme equipment and properties on the one hand and providing security and safety for the population in the new settlement on the other. So police stations, army units, and court councils were established in Kenana Scheme to maintain order and security and provide judicial services on the Estate.

In 1984, the Kenana main police station consisted of forty-one policemen, led by a chief of police and two police lieutenants. At that time, forty recruits were undergoing six months of training and preparation to be graduated to join Kenana police force. There was also an army unit of forty military personnel stationed at Kenana to support the police and security forces during the peak time of the production season. However, the main objectives of the army unit in Kenana are:

1. To guard the Scheme.

2. To prevent any sabotage directed against the Estate in general and against the refinery in particular.

3. To discourage people who illegally possess rifles or shotguns on the Estate.

Although the police force and the army unit share the same responsibilities concerning the guarding and protection of the Estate properties, equipment, and cane fields, the police force is further responsible for keeping order and security in Kenana township and the labor camps. This task of keeping order proved to be very laborious for the police forces, especially in Camps 4, 5, and Shandi Foug, where quarrels, disputes, stealing, and murder have occurred. This disorder is thought to be a reflection of the ethnic and cultural heterogeneity of these particular areas.

Before the declaration of the Islamic sharia law in September 1983, the labor camps, especially Camp 5 (Campo Khamsa), were the scene of the sale of liquor, prostitution (Farig Eshok), and a trade in hashish (locally known as bungo). During the first weeks of the sharia implementation, such activities slowed down in Camp 5. This suppression only gave a big boost to these illegal activities beyond the control of the Kenana police force. During my field work in Kenana (February 1983 through February 1984), the police forces reported nearly a thousand crimes.

According to Kenana police station, the number of crimes on the Estate is increasing rapidly, especially in the production season. The major crimes on the Estate are murder, attempted murder, assault, and burglary. The bulk of the crime takes place in Camp 5, especially Farig Eshok, where people may be intoxicated and likely to engage in fighting because of women and hashish. The KSC administration and the Kenana police force are concerned about the security on the Estate. It appears that efforts are needed to increase the size of the police force and equip it with effective means of transportation.

Table 7.5

CRIME REPORT - KENANA POLICE STATION

Type of Crimes	Number of Crimes Committed
Murder	3
Serious injuries (Assault)	12
Minor injuries (battery)	331
Prostitution and processing of liquor	154
Theft (including 5 vehicles from KSC)	292
Cheating (Money)	18
Illegal possession	17
Destruction by fire (Arson)	3
Damage of cane field by nomads	3
Burglary	44
Burglary of staff houses (servants)	20
Attempted murder	48
Rape	3

The KSC administration and the police force are concerned about the use and abuse of alcohol and narcotics on the Estate. The police make raids on the suspected sellers of local beer and liquor, arrest prostitutes, and also try to track down the drug traffickers who bring hashish from the southern part of the Blue Nile Province. These drug traffickers use the Damazine-Kenana road. Locally, this road is called "the smoke line" because of the large amount of hashish that is carried undetected from the Damazine region to the Kenana Estate.

To keep the situation under control, the police force needs to be increased. At the same time, help from the army unit is crucial when there is an incident that needs the collaboration of a larger force than the police have available. The KSC administration has increased the number of personnel working in the section of safety and security. Their job is to give advice to employees and workers who are using machinery to guard the Estate property and equipment and to draw attention to any person suspected of being drunk or intoxicated by drugs during working hours. They issue and check gate passes to control admission to the factory. They wish to make sure that there is no unidentified person inside the factory yard or within close range of the refinery area.

MARKETS AND SHOPPING SERVICES

Economic transactions in the Kenana market place have increased rapidly. The processes of selling, buying, and retailing are becoming an everyday activity in the new market economy. All the categories of people in the Kenana community participate in visiting the markets of Sug el Zink and Camp 5, which are congregations of private shops and services on the Estate. There are smaller markets such as those in Camp 4 and Shandi Foug, which provide goods and services for labor camp dwellers who live in the immediate vicinity.

The KSC administration introduced a number of shops and a cooperative to meet its staff consumption needs. There is a senior staff shopping center—a supermarket— which is restricted only to the senior staff. The field staff buys at the farm shop, which sells meat, poultry, eggs, and dairy products to Kenana employees. They buy their basic staple goods like sugar, tea, oil, soap, etc. from the Kenana cooperative shop. The restriction of Kenana supermarket, the farm shop, and its cooperative to KSC employees only, leaves the poor population (cane-cutters, service and self-employed migrants, peasants and nomads) to buy in the private shops. There, profit is the main goal. The private shop owners may hike the price of commodities 25 percent to 50 percent without the knowledge and recognition of a less-informed and less-experienced population, which is new to the idea of buying and selling.

The monthly payroll at Kenana is two million Sudanese pounds. A part of this is spent on food, rent, and other immediate consumption goods. A considerable part of it goes to entertainment. The rest is diverted to the obtaining of such expensive appliances as cassette recorders, TV sets, and refrigerators. These are purchased in the Rabak and Kosti Markets, which are the major towns in the region. They can be easily reached by all-weather road from the Kenana Scheme.

An increasing number of Kenana people are shopping in Rabak and Kosti. This is due to the limited availability of markets and shopping centers on the Estate, and the large number of badly managed and disorganized shops in the scheme.

A number of things could be done to improve the market sector at Kenana.

1. Expand the service of the produce farm and the cooperative to satisfy the basic needs of the entire population.

2. Monitor private shops by police or security forces to discourage black marketeering and illegal increasing of prices.

3. Private shop owners should be urged to put a price tag on the goods that they display.

4. Health authorities should provide guidance to the owners of the restaurants and cafes on the Estate. The present poor and unhealthy conditions are hazardous to customers who are served in these places.

5. Check trade licenses of the petty traders during the first week of each month. The goods displayed by these sellers are sometimes obtained illegally (stolen) and sold at a high price.

6. Extend the development of cooperatives in the Kenana residential areas, labor camps, and the nearby villages to stop the exploitation of the low-income groups by the shop owners.

CHAPTER SEVEN NOTES

1. Kenana scheme administration annually allotted L.S. 100,000 to upgrade the social services in the villages around Kenana to achieve "better relations with neighbours." but the money has not yet been put into the improvement of village systems of service.

2. A traditional way of collecting water from the White Nile by using donkeys or camels as carriers of tins and water-skins.

3. Coseley is a prefabricated house assembled for the Kenana top management, known as Type 1.

4. T2: Type 2, built to accommodate Kenana senior staff.

5. Junior staff residential areas, known as Type 4 or T4.

6. Junior staff housing, known as Type 4 or T4.

CHAPTER EIGHT

A SOCIETY TRANSFORMED

ENVIRONMENT AND ECOLOGICAL CHANGES

The Kenana region is a part of the "clay plains" that constitute the bulk of the White Nile Province. The most important natural feature of the region is the White Nile River, which is the key to the region in terms of human subsistence. The Kenana area has a vegetation complex known as the "open savannah woodland," with acacia trees and short to medium grass that flourishes in the rainy season (average precipitation 400mm) to provide the pasturage of Dar Muharib.

Prior to the late 1960s and early 1970s, the balance between the available resources of the Dar Muharib environment and the requirements of the nomads, peasants, and the wildlife appeared indefinitely sustainable. The nomads, peasants, and the wildlife lived in a close balance with the land. The nomads and their livestock made seasonal movements, which averted exhaustion of the land as well as using resources available at certain times. The peasants practiced shifting, or bush cultivation, for the same purpose and, in addition, to give sorghum fields time to regain their fertility. The open savannah woodland was the home of an enormous variety of species of wildlife, including hyenas, wild cats, gazelles, antelopes, monkeys, different varieties of snakes, eagles, hawks, hay-cocks, guinea fowls, water fowls, and crows. These species and others maintained a sustainable relationship with the human uses of the environment.

In the early 1970s, two million Feddans of the "clay plains" were assigned to rain-fed mechanized farming, and by 1977, four million Feddans were under mechanization. The mechanization program brought serious problems, environmental, social and economic. These problems became more complicated with the establishment of large-scale irrigated schemes like the Assalaya and Kenana Sugar Scheme.

The politicians, planners, and developers remain dangerously unaware of the magnitude of environmental degradation and the plight of the rural masses that has been caused by the mechanization program and the "breadbasket strategy." In Kenana region, 150,000 Feddans were cleared by KSC, shrubs and acacia trees were burnt, and 80,000 Feddans were leveled to become irrigated cane-fields.

As a result, the tribal land holding in Dar Muharib has been disrupted to accommodate the new development scheme. This process has led to the eviction of the nomads and peasants of the area. The affected nomads and peasants have been pushed into poor, marginal, and fragile ecosystems, which can only lead to more deterioration and disruption of these habitats. There is also the danger that the constant cultivation without rotation will expose the soil to erosion, salinization, and other damage.

When the main goal of development scheme is production and more production, the people and the environment risk being caught in a rapid downward spiral of degradation, often leading to losses in the international market and the national subsistence economy as well.

According to Eckholm:

Export crops, a principal source of foreign exchange for many arid countries, can bolster economic progress. But if their expanded cultivation is not accompanied by careful land use planning and if a major share of the income produced is not earmarked for rural development, the lot of the rural poor may deteriorate and environmental stresses intensify. All too often, the foreign exchange and taxes collected from export crops wind up mainly supporting bloated government bureaucracies and the pampered urban elite (1980:49).

As Eckholm noted, any development or expansion of agriculture in the absence of "careful land use planning" can create problems ranging from rural poverty to environmental degradation. The careful land use planning was absent when the Kenana project was in the process of construction. The main concern then was the clearance of the bush, pulling down of trees, excavation of irrigation canals, and the leveling, and preparation of the land for the cane crop. The first effect to be felt in the region as the result of the mass clearance of bush and forests was a "firewood crisis."

The firewood crisis hit the Kenana rural community hard, because wood is the main fuel for cooking and other domestic purposes. Now the rural people go long distances in search of wood for their cooking fires. The resulting rise in demand for charcoal drove the price of a sack of charcoal from L.S. 1 in 1976 to L.S. 7 in 1984. In 1985, it more than doubled to L.S. 15 a sack. To many environmental experts a firewood crisis is an alarming sign of desertification and drought in the arid and semi-arid third world countries. It may be overcome only by massive measures like reseeding, reforesting, and construction of green belts, usually with the help of technically advanced countries. It also requires enlightenment campaigns to help people be aware of their environment and prevent them from misuse and abuse of natural resources around them.

The problem of desertification and desert encroachment in the Sudan poses a serious threat to man and nature. It continued unchecked until, by the late 1970s, things had deteriorated to an alarming degree. Ibrahim (1978) states that 500,000km² were directly affected by desertification, which he attributed to the close connection between overgrazing, overcultivation, and deforestation.

The problem of desertification is probably man made, occurring where the land and its resources are excessively used by man. When the problem began to have its adverse effect in the Sudan, politicians and developers easily targeted the nomads, peasants, and the rural settlers as the source of the problem. As a matter of fact,

The popular notion that nomads wander aimlessly has little basis in fact: nomadic movements nearly always harmonize with the seasonal rhythm of climate and plant life (Eckholm 1980:48).

The nomads' high rate of mobility, which includes traveling long distances annually, suggests that nomads do not stay in a particular place for too long. This is because they are in a continuous search for adequate water supplies and green pastures for their animals. So the notion that nomads exploit the land until it is caught in a deteriorating cycle is not true. On the contrary, nomadic seasonal movements, made in a wide radius, can benefit fragile ecosystems and arid lands. When the animal droppings are spread in a wide range of areas, seeds in them germinate and reproduce different species of grasses and bushes in the wet season, which helps conserve the fragile soil.

As for the peasants and the rural cultivators, until the mid 1960s their farming activities were very much geared to shifting and bush cultivation. So the peasants and rural cultivators, like the nomads, lived in harmony with the environment around them.

Overgrazing, overcultivation, and deforestation are the kind of environmental problems that were accelerated by the absence of "careful land use planning." when the former government (1969–1985) launched large-scale agricultural programs. Land expropriation forced the nomads as well as the peasants from their original land. They were thus driven to search for new locations. They end up roaming because they try to cultivate poor, marginal, arid lands. Evicted rural cultivators and peasants have extended their northern boundaries of cultivation 200km too far north. While the limit of the agronomic dry boundary coincides with the 500mm-isohyet, cultivation activities now extend as far as the 250mm-isohyet (Ibrahim: 1978). The peasants and nomads are using arid and fragile ecosystems, which put them at serious risk and exacerbate the problem of desertification.

In Sudan, the development schemes have been accompanied by a non-rational land use method if we consider conserving the natural habitat. For example, the establishment of the Kenana Sugar Scheme was accompanied by large-scale clearance of the bush and acacia trees. One hundred fifty thousand Feddan were cleared. With an increasing population coming to Kenana looking for work and settling down, the demand for firewood and charcoal increased rapidly. Thus more of the scrubland and bush in the vicinity of Kenana were stripped clean. As the firewood crisis developed, a group of merchants and former government bureaucrats took advantage of the situation. They attacked the forested islands of the White Nile and the silt-banks (gerf) and basins of the river which contain a climax forest of Sunt (Acacia arabica Del) and Sidir (Ziziphus spinachristi wild). The process of deforestation that took place is unprecedented, leaving the whole province without a single "forest reserve." In the search for charcoal and profits the riverine environment was left open to erosion and sand accumulation.

CHANGE IN SOCIAL LIFE AND DOMESTIC ORGANIZATION

THE NOMADS

Dar Muharib nomads dwell in tents that accommodate their elementary families. The cluster of tents is known as a Farig (camp). Every tent is the physical and social property of kin who are usually a nuclear family that includes the father, mother, and their unmarried children. The nomadic household (tent) is the center of domestic, social, and economic activities in the Kenana pastoral society. The tent is the place where children are socialized and come to be fully aware of their role towards their family members, especially the father, who is seen as solely responsible for the economic maintenance and the welfare of the household. He is the main owner of the herd, although individuals from the household may hold separate title to a number of livestock. After the father's death, inheritance goes according to the Islamic law in which a son will have double the share of his sister.

The nomadic family household, or tent, is an important unit of the pastoral camp. Such a tent cluster is led by a Shaykh, to whom the cluster members are tribal kin. The structure of the nomadic camp often changes from one year to the next: young daughters marry and leave the camp to join their husband's kin camp, bachelors marry and bring their wives to be new members of the camp.

In the dry season, the Dar Muharib tribal camps move southward until they reach the northern fringes of the swamp grassland (Machare

Marshes). In the beginning of the wet season, Dar Muharib nomads travel north again and pitch their camps in the Kenana region. During this period, the household may release some of its members from herding to cultivate a small sorghum field to meet the family need for grain. The nomadic camp in Dar Muharib is not only a migratory unit, but it is also a social, political, and economic unit as well, in which people carry out their lives in full collaboration, mutual help and generalized reciprocity to achieve a self-sustaining pastoral economy.

The transformation of the land into cane fields not only disrupted the pastoral nomadic life of the indigenous population, but their domestic life and social organization as well. The largest part (70 percent) of the nomads left the area, hoping to continue to practice the nomadic life that they could no longer practice in the Kenana region. For these nomads who have out-migrated from the Kenana region there is no claim to land in other areas that belong to other nomads and peasants. As long as they wander without title or claim to land, their nomadic social life and domestic organization is threatened and may easily disappear.

The smaller portion of the former nomads (30 percent) congregated inside and around the Kenana Sugar Scheme. The first sign of change in their life is the end of their regular migration. They still live in the same kind of dwelling, but now they are part of a settled village. They manage to keep a few animals to produce dairy products, but there is no more family labor system in which every member of the household contributes to subsistence. There are too few animals to support family needs for dairy products and cash. With the high rate of unemployment among the displaced nomads, a family would be lucky if an elder son finds a seasonal manual job with the Kenana Scheme.

Most of the displaced nomadic heads of household are no longer in a position to be the economic provider for their family as they used to in the past. Their sons must do it. If they are lucky, these young men may work on seasonal basis with the Kenana Scheme. Otherwise, they will leave the area to work as agricultural laborers elsewhere. Most of the wages earned by the nomads' sons is given to the father to run the family affairs. Most of the heads of household try to sell whatever the nomadic family can produce, especially dairy products and basketry. Other items sold include firewood, charcoal, and green grass for other peoples' animals. Although the economic status of heads of household is deteriorating, there is no sign that the father's seniority and authority is declining. He still gains the ultimate respect of his family members, and his role as a guardian has increased and tends to overshadow his declining role as the person who is in charge of economic maintenance.

One of the most important features of the nomadic domestic organization and social life is the system of reciprocity that cements kinship bonds, individual and family relationships for centuries. With the disappearance of the self-sustaining nature of the nomadic mode of subsistence and the emergence of a market economy, goods which used to be given in reciprocal exchanges are gaining commodity value in the new cash economy. In order to make a living, all the family's limited products and labor must be put into the market to generate enough cash to buy sorghum, a commodity they can no longer grow in the present situation. The utilization of traditional tribal land by the Kenana Sugar Scheme and the introduction of a cash economy has put a lot of pressure on the nomads to change their organization of traditional reciprocity to an impersonal approach, except among nuclear family members.

THE PEASANTS

The peasants of Dar Muharib are derived originally from the tribes of Western Sudan. They established themselves in the region as cultivators, keeping only a few animals for times of urgent need. They were allowed to claim as much land as a family could manage to clear and cultivate, weed, guard against birds, and harvest. Although the land the peasants claimed was entrusted to certain nomadic Shaykhs, there was no obligation for the peasants to pay anything for it. However, after harvest, a peasant might give the concerned Shaykh a sack of sorghum as a gesture of respect to a neighbor who has allowed him to use the land.

In the dry season, peasants congregate at their villages along the White Nile banks. They cultivate the grerf to produce vegetables, engage in fishing, and work for wages in the nearby cotton schemes and urban centers. In the wet season, peasants move to their villages in the rainlands east of the White Nile to cultivate sorghum. After the harvest season ends, they return again to their dry season villages.

The peasant family depends on family labor on the land for subsistence. In the dry season villages, families usually cultivate small plots irrigated from the White Nile. After the vegetables are harvested and sold, many families seek work of picking cotton and move temporarily to cotton schemes, where they live in camps. Prior to the annual movement to the wet-season villages, the villages along the White Nile become socially active. People who have been away in employment are back and the village dwellers prepare the seeds and their agricultural tools for the rainy season. During this time of the year, social collaboration and mutual help are common. This might include exchanges and gifts of agricultural seeds, mending of agricultural tools, and construction of the field huts in the rainland. Cleaning the sorghum fields is also done through such mutual help.

With the establishment of mechanized schemes and large scale irrigated schemes in the area, the peasants, like the nomads, lost their land. Their source of subsistence was cut off and further intervention claimed their gerf at the banks of the White Nile. Thus, the peasants have left their villages to fall to ruins because they have nothing to live for in their original places. Waves of peasants and their families have migrated, seeking to become agricultural laborers; others have moved to the outskirts of urban centers to dwell in straw camps. Every morning, the peasant families walk into town in hopes of finding a job and hence a way to subsist. Newly arrived peasants are not trained or equipped to do jobs in town that attain them and their families any semblance of economic security or even subsistence. Having nowhere to turn, these "urban nomads" wander aimlessly in towns in severe economic distress, which contributes to the collapse of peasant social organizations, family, and domestic life.

A CHANGING POLITICAL SYSTEM

In an earlier chapter, the complex political history of the White Nile Province was briefly reviewed. It was noted that the Baggara Arabs of the region had long competed with each other to establish dominance over parts of the region. In the nineteenth century the Turco-Egyptian rule of the area was established (1821–1885). Heavy taxes were imposed, and the local leaders were punished for resistance. There was further heavy fighting and many losses during the Mahadiyya period. The economy was destroyed by Mahadist conflicts and the political system was shattered. Losses were so heavy that those few who remained dispersed throughout the region in small groups based on segmentary lineages. Such dispersal was facilitated by the pastoral character of the economy and, by coincidence, fit very well with the governing interests of the Anglo-Egyptian Condominium of this period. Any large tribal confederation was seen by this regime as containing the threat of a revolution.

In 1921, the Milner Commission Report recommended that decentralization of administration should be instituted. It was argued that a considerable part of the civil administration should be left in the hands of the (native) local authorities.[1] As a result, "The Power of Nomad Shaykhs Ordinance" was passed in 1922. The Power of Nomad Shaykhs Ordinance was the beginning of Native Administration in Sudan. The colonial government selected certain nomad Shaykhs and religious leaders who had sided with the Anglo-Egyptian regime. The implementation of the Nomad Shaykhs Ordinance triggered disputes and conflicts on two levels. First, it created conflicts and a constant struggle for power between rival tribes in the same territory. Second, internal disputes between lineages within tribes broke out, since the government gave power and support to some Shaykhs and omitted the others. This alignment of tribes and lineages against each other weakened the power of resistance against the Anglo-Egyptian regime and, at the same time, gave the Government the chance to increase its hold on the country.

The Condominium Administration set up a "cattle Nazirate"[2] in Dar Muharib region, to facilitate administration and payment of taxes to the colonial government. The leader of the Kibayshab tribe, Balla Wad Suliaman, was installed as Nazir. He was assisted by Omdas[3] and Shaykhs to carry out his duties and obligations as they were assigned by the Anglo-Egyptian regime. The installation of Balla Wad Suliaman, a Kibayshabi Shaykh, as a Nazir had its implications in terms of control and subjection of other nearby tribes. The position of the Nazir had great power, because appointment came from Khartoum and was confirmed by the District Commissioner. The Nazir enjoyed the backing of the colonial government, but at the same time gained the dissatisfaction and hostility of the tribes that shared the same area.

Other Baggara tribes in the region not only were dissatisfied but demanded their own Nazirate, which put the colonial government in a very precarious situation. To avoid unrest and rivalry in the area, the Nazirate was transferred to the tribe of El Gim'e on the western bank of the White Nile. The Anglo-Egyptian regime kept rotating the position of the Nazir among different tribes, and this served to keep them disunited and in competition with each other. Decision-making was mostly one-sided. The District Commissioner of the White Nile Province in Ed Deum transmitted central government decisions and his own provincial actions to the Nazir, who would take them to the Omdas (assistants) and the Shaykhs (agents). They were then passed to camp headmen and to the people of the camp. Decision-making passed from the upper Colonial Administrative apparatus to the natives; nothing went in the other direction.

After independence, the traditional authority of the Nazirs and Omdas continued and was strengthened because they joined the newly established parties. The tribes of Dar Muharib joined the Omma party, the Ansar: "followers of the Mahadi."

In May 1969, a military regime assumed power in Sudan. They regarded the Native Administration as a form of reactionary force and said that it did not serve the needs of the Sudanese people. It was abolished, and the military government directed all people to join together to form a one-party system, "the Sudanese Socialist Union," and hence become members of the village and rural councils in their own areas.

In Dar Muharib as well as in other parts of Sudan, the Native Administration was difficult to abolish. The figures who held power, such as the Nazirs, Omdas, and Shaykhs, had acquired not only political power over their followers through time but economic power as well. So the military government found it difficult to oust these figures who enjoyed the support of their tribal people. Many important people from the Native Administration were recruited as heads of villages or heads of rural councils and as members of the provincial council.

Because of the traditional nature of tribal politics, and little exposure to and experience in state bureaucracy, the tribal leaders had only a secondary and unimportant role in affecting the process of decision-making, even at the local level. For example, the rural councils were largely controlled by the new government bureaucrats. Although the tribal Shaykhs were unable to affect political events on the national level, they remained strong among their own tribesmen.

The abolition of Native Administration in 1969 was accompanied by the introduction of the one-party system. There were elections to newly-formed village councils, rural councils, town councils, and provincial councils. The People's Assembly and the Central Committee were also created. It was very confusing to the nomads and the peasants, but to please the military government, they elected representatives in what has been called "camp politics." They saw this as a way to retain their traditional political system and their economic power.

The position of the tribal Shaykhs of Dar Muharib has remained very important even after the abolition of the Native Administration. The pastures and the sorghum fields are entrusted to the Shaykh of the tribe. No one may use the land unless he is a member of the tribe or an accepted peasant who has an established connection with the involved tribe. Claim to use or title to tribal land is always through the Shaykh. After harvest, heads of lineages (sub-shaykhs) bring their contributions to the Shaykh. These may include livestock as well as grain. Peasants, using the land, also do the same. The contributions and gifts that are gathered by the tribal members and peasants and given to the Shaykh form a part of the traditional system of exchange. It is based on the view that the Shaykh represents the tribe. Thus, he must have the resources to impress other Shaykhs and government bureaucrats by showing his generosity and hospitality. He must also act as a host to many tribal members and other Shaykhs seeking advice or acting as mediators in lineage or tribal conflicts.

A Shaykh may also claim labor from his followers if he is a willing and generous host whose hospitality includes food, tea, and coffee. Such a Shaykh's generosity and hospitality may draw a wide range of supporters from his own tribesmen and outsiders. His supporters and followers congregate around him as long as they receive at least a meal a day. They may take care of his herds and cultivate his sorghum fields.

Another form of Shaykhs who have free access to labor are the Muslim Saints (El Fugara), who teach Quran and Hadith to a big gathering of Islamic students. Since the students live with such a man in his Dar, and he caters for their economic subsistence on a daily basis, they work in his sorghum fields and herd his livestock. Their return for this labor is received as both the spiritual support of his Islamic teaching and the subsistence support of the Shaykh.

Kinship position and inherited property can play a significant role in making a certain Shaykh an influential personality among his own tribesmen and the nearby tribes. However, the core of influence, power, and authority is the support of the Shaykh's followers. The more followers the Shaykh has, the better his chance of accumulating wealth through production of sorghum, growth of his herds, and receiving of gifts in traditional exchange relations.

If the Shaykh is successful in drawing more supporters, his influence, social status, and prestige grows, the government might trust him with the unpopular job of collecting taxes from his tribesmen. The Shaykh arranges to have his agents (Wakola) collect the taxes. Thus he has no need to confront his supporters directly when tax collection time approaches. The Shaykh is allowed to keep about 5 percent if the collection is poor, and 10 percent if the collection of taxes is good.

Before the establishment of the Kenana Sugar Scheme, the market economy and transactions utilizing cash were extremely limited in the Kenana region. Much of the Shaykh's accumulation of wealth was not transformed into any form of material assets or capital but was directly expended on his followers and supporters. Such followings were the vehicle to power, social prestige, and prosperity.

When the transformation of the land began in 1976, the nomads and the peasants were confident that their tribal Shaykhs would make the right move to save their pastures and sorghum fields, and thus their social order would be preserved.

When the Dar Muharib tribal Shaykhs met with the Kenana Sugar Administrators, they were clearly promised compensation, priority of job opportunities, a big canal to be extended outside the irrigated area to water the affected livestock, and a distribution of plots of land for cultivation by people who had lost their original holdings. Although the Shaykhs and their supporters were murmuring with dissatisfaction, they could do nothing. They had to accept the new situation since they could not stop the state intervention.

With the coming of the first production season in 1980–1981, the local population was ignored when hiring took place. They were also brutally prevented from following their former mode of subsistence. The promises of land, water, and compensation turned out to be fake. The Shaykhs were disillusioned and angered, and their supporters were disoriented and frustrated.

It became apparent to their followers that the Shaykhs could no longer preserve the formal structure of the old social order, nor affect the present sequence of events. Desperate people turned against their Shaykhs and held them accountable for the tragic sequence of events. Although people acknowledged that El Howkoma (the government) is responsible for their plight, it seems no one wanted to risk imprisonment, fines, or the hands of repressive military personnel. So the Shaykhs were made easy scapegoats. After they lost the land and herds which were their original sources of authority and power, they became no better than commoners. As the authority and power of the tribal Shaykhs began to decline, so did the numbers of their followers, which were very crucial for a prestigious Shaykh. The present position of the Shaykhs discourages new supporters because their economic resources are either lost or sharply depleted, which puts great limitations on their ability to be generous or hospitable. Like their subjects, some of the Shaykhs migrated outside Kenana region in hope of finding a way to subsist. Others stayed behind looking for work with Kenana Sugar Scheme, or have had to seek casual work outside the irrigated agricultural sector.

The government intervention to develop the area not only changed the traditional political system of Dar Muharib, it liquidated the system. When land was expropriated resulting in the displacement of the local population, it destroyed the Shaykhs. This set the stage for government bureaucrats to assume power in a newly emerging social and political order.

CHANGE IN THE MODE OF PRODUCTION: FROM SELF-SUFFICIENCY TO MARKET ECONOMY

The traditional subsistence pursuits of Dar Muharib are family enterprises within the context of tribal communities. All the economic activities are carried out by family members who work on a continuous annual cycle to secure the household needs in both the nomadic and the peasant communities. The indigenous population of Kenana was engaged in a pastoral-agriculturalist mode of production.[4] The means of production and the relations of production were directed to serve and satisfy the family needs and strengthen the bonds of the tribal society. All means of production, especially land, pastures, and sorghum fields were run on the basis of communal ownership. The land was basically trusted to the Shaykh of the tribe, but he had no authority to force any decision concerning an eviction of a tribesman from the use of the land, nor had he the right to allocate any plot of land to a relative or a family member without communal agreement of his subjects. So the Shaykh's responsibility was to regulate the use of the tribal land with the full consent of his fellow tribesmen.

In the traditional society of Dar Muharib, the relations of production were free from exploitation found in feudal or capitalist modes of production, where there is conflict of interest between the owners of the means of production and the direct producers. In the traditional society of Kenana, the relations of production were based on ties of kinship and affinity. In such a situation, there may be a harmony of interests between the family members who are working together to secure and satisfy their basic needs. We have also seen that communal relations of production existed in a camp or a village in the form of voluntary exchange of labor parties among households during the peak times of labor demand.

So the indigenous mode of production of Dar Muharib was directed towards self-sufficiency in a system where the market economy and cash transactions were extremely limited. According to Claude Meillassoux[5] (1978), in such a system, where there is absence of exchange in the economic sense, the result is an absence of transformation of land and produce into value. Since the absence of money and exchange value is inherent in the traditional economy of Dar Muharib, a system of prestations and counterprestations, redistribution, and generalized reciprocity was developed as a mechanism to deal with food shortages, scarce goods, and emergencies.

For centuries, the traditional users of the land in Kenana region were economically independent and self-reliant. They maintained their families, kinship ties, domestic organizations, political systems, and tribal cultures. We have previously reviewed the numerous catastrophes of the past ranging from wars and counter-wars to forcible recruitment in the Khalifa armies, to difficulties of famines, drought, and economic hardship. The traditional population managed to survive such difficulties and come back, re-populating their Dar and continuing their traditional economy. However, the forced commercialization of irrigated agriculture in the region, and the eviction of the traditional users of the land, gives a new dimension to change. The coercive intervention policy of rural development is marginalizing and victimizing the dwellers of rural Sudan in general, and Kenana region in particular.

According to the Sugar Agreement of 1972, the former military government agreed to lease Kenana Sugar Company (KSC) 150,000 Feddans with a symbolic rent of 10 piasters per Feddan, free of obligations or duties to the indigenous population of the region.[6] When the land was cleared and transformed the Kenana Sugar Company not only turned a blind eye and a deaf ear to the traditional population, but it demanded another 150,000 Feddans with the same symbolic rent in the same region, and free of charges or costs due to the expropriation process. It was no coincidence that the State deployed and reinforced the army, the police, and the security forces to protect the KSC. Such an agreement was ruinous to the local people who, it is well to remember, remained the main stream in the Mahadist movement.

The forced "development" in the Kenana area gave the military government and KSC administration the ideological basis on which to confiscate communal tribal property and to drive the tribesmen out of their ancestral homes. Rural development has been catastrophic not only for the traditional users of these lands, but is also a threat to the population in general. It can be a national disaster when transformation and social change in the rural areas is carried out through the forcible seizure of the means of subsistence and the displacement of the indigenous population. It leaves people starving at home or foraging into distant territories, or settling on the outskirts of towns facing the limited and undependable option of making a living by poorly paid casual labor.

The Kenana Sugar Scheme is a clear example of state intervention, which destroys traditional communities. This was done in the name of integrated rural development and the breadbasket strategy. It replaces local economic autonomy with a commercial venture to boost the export-oriented economy. The result has been massive indebtedness.[7] a sinking economy, environmental degradation, rural poverty, shortage of food, and unemployment in urban centers. All these factors contributed to the national wave of dissatisfaction, antagonism and political upheaval that succeeded in overthrowing the former military regime (1969–1985) and replaced it with the newly elected government.

The overriding goals of the new government are to provide and maintain security and justice all over the Sudan, to revive the national economy, and to take measures to deal with the increasing numbers of starving people. This will require a careful evaluation of the structurally deformed economic development projects such as the Kenana Scheme. It should begin with a resolve to preserve and respect the right of self-sustaining communities that held title or claim to land. Reconsideration of actions which have deprived these communities of their ability to support themselves is urgent.

FINAL THOUGHTS ON "DEVELOPMENT"

In the 1970s, the former Sudanese government (1969–1985) earmarked considerable resources and finance to start the so-called "breadbasket strategy." The aim of the breadbasket strategy was to make the Sudan the largest agricultural producer in Africa and the Middle East. The strategy generated a lot of enthusiasm among politicians and developers, who could see the Sudan not only as self-sufficient but a net exporter of food and grain to Africa and the Arab world.

The central rainland of the Sudan is the site for the breadbasket strategy. These central claylands of the Sudan traditionally are the homeland of the nomads and the peasants. They have depended on these lands for centuries as pastures and sorghum fields, besides making use of other benefits like hunting and collecting acacia products such as gum arabic to be sold in the market.

The present era of sugar industry in the Sudan began with the establishment of El Geneid Scheme in 1962, followed by the sugar schemes of New Halfa, Sennar, Melut, Assalaya, and the Kenana. The idea of establishing the Kenana Scheme and refinery was developed when the Sudan was importing thousands of tons of sugar. It was decided a successful sugar scheme would not only satisfy the need at home, but could help the economy by exporting sugar and earning hard currency.

The Kenana Sugar Scheme displaced 40,000 people. Another 35,000 have been severely affected. All this has happened in the name of the "breadbasket strategy" and "integrated rural development." which have proved to be synonymous with marginalization and proletarianization of nomads and peasants in rural Sudan. The dreams of commercial success and high export earnings have slipped away in cost overruns. Ownership by the government was gradually lost to foreign firms and governments. Employment at the Scheme has reached only 14,000 of which 8,000 gain only seasonal jobs. Crime and profiteering have proliferated. It is indeed difficult to find any benefits to offset the staggering financial and social costs of this form of so-called development.

CHAPTER EIGHT NOTES

1. Cited in Shaykhs and Followers by Abdel Ghaffar M. Ahmed, 1974, p. 108.

2. Cattle Nazirate during the colonial time refers to the Baggara Arab political districts. The Nazirate was administered by a Nazir, a tribal Shaykh who was nominated by the District Commissioner and confirmed by the Governor General in Khartoum.

3. Omdas were the assistants of the Nazir, who supervised nomadic camps or villages.

4. See Chapter 3.

5. See the Economy in Agricultural Self-Sustaining Societies: A Preliminary Analysis, p. 131, 1978.

6. See Chapter 4.

7. An estimation of four to seven billion dollars in 1982–1983.

BIBLIOGRAPHY

Ahmed, Abdel Ghaffar M.	1972	The Rufa'a al-Hoi Economy. In (eds.) Ian Cannison and Wendy James, Essays in Sudan Ethnography. London: C. Hurst & Company.
—	1974	Shaykhs and Followers: Political Struggle in the Rufa'a al-Hoi Nazirate in the Sudan. Khartoum: Khartoum University Press.
—	1977	The Relevance of Indigenous Systems of Organization and Production to Rural Development: A Case from Sudan. In (ed.) Ali Mohamed El Hassan, Essays on the Economy and Society of the Sudan, v.l. Khartoum: Economic and Social Research Council. Pp. 57–66.
Amir, ELTigani,	1980	White Nile Past and Present. (In Arabic) Khartoum: Dar El Sahafa.
Amin, Samir.	1974	Introduction. In Amin (ed.) Modern Migration in West Africa. Oxford: IAF.
—	1977	Imperialists and Unequal Development. New York: Monthly Review Press.
Ansari, Awahid.	1980	The Changing Village, India. New Delhi: Chetana Publications.

Arrighi, Giovanni,	1973	Labour Supplies in Historical Perspective: A Study of Proletarianization of the African Peasantry in Rhodesia. In Arrighi, G. And J. Saul (eds.), Essays on the Political Economy of Africa. New York: Monthly Review Press.
Asad, Talal.	1970	The Kababish Arabs: Power, Authority and Consent in a Nomadic Tribe. New York: Praeger Publishers.
Harriett, Don.	1973	Peasant Types and Revolutionary Potential in Colonial Africa. Richmond: LSM Press.
Barnett, Tony.	1977	The Gezira Scheme: An Illusion of Development. London: Frank Cass.
Beltrame, Fr. G.	1961	Some Notes on the Distribution of Nilotic Peoples in the Mid-Nineteenth Century. Sudan Notes and Records. Vol. XLII, pp. 118–122.
Biesanz, Mavis Hiltunen and Biezanz, John.	1973	Introduction to Sociology. Englewood Cliffs: Prentice-Hall.
Boserup, Ester.	1965	The Conditions of Agricultural Growth. New York: Aldine.
Burns, Emile.	1982	The Marxist Reader: Works that Changed the World, Karl Marx, Friederich Engels, V.I. Lenin, Joseph Stalin. New York: Arenel Books.

Bussey, Ellen M.	1973	The Flight from Rural Poverty: How Nations Cope. Toronto: D.C. Health and Company.
Campbell, Angus, and Converse, Philip E.	1972	(eds) The Human Meaning of Social Change. New York: Russell Sage.
Chambers, Robert.	1969	Settlement Schemes in Tropical Africa: a Study of Organizations and Development. London: Routledge & Kegan Paul.
Collins, Carol.	1981	Sudan: Colonialism and Class Struggle. MERIP Report No. 46.
Colson, Elizabeth.	1971	The Social Consequences of Resettlement. Cariba Studies IV. Manchester: Manchester University Press.
Comte, Auguste.	1964	The Progress of Civilization through Three States. In (eds.) Amitai Etzioni and Eva Etzioni, Social Change: Sources, Patterns, and Consequences. New York: Basic Books.
Coquery-Vidrovitch, Catherine.	1978	Marxism and Anthropology: A Preliminary Survey. In (ed.) David Seddon, Relations of Production. Padstow: T.J. Press.
Copans, Jean and Seddon, David.	1978	Research on an African Mode of Production. In (ed.) David Seddon, Relations of Production. Padstow: T.J. Press.

Cunnison, Ian. 1966   Baggara Arabs: Power and the Lineage in a Sudanese Nomadic Tribe. Oxford: Clarendon Press.

Dahrendorf, Ralf. 1964   Toward a Theory of Social Conflict. In (eds.) Amitai Etzioni and Eva Etzioni, Social Change: Sources, Patterns and Consequences. New York: Basic Books.

Deng, Francis. 1978   Africans of Two Worlds. New Haven: Yale University Press.

Development Studies and Research Center. 1981   A Comprehensive Social Development Programme for Geneid, New Halfa, Sennar and Assalaya Sugar Estates. Report prepared for Ministry of Finance and National Economy. Khartoum, Sudan.

Eckholm, Erik. 1980   Man-Made Deserts: Man-Made Sorrow. In (ed.) Kathleen Courrier, Environmental Choice We Can Live With. Andover: Brick House Publishing Company.

Edquist, Charles and Edquist, Olle. 1979.   Social Carriers of Techniques for Development: A Comparative Economic Systems Approach. In Appropriate Technology, Myths versus Reality. SAREC Report #3. Stockholm, Sweden,

Ernst, Klaus.   1976   Tradition and Progress in the
                                     African Village: Non-Capitalist
                                     Transformation of Rural
                                     Communities in Mali. New York: St.
                                     Martin's Press.

Etzioni, Amitai   1973   Technological Shortcuts to Social
and Remp,   Change. New York: Russell Sage.
Richard.

Fitzsimmons,   1981   Rural Community Development:
Stephen J. and   A Program, Policy and Research
Freedman,   Model. Cambridge: Abt Books.
Abby J.

Fromm, Erich.   1961   Marx's Concept of Man. New York:
                                     Frederick Ungar Publishing Co.

Galal el Din, M.   1978   Immigration and Internal Migration
El Awad and   in Sudan. (In Arabic) Khartoum:
Mohammed   Economic and Social Reserach
Yousif El   Council, National Council for
Mustafa.   Research.

Godelier,   1973   Perspectives in Marxist
Maurice.   Anthropology. London: Cambridge
                                     University Press.

Godelier,   1978   The Concept of the Asiatic Mode
Maurice.   of Production and Marxist Models
                                     of Social Evolution. In (ed.,) David
                                     Seddon, Relations of Production.
                                     Padstow: T.J. Press.

Green, Arnold   1956   Sociology: An Analysis of Life
W.   in Modern Society. New York:
                                     McGraw-Hill Book Company.

Hassaballa, Hassaballa Omar.	1983	An Approach to Rural Urban Migration and Development in Africa: A Case Study of Sudan and Ghana. Bulletin No. 100. Khartoum: Economic and Social Research Council, National Council for Research.
—	1984	Kenana Project and its System of Social Infrastructure. (In Arabic) The Second National Economic Conference. Khartoum, 19–24 March 1984.
Hassan, Yusuf Fadl.	1971	The Arab and the Sudan. Khartoum: Khartoum University Press.
Heimer, Franz-Wilhelm.	1973	Social Change in Angola. München: Weltforum Verlag.
Hill, Richard.	1959	The Period of Egyptian Occupation: 1820–1881. In Sudan Notes and Records, Vol. XL, pp. 101–06.
Holt, P.M.	1959	The Place in History of the Sudanese Mahadia. Sudan Notes and Records, Vol. XL, pp. 107–12.
Holt, P.M. and Daly, M.W.	1961	The History of the Sudan. London: Weidenfeld and Nicolson.
Hyden, Goran.	1980	Beyond Ujamaa in Tanzania: Underdevelopment and an Uncaptured Peasantry. Berkeley: University of California Press.

Ibn Khaldun.   1967   The Muqaddimah: An Introduction to History. (Translated from Arabic by Granz Rosenthal). Bollingen Series. Princeton: Princeton University Press.

Ibrahim, Fouad N.   1978   The Problem of Desertification in the Republic of the Sudan, with Special Reference to Northern Darfur Province. Monograph #8, Development Studies and Research Centre. Faculty of Economic and Social Studies. University of Khartoum.

IDS Bulletin.   1977   Lonrho Revisited: Witch-hunt, Crusade, Quest for El Dorado, Road to Darien? In Imperialism: New Tactics. Vol. 8, #3. Sussex University.

Iliffe, John.   1983   The Emergence of African Capitalism. Minneapolis: University of Minnesota Press.

Jackson, J.K. and Shawki, M.K.   1950   Shifting Cultivation in the Sudan. Sudan Notes and Records. Vol. XXXI, Part II, pp. 210–22.

Jagannadham, V.   1978   Administration and Social Change. New Delhi: Uppal Publishing House.

Keddeman, Willem and Ali, Abdil Gadir.   1978   Employment, Productivity and Incomes in Rural Sudan. Khartoum: Economic and Social Research Council and International Labour Organization.

Kenana Sugar Company.	1978	Kenana Sugar Project: Information Circular.
—	1980	Conditions of Employment.
—	1980	Green Gold at Kenana. (In Arabic).
Kerblay, Basile.	1971	Chayanov and the Theory of Peasantry as a Specific Type of Economy. In (ed.) T. Shanin, Peasants and Peasant Societies. London: C. Nicholls.
Lebon, J.H.G.	1961	Some Concepts of Modern Geography Applied to Sudan. Sudan Notes and Records. Vol. XLII, pp. 3–28.
Lele, Uma.	1975	The Design of Rural Development: Lessons from Africa. Balitmore: Johns Hopkins University Press.
Lonrho Ltd.	1973	Kenana Sugar Project: Feasibility Study. Vol. 3.
Manger, Leif O.	1981	The Sand Swallows Our Land: Overexploitation of Productive Resources and the Problem of Household Viability in the Kheiran a Sudanese Oasis. Occasional Paper #24. African Savannah Studies. Department of Social Anthropology, University of Bergen.

Marx, Karl and Engels, Friedrich.	1967	The Communist Manifesto. With an Introduction by A.J.P.Taylor. Harmondsworth: Penguin Books Ltd.
Marx, Karl.	1976	Capital: A Critique of Political Economy. Introduced by Ernest Mandel; translated by Ben Fowkes. Vol. 1. New York: Vintage Books.
McClelland, David C,	1964	Business Drive and National Achievement. In (eds.) Amitai Etzioni and Eva Etzioni, Social Change: Sources, Patterns and Consequences. New York: Basic Books.
Meillassoux, Claude.	1978	The Economy in Agricultural Self-Sustaining Societies: A Preliminary Analysis. In (ed.) David Seddon, Relations of Production. Padstow: T.J. Press.
—	1978	The Social Organization of Peasantry: The Economic Basis of Kinship. In (ed.) David Seddon, Relations of Production. Padstow: T.J. Press.
Mitchell, J.C.	1959	Labour Migration in Africa South of the Sahara: the Causes of Labour Migration. Bull. International Labour Inst. 6 (1).
Mukherjee, R.	1975	Social Indicators. Meerut: Prabhat Press.

Nimeri, Sayed.   1977   The Five Year Plan (1970–1975):
                          Some Aspects of the Plan and
                          its Performance. Monograph
                          No. 1, Development Studies
                          and Research Centre. Faculty
                          of Economic and Social Studies,
                          University of Khartoum.

O'Brien, John   1980   Agricultural Labour and
James.   Development in Sudan. PhD
                          Dissertation. University of
                          Connecticut.

Oburn, William   1974   Social Changes During Depression
F.   and Recovery (Social Change in
                          1934). New York: Da Capo Press.

Oesterdiekhoff,   1983   The "Breadbasket" is Empty: The
Peter and   Options of Sudanese Development
Wohlmuth,   Policy. Canadian Journal of African
Karl.   Studies Vol. 17.

Ominde, S.H.   1968.   Land and Population Movement
                          in Kenya. Evanston: Northwestern
                          University Press.

Parsons, Talcott, 1964   A Functional Theory of Change.
                          In (eds.) Amitai Etzioni and Eva
                          Etzioni, Social Change: Sources,
                          Patterns, and Consequences. New
                          York: Basic Books.

Qabudan, Salim.   1842   The First Trip Looking for the
                          Origin of the White Nile (in
                          Arabic) tranlated to Arabic from
                          French in 1922 in Cairo.

Reid, J.A.   1930   Some Notes on the Tribes of the
                          White Nile Province. Sudan Notes
                          and Records, Vol. XIII, Part II, pp.
                          149–213.

Rempel, Henry.   1978   Seasonal Outmigration and
                          Rural Poverty: Causes and Effect.
                          Paper presented at a conference
                          organized by the Institute of
                          Development Studies and the Ross
                          Institute of Tropical Hygiene.

International   1976   Growth, Employment and Equity:
Labour   A Comprehensive Strategy for
Organization.   Sudan. Geneva: International
                          Labour Office.

Rostow, W.W.   1964   The Take Off into Self-sustained
                          Growth. In (eds.) Amitai
                          Etzioni and Eva Etzioni, Social
                          Change: Sources, Patterns and
                          Consequences, New York: Basic
                          Books.

Saul, John and   1971   African Peasantries. In (ed.) T.
Wood, Roger   Shanin, Peasants and Peasant
                          Societies. London: C. Nicholls.

Schapera, I.   1956   Migrant Labour and Tribal Life in
                          Bechunaland. In Inter. Am. Inst. Bull.,
                          pp. 205–208.

Seddon, David.   1978   The Relations of Production. In
                          Marxist Approaches to Economic
                          Anthropology. London: Frank Cass
                          Company.

Seidman, Ann.	1974	Planning for Development in Sub-Saharan Africa. New York: Praeger Publishers.
Seligman, C.G.	1932	Pagan Tribes of the Nilotic Sudan. London: George Routledge & Son.
Shanin, Teodor.	1971	Peasants and Peasant Societies. London: C. Nicholls.
Sheibeika, Mekki	1971	The Expansionist Movement of Khedive Ismail to the Lakes. In (ed.) Sudan in Africa. Khartoum: Hassan Yusuf Fadl.
Simpson, I.G. and Simpson, Morag C.	1978	Alternative Strategies for Agricultural Development in the Central Rainlands of the Sudan, with Special Reference to the Damazine Area. Rural Development Study No. 3. University Printing Service: University of Leeds.
Smith, Alan D. and Welch, Claude E.	1978	Peasants in Africa. African Studies Association. Waltham: Brandeis University.
Sobat, R.H.	1979	Economic Development and Urban Migration: Tanzania 1900–1971. Oxford: Clarendon Press.
Sorokin, Pitirim A.	1959	Social and Cultural Mobility. London: Collier-Macmillan Limited.
Spencer, Herbert.	1907	The Evolution of Society (ed. by Robert L. Carneiro). Chicago: Universtiy of Chicago Press.

Spengler, Oswald.	1964	The Life Cycle of Cultures. In (eds.) Amitai Etzioni and Eva Etzioni, Social Change: Sources, Patterns and Consquences. New York: Basic Books.
Spradley, James P. and Brenda, Mann.	1979	The Ethnographic Interview. New York: Holt, Rinehart and Winston.
Spradley, James P.	1980	Participant Observation. New York, Holt, Rinehart and Winston.
Steward, Julian H.	1964	A Neo-Evolutionist Approach. In (eds.) Amitai Etzioni and Eva Etzioni, Social Change: Sources, Patterns and Consequences. New York: Basic Books.
Theobald, A.B.	1950	The Khalifa Abdallahi. Sudan Notes and Records, Vol. XXXI, Part II.
Thornton, Douglas,	1977	Rural Development: The Role of the Agricultural Economist. In (ed.) Ali Mohamed El Hassan, Essays on the Economy and Society of the Sudan. Vol. I. Khartoum, Economic and Social Research Council. Pp. 1–14.
Todaro, M.P.	1971	Income Expectations, Rural-Urban Migration and Employment in Africa. Inter. Lab. Rev. 104 (4): 387–413.

Toynbee, Arnold.	1964	The Nature of the Growth of Civilizations. In (eds.) Amitai Etzioni and Eva Etzioni, Social Change: Sources, Patterns and Consequences. New York: Basic Books.
Van den Berghe, Pierre L.	1979	Human Family Systems: An Evolutionary View. New York: El Sevier North Holland, Inc.
Vasudeva, Promila.	1976	Social Change: An Analysis of Attitudes and Personality. New Delhi: Sterling Publishers.
Weber, Max.	1968	On Charisma and Institution Building, (ed. with an Introduction by S.N. Eisenstadt). Chicago: University of Chicago Press.
Whiting, Larry R.	1973	Rural Development: Research Priorities. Ames: Iowa state University Press.
Wilson, F.	1972	Migrant Labour in South Africa. Johannesburg: South African Council of Churches.
Winans, Edgar V.	1962	Shambala, the Constitution of a Traditional State. Berkeley: University of California Press.
Wohlmuth, Karl.	1983	The Kenana Sugar Project: A Model of Successful Trilateral Cooperation? (ed.) Peter Oesterdiekhoff and Karl Wohlmuth. Miinchen: Weltforum Verlag.
Wolf, Eric. R.	1966	Peasants. Englewood Cliffs: Prentice-Hall.

APPENDIX I*

KENANA SUGAR COMPANY LIMITED
CONDITIONS OF EMPLOYMENT
SECTION-I
PRELIMINARY PROVISIONS

TITLE AND COMMENCEMENT

1.1   The regulations may be cited as "The Employment Conditions of the Kenana Sugar Company Limited" and shall come into force on 1.10.1980.

REPEAL

1.2   All regulations, circulars, letters and instructions which previously regulated the employment of the company's employees and which are relevant to these regulations are hereby repealed.

APPLICABILITY

1.3   Permanent employees are subject to the regulations in their entirety.

1.4   Non-permanent employees are entitled to benefits, as are provided by the law or in terms of their contract.

DEFINITIONS

1.5 In these regulations, unless the context otherwise requires, the following definitions apply.

<u>The Company</u> Limited	:	Kenana Sugar Company
<u>The Managing</u>	:	The person appointed in pursuance to article 103 of the Company's Articles of Association.
<u>Unit</u>	:	Department, Division, or Section according to the company's organisation.
<u>Employee</u>	:	A person who has entered into a contract of service with the Company.
<u>Permanent employee</u>	:	A person employed on a permanent basis under a written contract.
<u>Non-permanent employee</u>	:	A person employed either on an hourly/daily basis, or for a period as pre-determined by a contract in writing.
<u>Family</u>	:	Dependent wife or wives, sponsored children under 19 years and dependent father and/or mother.

Basic rate of pay	:	The basic rate of remuneration payable to an employee, but excludes all other remuneration.
Monthly pay	:	Basic rate of pay expressed in monthly terms.
Daily pay	:	Monthly pay divided by 30.
Hourly pay	:	Monthly pay divided by 240.
Month	:	A month according to the Gregorian Calendar.
Leave year	:	The year from 1st October to 30th September.
Company Medical Board	:	A Board comprising of the Company's Chief Medical Officer and at least one other medical practitioner registered in the Sudan nominated by the Company.

SECTION II

MEDICAL EXAMINATION

2.1 All applicants for permanent employment are required to pass medical examinations by the Company's medical officer prior to appointment.

PROBATION

2.2 The initial period of probation to determine the suitability of an employee is three months minimum, but any probationary period may be extended for a period not exceeding 12 months. The precise length of the period of probation is determined by the grade and nature of the post.

2.3 If the employee's performance is satisfactory by the end of the probationary period, he is confirmed in the job, with retroactive effect, by a letter signed by the Unit Head.

HOURS OF WORK

2.4   Normal Work Day

a) For industrial shift operations:

The standard hours of work for shift employees shall be 8 hours per shift, excluding any handover time which is not counted towards overtime, in accordance with the Company's shift schedules. It is recognised that because of the shift rotas, the weekly day of rest may not coincide with Friday.

In order to maintain the continuity of operations, all shift employees shall remain on duty until relieved by the succeeding shift or until permitted to leave by the shift supervisor in charge.

Shift workers, while they are eligible for the statutory half-hour rest, they are bound not to abandon their point of work unless permitted by the supervisor, who shall arrange that in such a way that there will be sufficient cover for operations.

b) For field operations.

Working hours in the field (agriculture) are determined by the Company noting that, while it is generally 8 hours, the exigencies of work may demand more than that.

c) For watchmen.

Hours of work are 12 hours per day. They are required to remain on duty until they are relieved.

d) For all other employees.

Eight hours commencing and finishing at times determined by the Company, which may vary according to operations. This includes a half-hour for rest or meal.

Working Extra Hours

2.5 Except in cases of extreme hardship, employees must comply with any request by the company to work extra hours.

Unit Heads should plan the schedules in such a way as to cut overtime work to the minimum.

2.6 No payment is made for extra hours unless the work performed has prior authorization by the unit head or his designate.

2.7 Senior Staff Grade 10 and above are expected to work extra hours as and when necessary without claiming overtime payment.

OVERTIME

2.8 Employees in Grade 1 to 8 inclusive qualify for overtime payment, after having completed 8 hours' work, at the rate of time and a half of the basic hourly pay in normal work days. Work on Fridays, the weekly day of rest, and public holidays shall be calculated at the rate of two times the basic hourly pay. Field permanent employees in Grades 7–9 who qualify for field allowance do not qualify for overtime during the normal days of work, but they may claim overtime for work on Fridays and public holidays. Staff in Grade 10 and above do not qualify for overtime.

2.9 SHIFT ALLOWANCE

Employees who work rotating shifts covering the 24 hours, whether divided into 2 or 3 shifts qualify for shift allowance at the following rates:

Grades 1 & 2	:	LS 5.00 per month
Grades 3, 4 & 5	:	LS 10.00 per month
Grades 6 & 7	:	LS 15.00 per month
Grades 8&9	:	LS20.00 per month
Grades 10 & above	:	LS 30.00 per month

Shift allowance is only paid when an employee is actually on shift. It stops when shift work stops.

2.10 Employees in grade 9 qualify for overtime at a flat rate of 750 mms per hour worked.

2.11 During Ramadan, Moslem shift employees who don't enjoy shorter hours *of work* shall be paid extra one hour— at the overtime rate.

2.12 Shift employees working beyond shift hours or on their scheduled day of rest or on a public holiday will be paid overtime when applicable along the lines stated above.

ALLOWANCES

2.13 Field Allowances

a) Field Allowance is paid to those grade 7 to 12 agriculturalists (excluding those who work in harvesting) whose work normally takes time beyond the usual office hours. It is paid at the following rate:

Grade 7 to 12   :   LS 20.00 per month

2.14 Meal Allowance

An employee who is required by the company to continue working after office hours for two hours or more qualifies for a meal allowance at the rate of 750m/mms.

2.15 Responsibility Allowance

Senior staff grade 10 and above qualify for responsibility allowance paid monthly at a flat rate of LS 30.00. This is meant to compensate for any extra hours they are naturally expected to put in as and when needed.

2.16 Cash Handling Allowance

An employee who is in charge of a safe and handles money as a daily routine shall be paid an allowance amounting to LS 30.00 per month. Those employees in the Pay Office who work regularly as Cashiers may at the recommendation of their Department Head be awarded half the rate of the above allowance.

2.17 On Call Allowance

An employee who is regularly on call during any particular month shall be paid on call allowance at the following rates:

Grades 1 to 6   :   LS 10.00

Grades 7 to 9   :   LS 15.00

Grades 10 and above :   LS 25.00

2.18 Infection Allowance.

Employees who are engaged in preventive medicine are entitled to Infection allowance at the following rates:

Grades 1 & 2 : LS 5.00 per month

Grades 3 to 6 : LS 10.00 per month

Grades 10 and above : LS 25.00 per month

Rates of Pay

2.19 Employees' jobs are classified into one integrated pay structure 14 grades set out in Appendix 'A.'

Job Classificaition

2.20 Jobs shall be basically classified according to the scales in Appendix 'B.' classifications on grades 11, 12, 14 & 14 are issued sepately.

Acting Pay

2.21 Employees who are authorized to act in a job of a higher classification for not less than one month qualify for acting pay which is expressed as:

The difference between the employees' current basic pay and (a) the minimum of the next grade, or (b) the next incremental step in the higher grade if any employee's own pay overlaps the next grade.

Housing

2.22 Company owned housing accommodation is provided free of charge to employees whenever it is available. If no accommodation is available, the following house subsidy is paid:

Grade 14 : LS 95.00 per month

Grade 13 : LS 85.00 per month

Grade 12	:	LS 75.00 per month
Grade 11	:	LS 65.00 per month
Grade 10	:	LS 55.00 per month
Grade 9	:	LS 45.00 per month
Grade 8	:	LS 35.00 per month
Grade 7	:	LS 30.00 per month
Grade 6	:	LS 25.00 per month
Grade 5	:	LS 25.00 per month
Grade 4	:	LS 20.00 per month
Grade 3	:	LS 20.00 per month
Grade 2	:	LS 15.00 per month
Grade 1	:	LS 15.00 per month

Employees working in Khartoum qualify for 25% of the above rate extra. Those in Port Sudan qualify for 20-extra.

The Company has the right to amend the above rates and to make such rates and regulations as deemed appropriate from time to time.

Transport

2.23 Where no Company transport is provided to and from office, a monthly allowance is paid at a rate on the cost of public transport and approved by the Company from time to time.

Mileage allowance:

An employee required by the Company to use his own car on Company business in a regular form is entitled to a mileage allowance at a rate approved by the Company from time to time.

TRAVELLING ALLOWANCE (ON DUTY)

2.24 When an employee is required to travel on duty in the Sudan, the Company will reimburse the cost of transport, and where an employee cannot be housed and fed in a company Rest House, also pays a daily subsistence at the following rates:

Grades 1 to 2	:	LS 2.00
Grades 3	:	LS 3.00
Grades 4	:	LS 4.00
Grades 5	:	LS 5.00
Grades 6 to 7	:	LS 6.00
Grades 8 to 9	:	LS 7.00
Grades 10 to 11	:	LS 8.00
Grades 12 and above	:	LS 10.00

2.25

(a) Annual leave is a paid leave and is earned after the completion of 12 months starting from the date of appointment in the permanent service according to the following rates:

Grade 1 and 2	:	25 days
Grade 3, 5, & 5	:	30 days
Grade 6, 7, 8 & 9	:	35 days
Grades 10–14	:	40 days

(b) With the approval of the Unit Head, leave may be granted in advance in the event of hardship or emergency or in the interest of the Company.

(c) Employees whose permanent domicile is in remote places may be granted up to a maximum of seven days per leave year according to the distance from their place of work.

(d) If an employee is prevented by the Company from taking his leave during any leave year, his leave will either be carried forward to the next year, or cash is paid in lieu of leave by mutual agreement at the discretion of the Head of the Department. In either case, the employee is entitled to leave travel allowance.

(e) With the Company's prior consent, an employee may defer his leave to the next leave year.

LEAVE TRAVEL ALLOWANCE

2.26 On the completion of 12 months' continuous service, employees shall be entitled to payment of Leave Travel Allowance equivalent to one month's basic pay.

SICK LEAVE

2.27

(a) An employee becomes eligible for paid sick leave after six months' continuous service.

(b) Paid sick leave is granted only on the production of a sickness certificate signed by Company doctor or, when this is practically impossible, by a registered medical practitioner.

(c) Payment within any 52-week period is limited to the following schedule:

i) six months at basic rate of pay.

ii) six months at half basic rate of pay.

(d) When an illness or accident occurs during a period of annual leave, sick leave does not commence until the annual leave has been exhausted.

(e) An employee who is injured in the performance of his duties shall be eligible for paid sick leave on the above lines or according to the Workmen's Compensation Act, whichever is more beneficial to the employee.

MATERNITY LEAVE

2.28 After 12 months' continuous service, a married woman is eligible for 56 calendar days' maternity leave paid at basic rate of pay, not less than 28 days of which must be taken after delivery date as certified by a registered medical practitioner or midwife. Any leave taken beyond 56 days will be treated as annual leave.

COMPASSIONATE LEAVE

2.29 With the prior consent and at the sole discretion of the unit head, compassionate leave at the basic rate of pay and not exceeding seven calendar days in any 52 weeks period may be granted in cases of emergency.

PILGRIMAGE LEAVE

2.30 Fifteen calendar days may be granted once only during service with the company and not before completion of one year's continuous service. This is paid at the basic rate of pay.

UNION DUTIES

2.31 Four employees holding executive positions in the main committee of a track union may be granted up to 30 calendar days in a leave year, paid at basic rate of pay, to attend interviews or other meetings officially sanctioned by the central union. This does not prejudice or contradict any statutory laws enacted.

NON PAID LEAVE

2.32 At the sole discretion of the Unit Head, leave without pay up to 45 calendar days in a leave year may be granted for a compelling personal reason.

MEDICAL CARE

2.33

(a) The Company provides a medical service—based on the national health programme—for all employees and their families, towards the cost of which employees are required to contribute at the following rate:

Grade 1–2	:	LS 0.20
Grade 3–8	:	LS 0.30
Grade 9 & above	:	LS 0.50

(b) The Company Medical Service does not cover:

i) normal deliveries

ii) circumcision

iii) artificial denture

iv) corrective glasses

v) hearing aids

The service is administered:

i) at Sufieya by the Company's Medical officers.

ii) at Khartoum and Port Sudan, by a medical practitioner appointed by the Company in those towns.

In cases where the company medical service cannot provide hospitalization or specialist treatment, employees will be referred by the Company Medical Officer to the government medical services.

(d) In case an employee is admitted to hospital, he shall be treated along the following lines:

Grade 1–2	:	in common wards
Grade 3–8	:	in second-class wards
Grade 9 and above	:	in first-class wards

The Company shall bear the expenses incurred thereof.

(e) An employee who is admitted to hospital during his leave, in order to accrue the benefits stated above, must report the fact to the Company as soon as possible and follow that by a medical report by a recognized practitioner.

(f) All employees must take all reasonable precautions to safeguard their health and that of their families and shall submit to such medical treatment as the Company's Medical Officer may from time to time consider necessary, including inoculations, vaccinations, and preventive treatment.

All employees must submit to medical examination when required to do so by the Company.

(h) The Company acknowledges the right of every employee to consult a medical practitioner outside the Company's medical service, but the Company accepts no responsibility for the consequences thereof or charges arising therefrom. The company accepts no responsibility for medical charges incurred outside Sudan.

SAFETY

2.34 It is the duty of each employee to acquaint himself with the Company Safety Regulations (issued separately).

Department Heads are responsible for obtaining safety gear for their employees whenever necessary and for ensuring that these are used at work.

2.35 No employee under 18 years of age will be required to work with, on, or close to dangerous machinery which is capable of injury.

CLOTHING ISSUES

2.36 Clothing is issued by the Company annually on a scale specified in Appendix 'D.'

2.37 Uniforms are Company's property throughout the year in which they are issued, and the employees will be responsible for their upkeep.

2.38 Employees who are issued uniforms should always wear them at work.

CODE OF CONDUCT

2.39

(a) Employees must behave decently and must not use any abusive language when addressing their superiors, colleagues, subordinates, and the members of the public with whom they deal.

(b) Employees are entrusted with the task of carrying out the duties of the company and are expected to earn for the Company the respect of those who deal with it. As such, they shall maintain high standards of honesty, integrity, and impartiality. They must conduct their official and personal relationships in a manner which commands respect and confidence and must avoid situations which might result in actual or apparent conflict of interest.

(c) An employee owes his duty entirely to the Company and shall not engage in any outside activity which is incompatible with the full and proper discharge of duties and responsibilities of his employment. He shall not, directly or indirectly, receive any directives in the fulfillment of his duties from any authority or source other than the Company.

(d) Employees must not engage themselves in any part time work to augment their income by private practice without the written consent of the Company.

(e) Except in the course of his duty, an employee shall not for the purpose of furthering a private interest, directly or indirectly, use or allow the use of information obtained in the course of his employment which is not available to the public generally.

(f) An employee shall be fully devoted to the performance of his duties and any other assignments as may be directed by the Company. He shall agree to serve in any place as determined by the Company, and shall comply with the rules and directives issued by his superiors.

(g) An employee shall adhere to the official working hours determined by the Company and shall agree to work outside the official working hours, if the exigencies of the work so require.

(h) Disciplinary code is appended to this regulation.

GRIEVANCE PROCEDURE

2.40 Any employee having a cause for grievance shall have the right to present his case for investigation and consideration, and the Company will endeavor to resolve it as quickly as possible. The procedure shall be as follows:

First step   An employee desiring to raise any complaint shall, in first instance, discuss the matter with his immediate supervisor, who will give his reply within 48 hours unless further investigation requires more time.

Second step   Failing to get a satisfactory solution, the employee may refer the matter to his senior supervisor, who will give his reply within four days

Third step   Failing to get a satisfactory solution, the employee accompanied by a union representative, if it is a major issue (involving dismissal) may take up the matter with the Personnel Department. The latter will give its reply within 15 days.

RETIREMENT

2.41 Normal retirement age is 60 years. However, service may be continued thereafter on a monthly or contract basis on such terms and conditions as the Company may specify, subject to satisfactory completion of a medical examination by the Company's Medical Officer.

RETIREMENT BENEFITS

2.42

(a) The Company shall maintain a Provident Fund Scheme in which both the Company and the employees contribute.

Company Contribution :

(b) The Company shall contribute 15% of each permanent employee's basic pay, and the amount of such contribution shall be transferred by the Company to the Trustees for deposit into the employee's "Provident Fund Account."

(c) In pursuance to (b.) above, any such Company contribution shall not be compounded with any similar benefits introduced by legislation. Accordingly, the Company shall deduct from its contribution any amounts paid by it to the public Social Insurance Funds.

Members' Contribution

(d) Members' contribution. Each employee in the permanent service shall contribute to the Provident Fund 20% or 15% or 5% of his basic pay. He may elect any one of these percentages in writing.

An employee may change the rate of his contribution only on the first of January each year after giving 30 days' notice of the intended change.

Deduction

(e) An employee's contribution shall be deducted from his pay by the Company on the payday and shall forthwith be paid together with the Company's contribution to the Trustees.

CERTIFICATE OF SERVICE

2.43 On retirement, resignation, or termination of service, the only certificate that shall be given is on the Company Standard Form (Appendix 'E').

Personnel Department will prepare this certificate of service.

If departments receive queries from third parties about ex-employees of the company, personnel Department should be informed and will be responsible for dealing with the query.

*I did not try to apply any change to the contents of the Conditions of Employment, to be sure that it is presented in its original form. Although I managed to get a copy of Kenana Sugar Company Conditions of Employment from the factory personnel office, I could not get the Appendix which is cited in the article on the grounds that it was either confidential or for internal use only.

Table I.I

Kenana Suger Company Limited, Employees Salary Scales in L.S.

Grade	Base	1st step	2nd step	3rd step	4th step	5th step	6th step	7th step	8th step	Increment
I	40	42.5	45	47.5	50	52.5	55	57.5	60	2.5
2	52	55	58	61	64	67	70	73	76	3
3	68	72	76	80	84	88	92	96	100	4
4	85	90	95	100	105	110	115	120	125	5
5	106	112	118	124	130	136	142	148	154	6
6	130	138	146	154	162	170	178	186	194	8
7	160	169	178	187	196	205	214	223		9
8	200	210	220	230	240	250	260	270		10
9	240	252	264	276	288	300	312	324		12
10	300	315	330	345	360	275	390	405		15
11	370	390	410	430	450	470	490	510		20

Source: KSC Conditions of Employment

APPENDIX II

KSC HOUSING

Senior Staff. Top Management; Type 1

The construction of this type consists of concrete foundations and block walls, floor, and galvanized steel roof covered with timber trusses. This type of house has a living and dining room, four or three bedrooms, kitchen, bathroom, and two enclosed verandahs with a total floor area of 128m². The house has board ceilings, tile floors, timber doors and windows, and framed verandahs (panels). Wardrobes and cupboard units are built into the bedrooms. The house is provided with all the necessary electrical installations, including overhead lighting and power outlets, and air conditioning in bedrooms and living room. The sanitary installation consists of bath, shower, w.c. lavatory, basin, and bidet. The kitchen is supplied with a stainless steel sink unit, floor and wall unit, and external laundry tub, all served by hot and cold water, with discharge connection to the main drainage system.

The other extra equipment supplied to the Type 1 houses are air conditioning units, water heater, an electric stove, a refrigerator, and TV.

The houses are detached, and each one has a fenced garden and car park.

Senior Staff. Middle Management; Type 2

This type of house consists of three bedrooms, each of approximately 18m², and a sala of the same size. Kitchen is approximately 10m², fitted with the necessary equipment. Also included are a shower room, a toilet, and an enclosed verandah of namlia panels on timber framing.

The house is supplied by all the necessary electric installations, plus running water, and the sanitary service. The extra equipment supplied are the ceiling fans, an electric stove, air coolers, and water heaters.

The houses are built in groups and include enclosed courtyards of approximately 230m².

Junior Staff (Top Junior Staff); Type 3

This type of house is constructed of concrete foundations. The house has two bedrooms, each of approximately 18m², a sala of the same size, a kitchen of approximately 10m², and a shower room and toilet. The house is supplied with the necessary installations, including an electric stove. The houses are built in groups; each house has a courtyard of 170m². This housing unit is surrounded by a 2.5 metre-high wall.

Junior Staff (Middle Junior Staff); Type 4

These houses are constructed on concrete foundations with block walls, galvanized steel roof covering on timber rafters, and timber doors and windows. The house consists of one bedroom of approximately 18m², a living area of 18m² opening on to a courtyard (70m²) on one side, and a kitchen of 13m². The house is provided with a washroom, and a toilet block built in the courtyard, with pipe water which is connected to the main drainage system. Also this unit is surrounded with 2.5 metre-high wall.

Seasonal Laborers; Type 5

This type of housing is made mainly for the seasonal laborers and workers. They dwell in these houses from October to April, the length of the production season. After that, or during the off-season, the houses are empty. These houses are constructed when the production season approaches. The houses are made of straw, in the shape of round thatched huts, with no equipment or furniture inside. These areas where the seasonal workers stay are called the labor camps (campo). The KSC administration provides water in storage tanks for drinking, while for other activities such as laundry or taking a bath the labor camp dwellers use the irrigation canals.

Table II.1
Number of Houses, Types and Occupants
In the Kenana Estate, November 1983

Senior Staff

Number of Houses	Types	Expatriates	Sudanese	Total number of occupants	Other
27	4 bedroom Coseley	48	11	59	3 rest houses
72	3 bedroom Coseley	43	46	89	Expatriate children's school
18	2 bedroom Coseley	16	2	18	
18	1 bedroom Coseley	17	1	18	
25	3 bedroom T2	16	6	22	3 rest houses
25	2 bedroom T2	26	–	26	
185		166	66	232	7

Number of Houses	Types	Expatriates	Sudanese	Total number of occupants	Other
35	EBCS	6	31	37	
42	Lessers	39	–	39	
14	Ovalavels	–	40	40	
91		45	71	116	

CNI Camp – Capper Neill

Number of Houses	Types	Expatriates	Sudanese	Total number of occupants	Other
198	Boyton	175	9	184	
26	Ovalavels	129	9	138	
1	Lesser house	4	–	4	
8	Roundavels	15	–	15	
233		318	18	336	

C9 Junior Staff Housing – El Alamiyya

Number of Houses	Types	Expatriates	Sudanese	Total number of occupants	Other
40	T3A	–	71	71	
77	T3	–	110	110	
386	T4	–	404	404	
503		–	585	585	

C10 Junior Staff Houing – Abdalla El Khidir

Number of Houses	Types	Expatriates	Sudanese	Total number of occupants	Other
40	T3A	–	40	40	
40	T3	–	40	40	
88	T4M	–	88	88	
100	T4A	–	100	100	
424	T4	–	495	495	
692		–	763	763	

Village 2

Number of Houses	Types	Expatriates	Sudanese	Total number of occupants	Other
3	T2B	–	3	3	
10	T3B	–	13	13	
148	4x4 rooms	–	168	168	
14	Barrakcks	–	37	37	
180		–	221	221	

Village 3

Number of Houses	Types	Expatriates	Sudanese	Total number of occupants	Other
3	T2B	–	3	3	
10	T3B	–	12	12	
3	T4B	–	2	2	3 mess
104	4x4 rooms	–	175	175	
120		–	192	192	3

Village 4

Number of Houses	Types	Expatriates	Sudanese	Total number of occupants	Other
4	T3B	–	8	8	
2	T4B	–	–	–	2 mess
6		–	8	8	2

(PSU) Pump Station 4 Housing Units

Number of Houses	Types	Expatriates	Sudanese	Total number of occupants	Other
56	T4B	–	52	52	5 service units
174	Camps huts	–	174	174	
11	Demech. Camp-ovals	35	–	35	
13	Camp oval huts	–	14	14	1 for the army
254		35	240	275	6
Grand Total					
2264		564	2164	2728	18

INDEX

Hassaballa Omar Hassaballa

Research Fellow/Professor of Sociocultural Anthropology

Made in the USA
Charleston, SC
21 December 2010